IMAGES
of America

STONEHAM

Joanne B. Harriman

ARCADIA
PUBLISHING

ISBN 978-0-7385-0222-9

Published by Arcadia Publishing
Charleston, South Carolina

Printed in the United States of America

Library of Congress Catalog Card Number: Applied for

For all general information contact Arcadia Publishing at:
Telephone 843-853-2070
Fax 843-853-0044
E-mail sales@arcadiapublishing.com
For customer service and orders:
Toll-Free 1-888-313-2665

Visit us on the Internet at www.arcadiapublishing.com

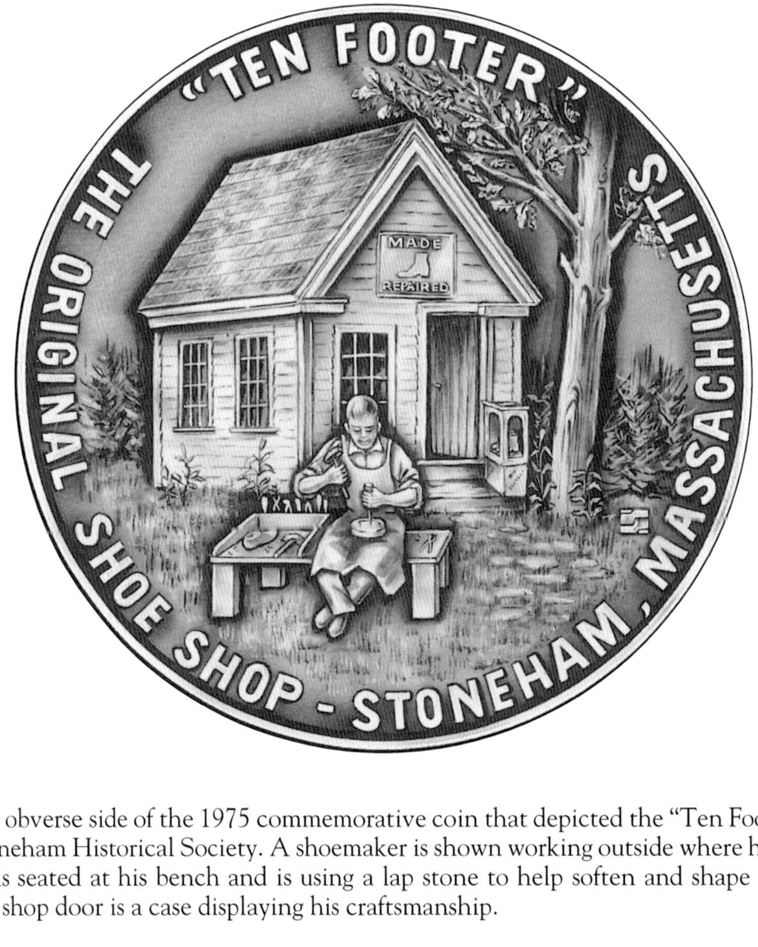

This is the obverse side of the 1975 commemorative coin that depicted the "Ten Footer" owned by the Stoneham Historical Society. A shoemaker is shown working outside where he has better light. He is seated at his bench and is using a lap stone to help soften and shape the leather. Beside his shop door is a case displaying his craftsmanship.

IMAGES
of America

STONEHAM

CONTENTS

ACKNOWLEDGMENTS

Books such as this are possible only because individuals and organizations are willing to share the images that they have preserved. Such individuals and organizations are the true authors, for without their images there could be no book. They selected the people and places to capture on film and preserve as examples of their age. This book is dedicated with gratitude to all those who helped create it. Individuals include the following: Ruth and John Angelosanto; Cameron Bain; Charlie Bamberg; Joe and Beverly Beane; Arthur Bennett; Kathy Bray; Helen, Norma, and Bob Lister; Bernice Lobdell; John Melkonian; Elaine Moore; Patricia Landry O'Neil; Ed Palmer; Ed Pearson; Paulene "Bee" Russo; Kay Sullivan; Beverly Mahn Surette; Ellen Swanson; Barbara Sweeney; Marilyn Worthen; Gail Wright; Linda Zibell; and Albert Zwicker. The organizations include the following: The Walker Transportation Collection at Beverly, Massachusetts Historical Society, Richard Symmes, curator; the Stoneham, Massachusetts Historical Society; the *Stoneham Independent*, Jason Fredette, former editor, and Bill Ryerson, photographer; Town of Stoneham, John J. Hanright, town clerk; Town of Stoneham, Selectmen's Office; and the Special Libraries of the University of Washington.

Introduction

The town of Stoneham is a residential suburban community lying less than 10 miles northwest of Boston. About one-third of the town's total area lies in the Middlesex Fells Reservation, including beautiful Spot Pond. Although early explorers of the region deemed it "an uncouth wilderness, full of timber," Charlestown laid claim to the area. It became known as Charlestown End, with the northwestern section being called Charlestown Farms. Most early settlers were farmers, with some arriving c. 1645. Growth was slow, since the area was remote and difficult to reach. It was not until 1725, when the taxable male population numbered 65, that a petition was presented to the General Court requesting that Stoneham be set off as a separate town due to its remoteness from Charlestown. This petition was granted on December 17, 1725, and Stoneham's first town meeting was held on December 24, 1725. A meetinghouse was established at the intersection of Summer and Pleasant Streets, where a school already existed. This became the first town center and remained as such for many years. A burial ground was established in 1726 on Pleasant Street, and many people, including slaves, were buried in unmarked graves. However, the headstones that remain intact portray the stylistic sequence of gravestone art for over a century.

Stoneham has never forgotten her duty to her country, and the military records of her citizens bear witness to this. After defending the Mother Country in the Colonial Wars, the residents of Stoneham united with their neighbors in opposition to the "Intolerable Acts" imposed on them by the British. A company of Minutemen was organized and drilled during the winter and early spring of 1775. They were ready to answer the call to Lexington and Concord and were thus engaged in the first battle of the Revolution. Interestingly, another Stoneham military company, exactly 86 years to the day after Lexington and Concord, participated in the first skirmish of the Civil War. While passing through Baltimore en route to Washington, the unit was taunted and attacked by a mob.

The building of the Medford to Andover Turnpike in 1806 caused the center of town to gradually shift westward to the present-day Main Street. The turnpike was Stoneham's first direct link to commercial trade. Large herds of cattle from northern New England were driven through town en route to slaughter houses in Boston. A large tavern for drovers with a fenced area for their animals existed near Elm and Central Streets. During the Federal Period (1775–1830) most residents still engaged in agriculture, though a large number also produced shoes in small shops. In the late 1830s central shops came into being and were often in conjunction with a general store.

In 1833 transportation improved greatly when a public stagecoach line from North Reading to Boston began to run through Stoneham along the turnpike. Gradually, the farmland adjacent to the turnpike was subdivided for homes built by shopkeepers, shoemakers, carpenters, and other craftsmen. In 1840 the Congregationalists erected their new building on Main Street, and the Universalists did the same at the northeast corner of Central and Common Street. Businesses such as the Stoneham 5¢ Savings Bank (1855) and John Hill's Factory (1858) were established on Main Street. The bank exists today, though at a different location, and the factory is now Love's Furniture.

The town was booming! The force of the Industrial Revolution was felt in Stoneham, as the home shoemaking industry was gradually absorbed by more than 40 shoe manufacturing plants. Shoe manufacturing and related industries such as tanneries and box factories became Stoneham's livelihood as reflected in the town seal. Stoneham's population increased nearly 600% between 1810 and 1860. Carpenters and craftsmen were in great demand to build dwelling places to house this population explosion. Among these houses were three built in the 1850s that followed the octagon fad.

In the town's earliest days, Spot Pond Brook was the overflow for Spot Pond, and the waters of this brook produced power for mills along its banks. Besides the usual gristmills and sawmills, many other industries were located here through the years, including snuff mills, a chocolate mill, a spice mill, a brass foundry, and, from c. 1858 to c. 1870, the Haywardville Rubber Works. Few traces of these early industries remain, and the area today is part of the Middlesex Fells Reservation.

The railroad reached Farm Hill in 1861 and was later extended with the opening of the Stoneham station at the corner of Pine and Franklin Streets in 1863. The railroad's tracks ran along a business route on the outskirts of downtown Stoneham. Beginning in 1910, passenger service to Boston was shared with the trolley that ran through the Fells. Increased automobile traffic had its impact, also, and railroad passenger service was discontinued in 1958.

In 1891 there were 27 boot and shoe manufacturers, each employing from 25 to 365 people. Almost all dealt in women's and children's shoes. However, by 1925 only 3 large shoe factories remained. As the shoe industry declined, the town's largest employer became the E.L Patch Company, a pharmaceutical firm established in 1888 and located on Montvale Avenue. A promising industry at the beginning of the 20th century was the manufacture of automobiles. Had a 1908 fire not destroyed the factory and plans, Stoneham might have become the "Detroit of the East." Although the town's actual nickname of "The Friendly Town" began in the 1930s, Stoneham might well be called an "Olympic Town," having produced not only shoes but a number of Olympic team members from 1932 to 1994.

In recent years, Stoneham has experienced rapid growth as a suburban community. This is attributable to a great extent to the town's excellent schools, fine local government services, and convenient location. Stoneham approaches the millennium with high hopes for continued growth and prosperity.

One

In the Beginning

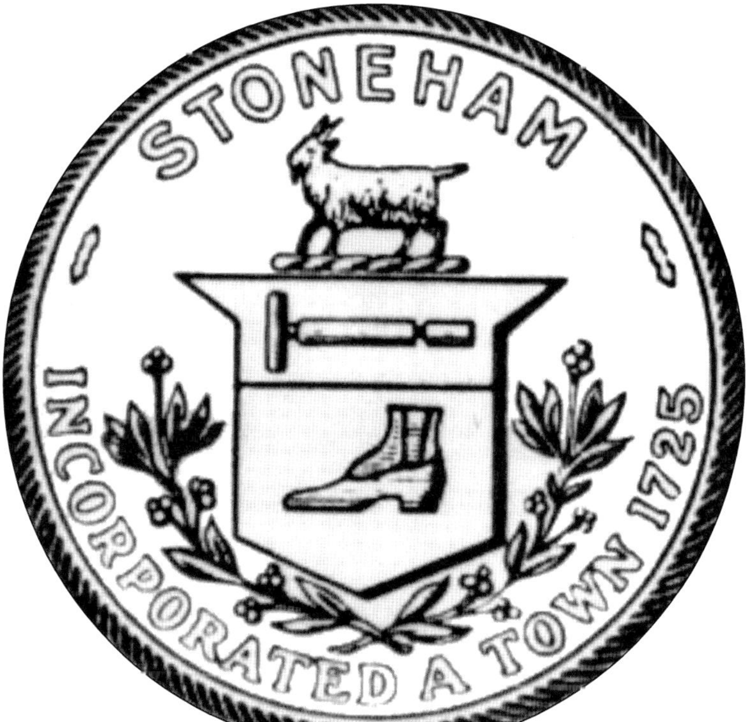

Stoneham's town seal reflects what for many years was the chief industry in Stoneham. The goat represents the tanning of hides, and the pegging hammer was used in making a shoe, the finished product. The seal also includes the year 1725, the date when Stoneham separated from Charlestown and became its own town. The plants or berries perhaps represent sumac, oak, hemlock, or mimosa, which were used in the tanning process.

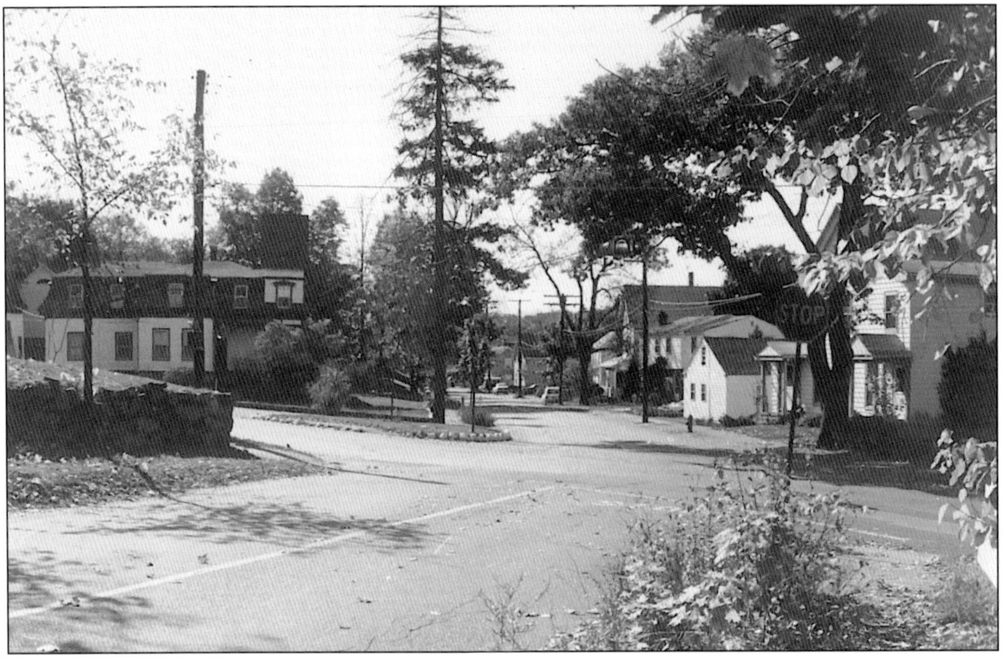

The original town center was near the junction of present-day Pleasant and Summer Streets. A school was erected at this site *c.* 1718, and here the town's first town meeting was held on December 24, 1725. The following year a meetinghouse (36 feet by 40 feet) was built nearby and is said to have been framed by Timothy Wright. Both church and town meetings were held in this building until 1803.

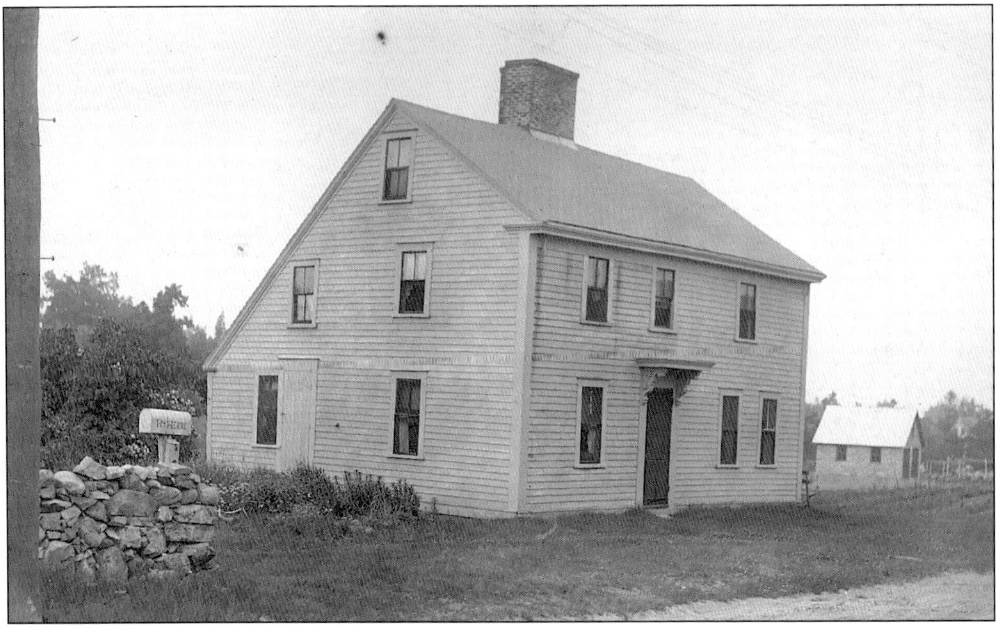

One of Stoneham's earliest houses is located on Green Street. Originally built for Thomas Millard, by 1725–26 it was the home of John Souther and meetings were held here to plan for building the first meetinghouse. For over 100 years the house was owned by the Green family. The early-18th-century form of this home is nearly intact.

The Old Burial Ground on Pleasant Street was established in 1726. The stone shown is that of Elder Daniel Green who died in 1759 in "ye 79th year of his age." Elder Green was a signer of the compact when Stoneham was organized in 1725. Over 300 headstones remain intact in this cemetery. In addition, many people, including slaves, were buried in unmarked graves.

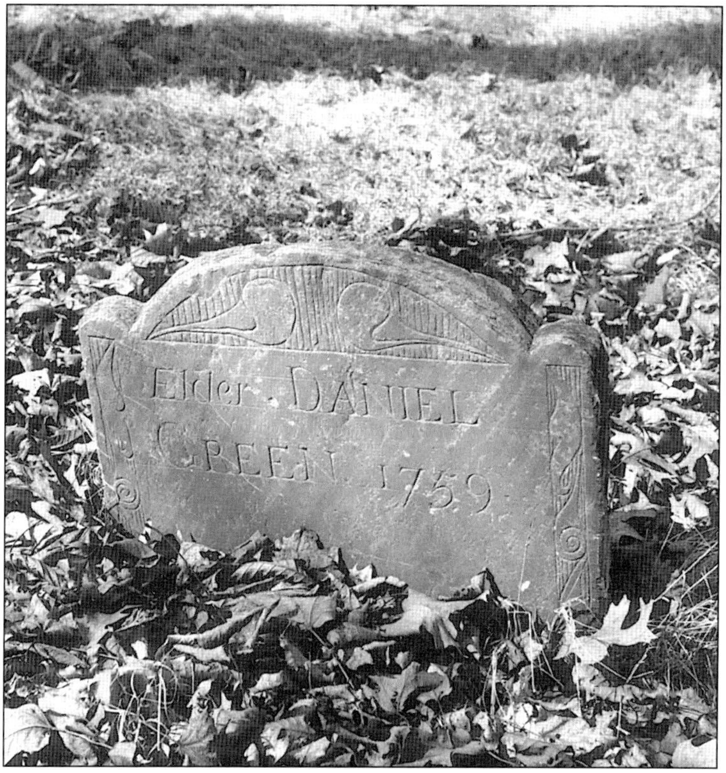

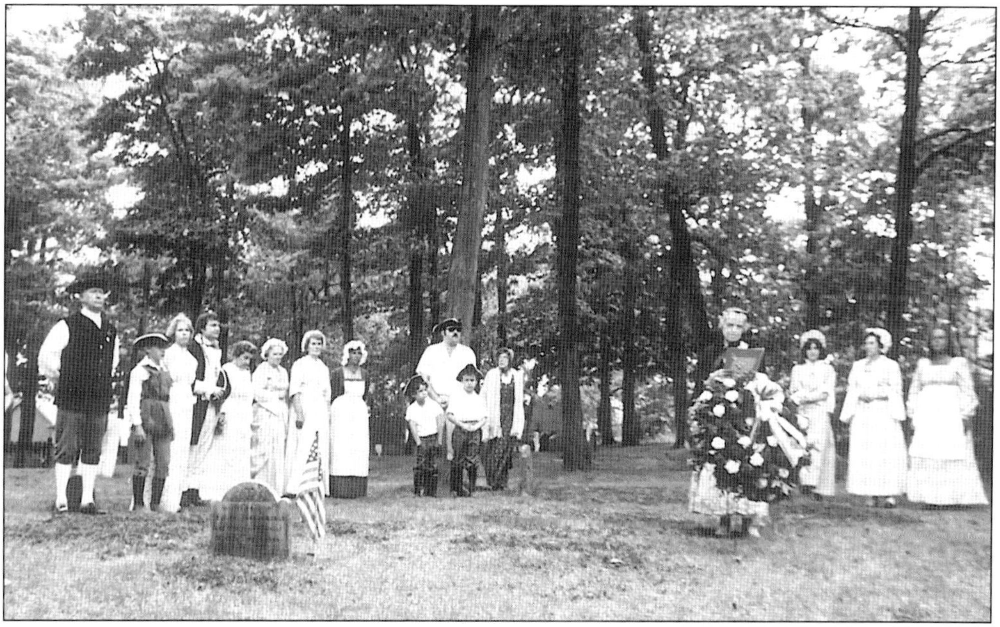

In celebrating Stoneham's 250th birthday in 1975, time was taken to commemorate those interred in the Old Burial Ground. The earliest marker is that of Lt. Timothy Wright, who died in 1728, and the most recent is that of Sarah Lynde, who died in 1924. Here lie veterans of the Colonial Wars, the Revolution, the War of 1812, and the Civil War, including a Civil War nurse.

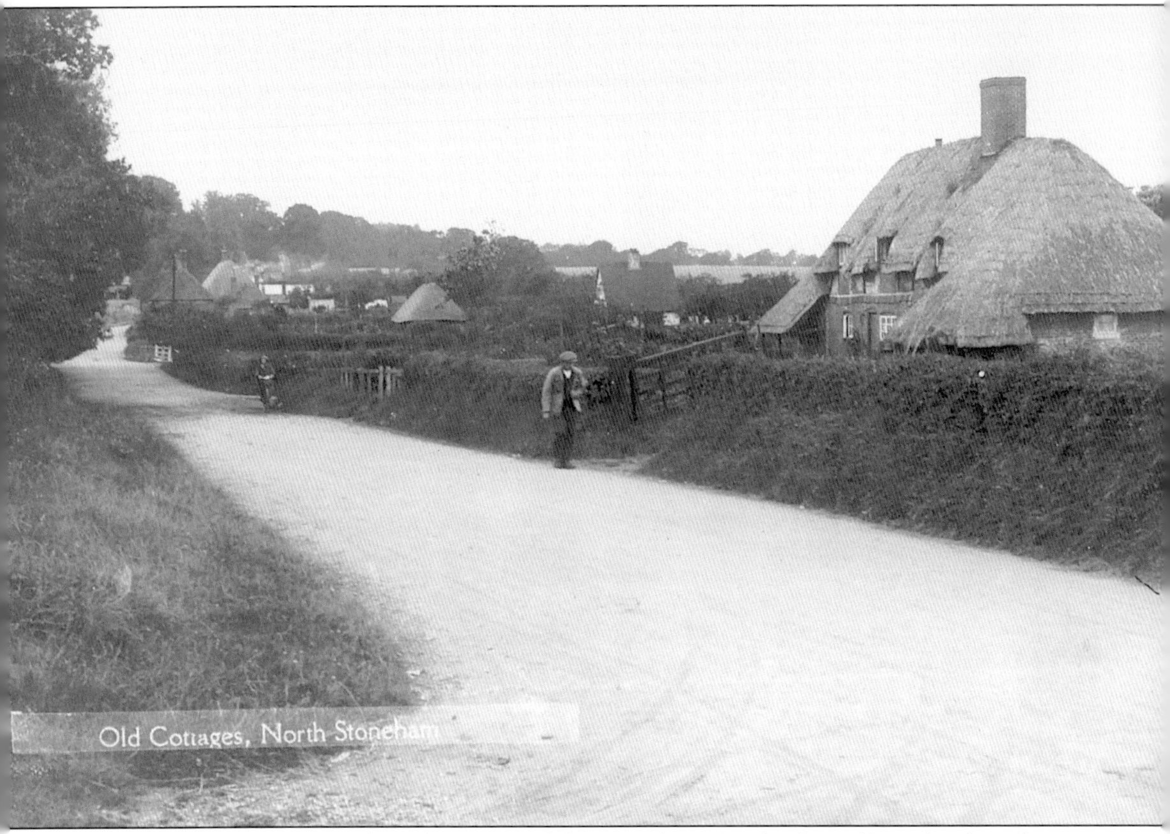

Stoneham is thought to have been named for Stoneham, England, a village that lies along an old Roman road about 5 miles north of Southampton. It is in one of the oldest inhabited parts of England and is believed to have been the ancestral home of Timothy Baldwin, Stoneham's first town clerk. Chestnut Avenue, a main thoroughfare of Stoneham, England, is shown in this 1930s view. This part of England was famous for its stones, which were used in buildings. In earlier years, Stoneham, England, was an important place and consisted of North Stoneham and South Stoneham. However, nearby Eastleigh developed as a railroad center, and in 1936, Stoneham, England, became a ward of Eastleigh.

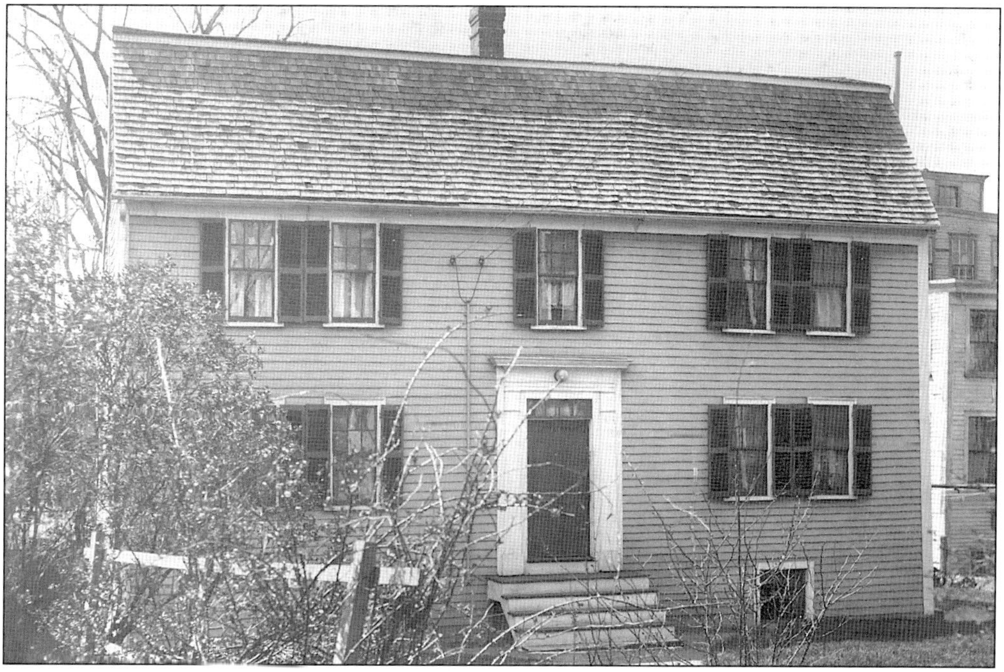

The church did not build a parsonage until 1747. It was located on the west side of present-day Central Street, and the first occupant was the second minister, Rev. John Carnes. In later years, this parsonage was purchased by Rev. John H. Stevens, who lived there while he served the local church from 1795 to 1827. The owner in 1889 moved the building to a back lot where it stood until it was razed c. 1958.

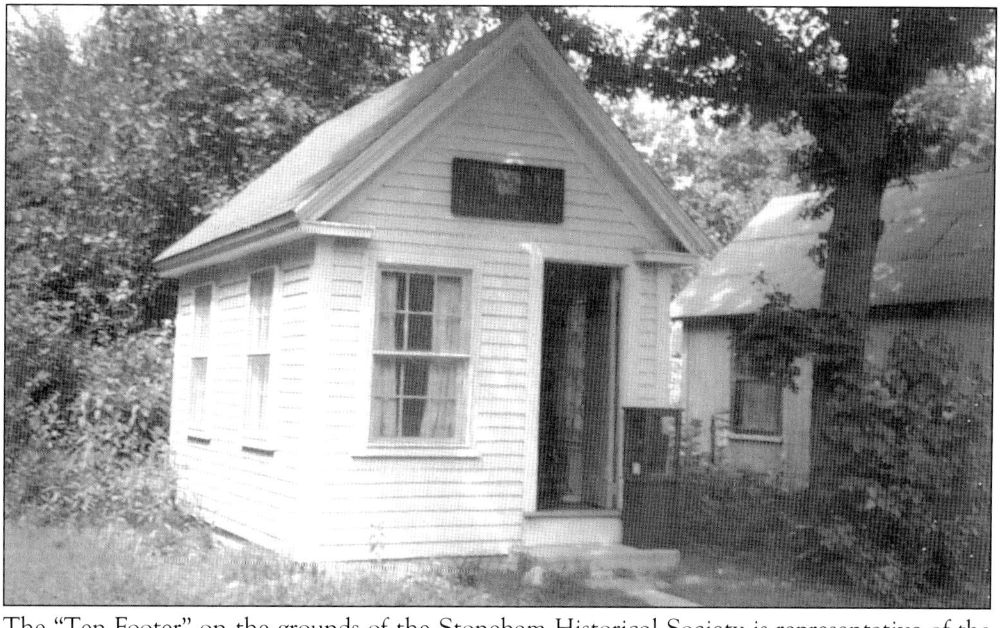

The "Ten Footer" on the grounds of the Stoneham Historical Society is representative of the early shops used by independent shoemakers in the late 18th to mid-19th century. It contains tools typical of the trade such as lasts, pegs, a lap stone, and awls, and the society has maintained the structure as a museum since May 1968.

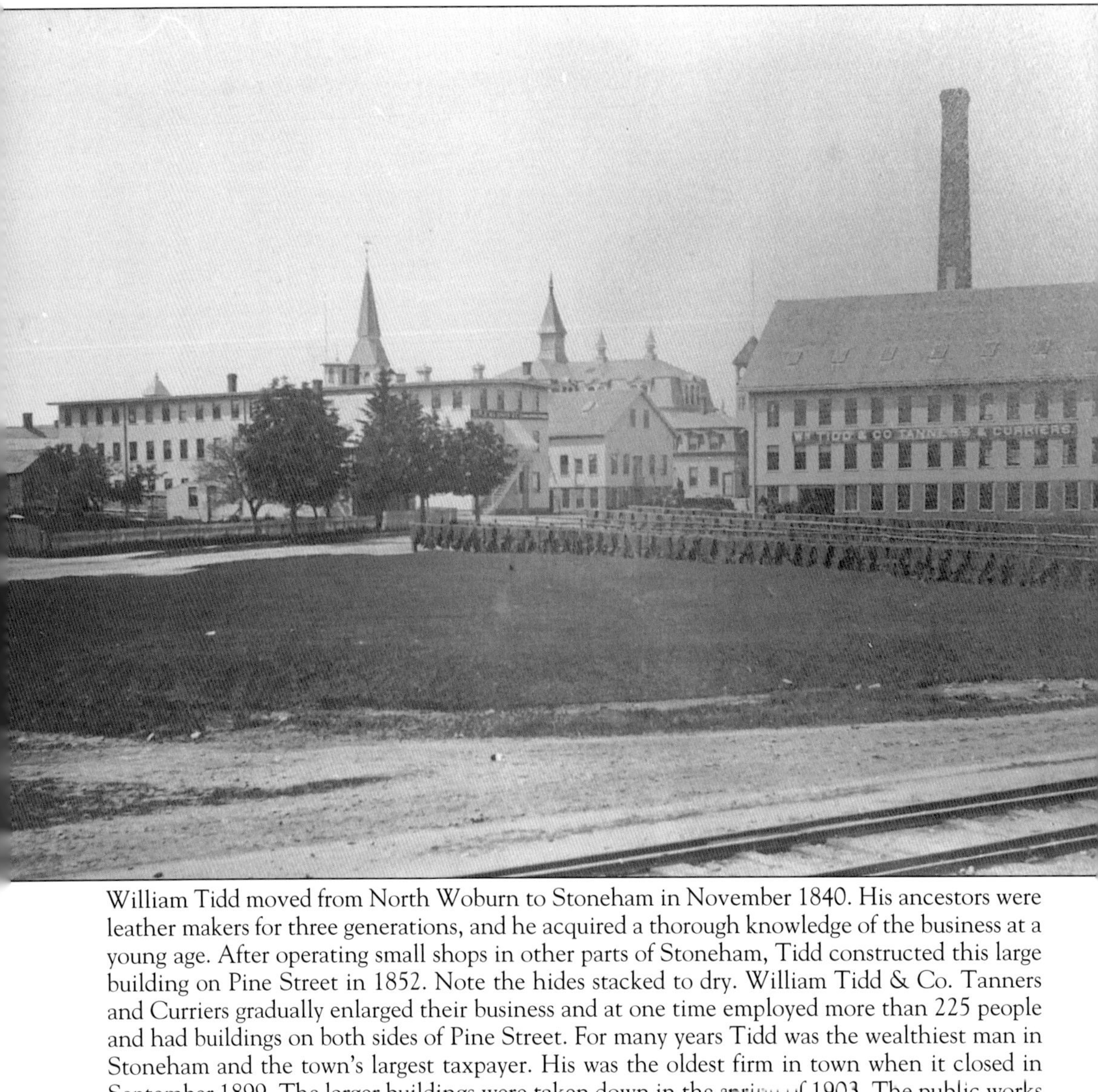

William Tidd moved from North Woburn to Stoneham in November 1840. His ancestors were leather makers for three generations, and he acquired a thorough knowledge of the business at a young age. After operating small shops in other parts of Stoneham, Tidd constructed this large building on Pine Street in 1852. Note the hides stacked to dry. William Tidd & Co. Tanners and Curriers gradually enlarged their business and at one time employed more than 225 people and had buildings on both sides of Pine Street. For many years Tidd was the wealthiest man in Stoneham and the town's largest taxpayer. His was the oldest firm in town when it closed in September 1899. The larger buildings were taken down in the spring of 1903. The public works department buildings currently occupy this site.

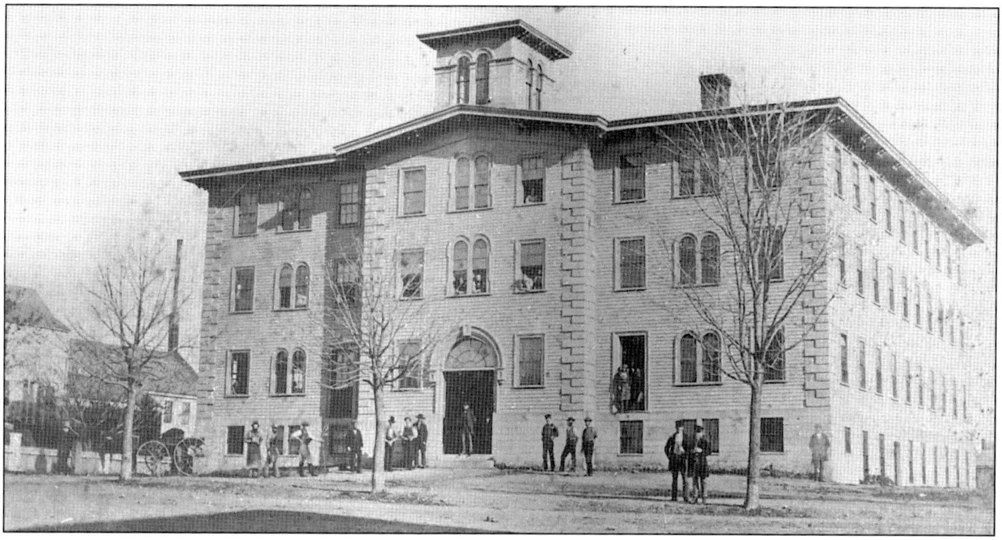

The John Hill Shoe Factory, built in 1858, was one of the first in the country to make an entire shoe in one building. The original building was four stories, but later was extended to the sidewalk and a fifth floor was added. Other manufacturers who operated in this building include A.E. Mann (1895–1902), Stone and Forsythe (1902–1912), Grover's (1912–1938), and Marilyn Sandal (1938–1967). Since October 1969, Love's Furniture Store has occupied this site.

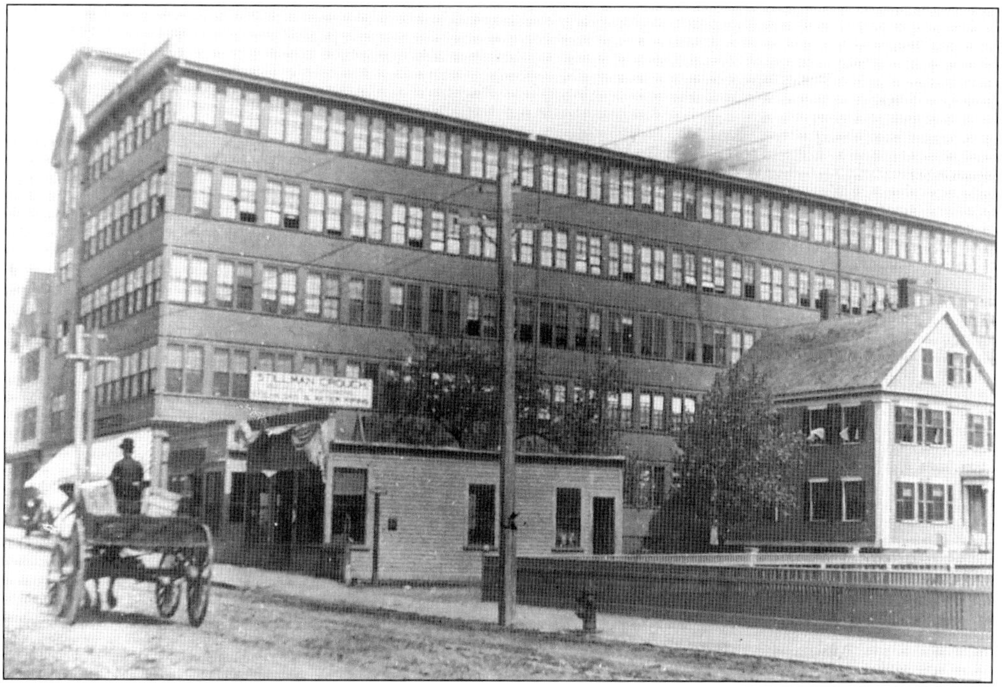

The T.H. Jones Shoe Factory, built on Franklin Street in 1890, was the last and largest shoe factory to be built in Stoneham. It was 175 feet long and 50 feet wide. Five floors and a cellar could house up to 500 workers. Six hundred windows in continuous bands provided light and ventilation. The building was razed in August 1939. In 1946, a garage was built there, but it was demolished to create a parking lot in 1999.

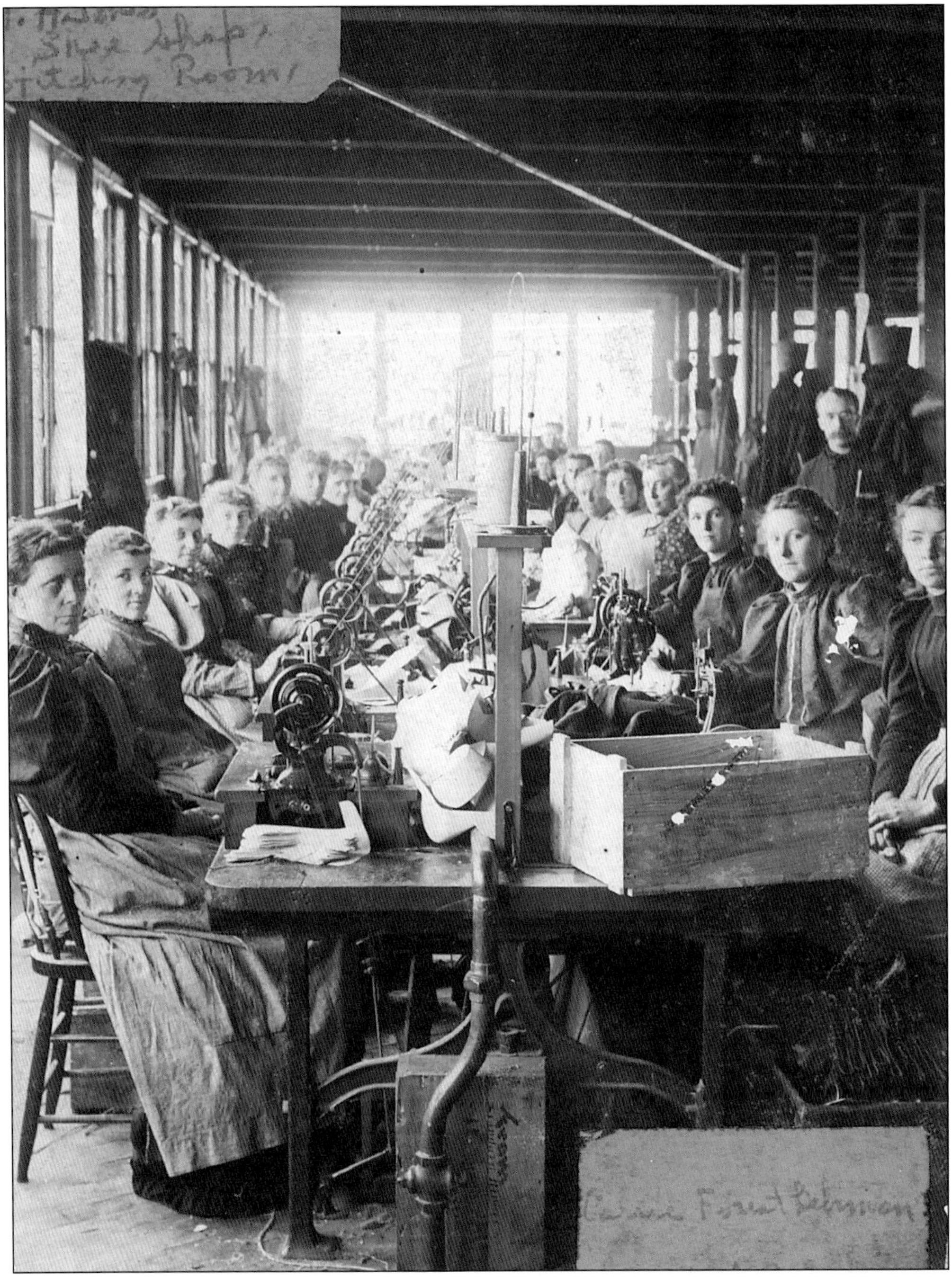

The task of sewing, or "binding," uppers was for many years done by women at home in their "free" time. Within a few years of the invention of the sewing machine, stitching machines appeared that could sew leather. These were introduced into factories *c.* 1858 and brought women into central shops. These machines were at first run by a foot pedal, but later mechanized. The women pictured are working in the T.H. Jones Factory. Women usually worked six days per week from 7 a.m. to 6 p.m. with one hour for lunch, and their typical daily pay was one dollar (about half that of a man).

Two

Round the Community

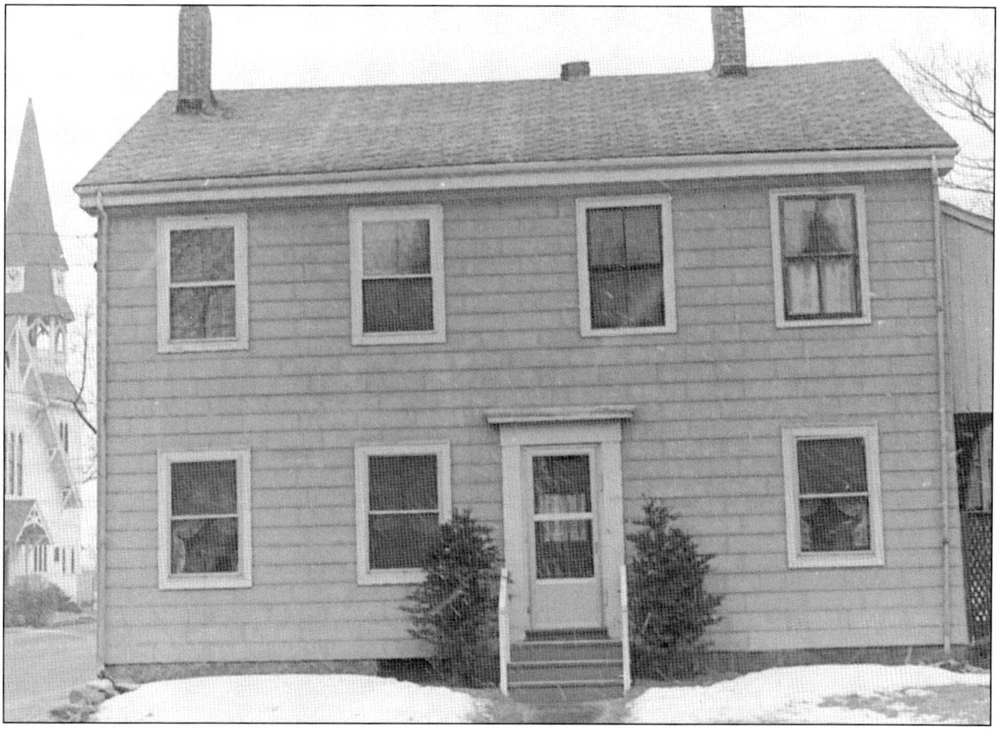

This home at the corner of Pleasant and Central Streets was built as Stoneham's first town hall in 1826. Classes were held on the first floor, and meetings on the second. Used only until 1847, this building has a colorful history. In March 1833 it was moved across Gould Meadow nearer the Medford to Andover Turnpike. Anti-slavery meetings held here became violent, concluding with the homicide of Timothy Wheeler in March 1837. Thereafter, no further meetings of that type were permitted.

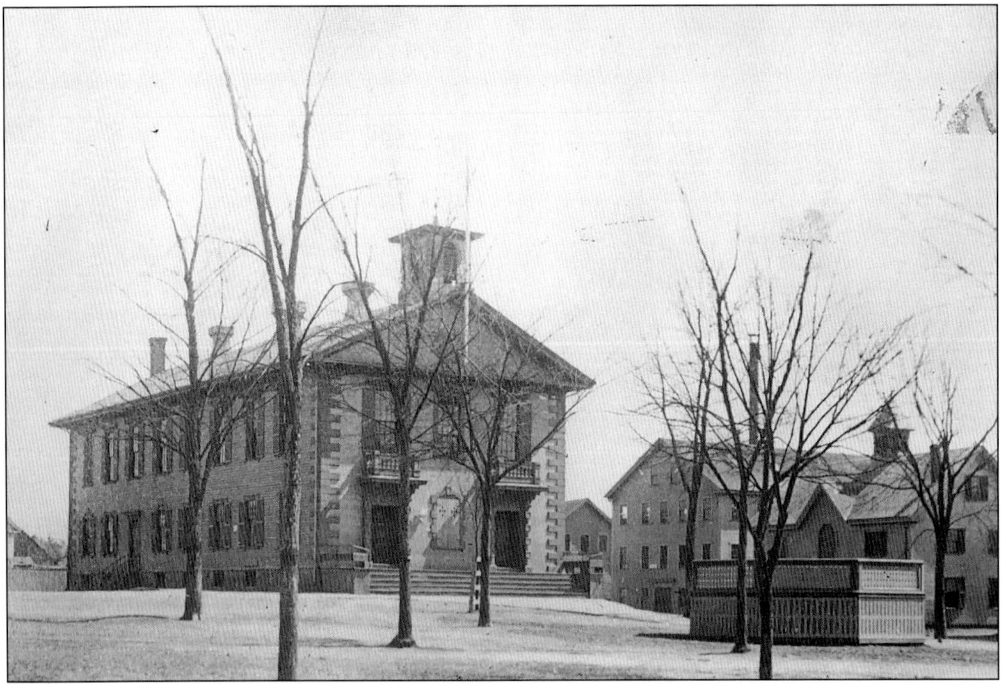

Stoneham's second town hall was built in 1847. High school classes were held on the first floor until a separate school building was constructed in 1871. From 1871 to 1929, the town hall housed elementary classrooms and was known as Center School. During some years the basement served as the town lockup, and fire equipment was also stored there. This town hall was demolished in 1934.

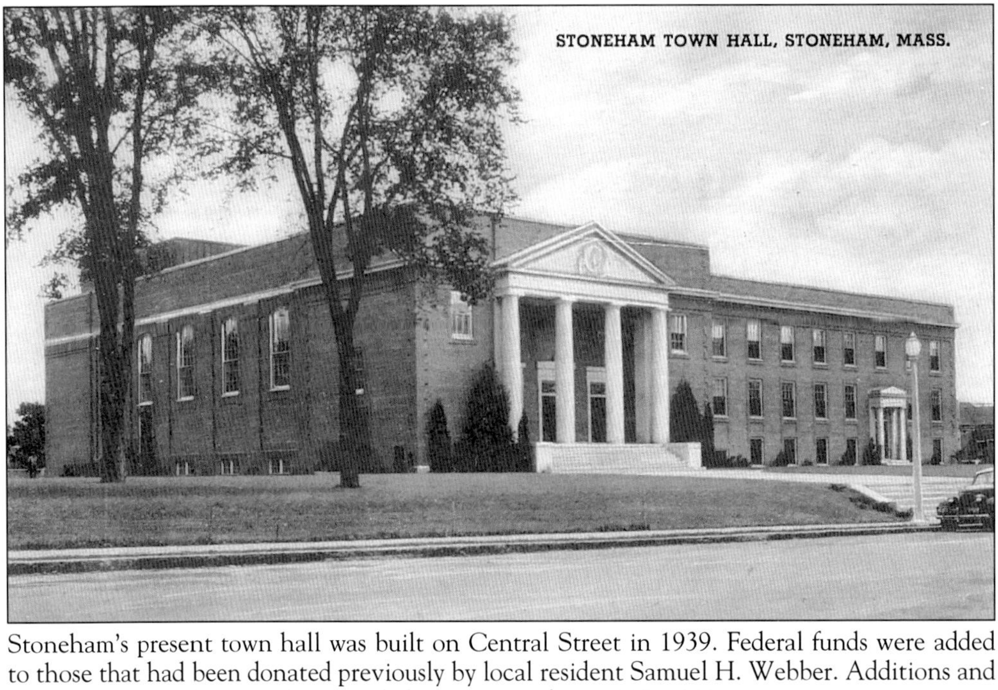

Stoneham's present town hall was built on Central Street in 1939. Federal funds were added to those that had been donated previously by local resident Samuel H. Webber. Additions and renovations have been made as needed, most recently in 1987–1989.

As a result of the June 30, 1938 town meeting decision to build a new town hall, the meeting's moderator appointed a building committee composed of the following, from left to right: (front row) Robert A. Newcomb, Chairman William D. Desmond, and George E. MacNeil Jr.; (back row) Everett C. Hunt, Secretary Charles A. Owen, and Percival H. Wardwell.

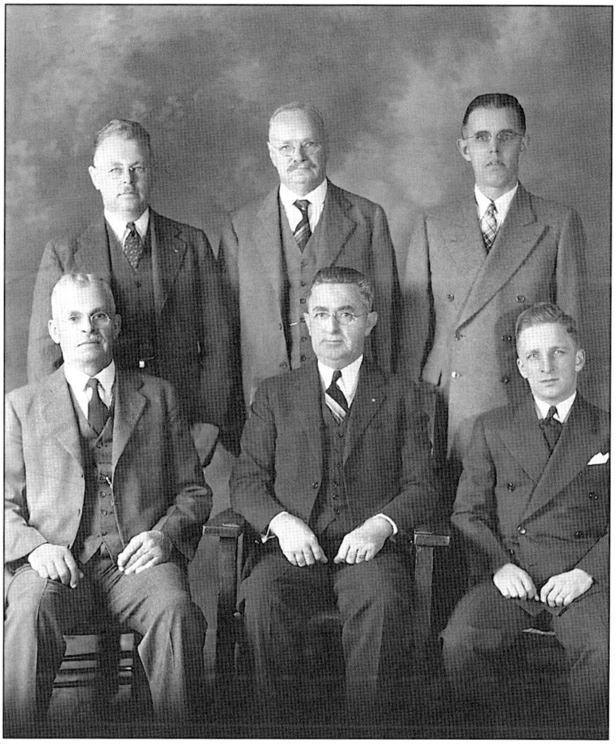

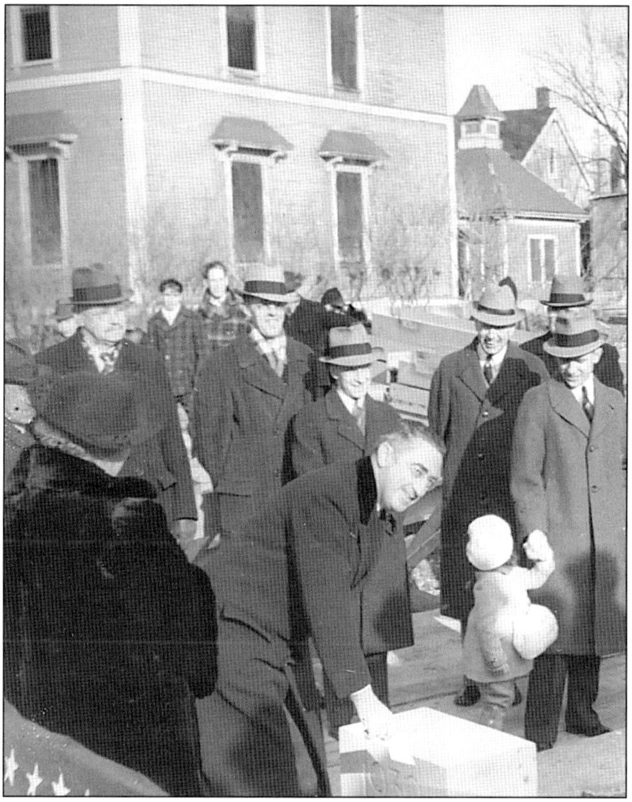

William D. Desmond, the chairman of the building committee, laid the cornerstone for the town hall on January 28, 1939. Some items placed in the cornerstone included a map, a copy of Steven's *History of Stoneham*, programs relative to the 1925 celebration, the town's by-laws, and pictures of town buildings, churches, and local scenes.

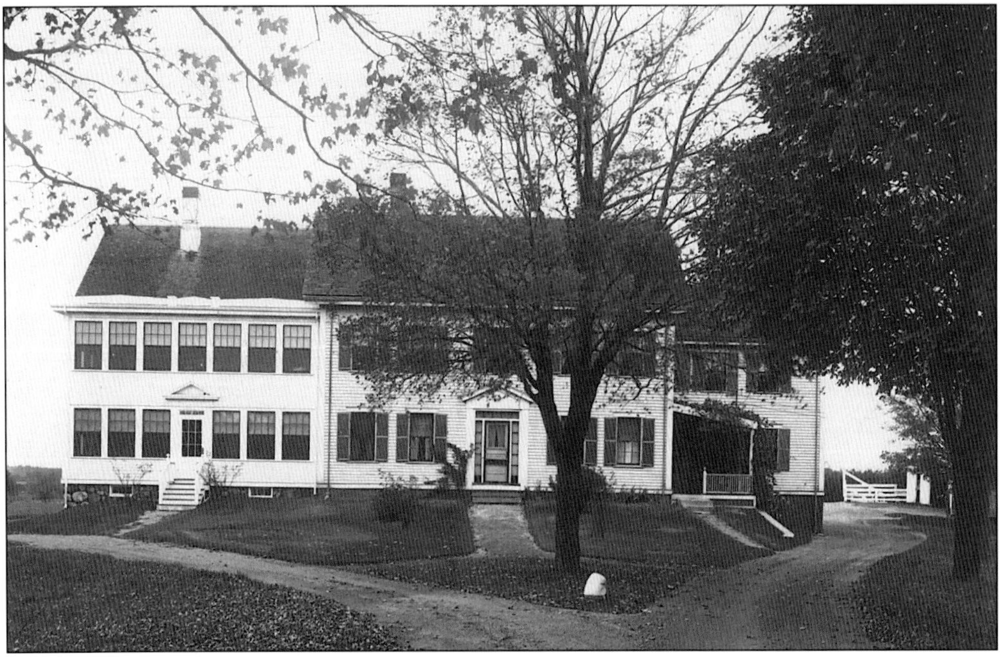

In 1852, an almshouse was built on Elm Street. It operated until July 1, 1968, with various name changes reflecting how people viewed those in need. Shortly thereafter it became a Senior Center. With extensive renovations it is today a welcome home away from home and provides many activities and services for older residents.

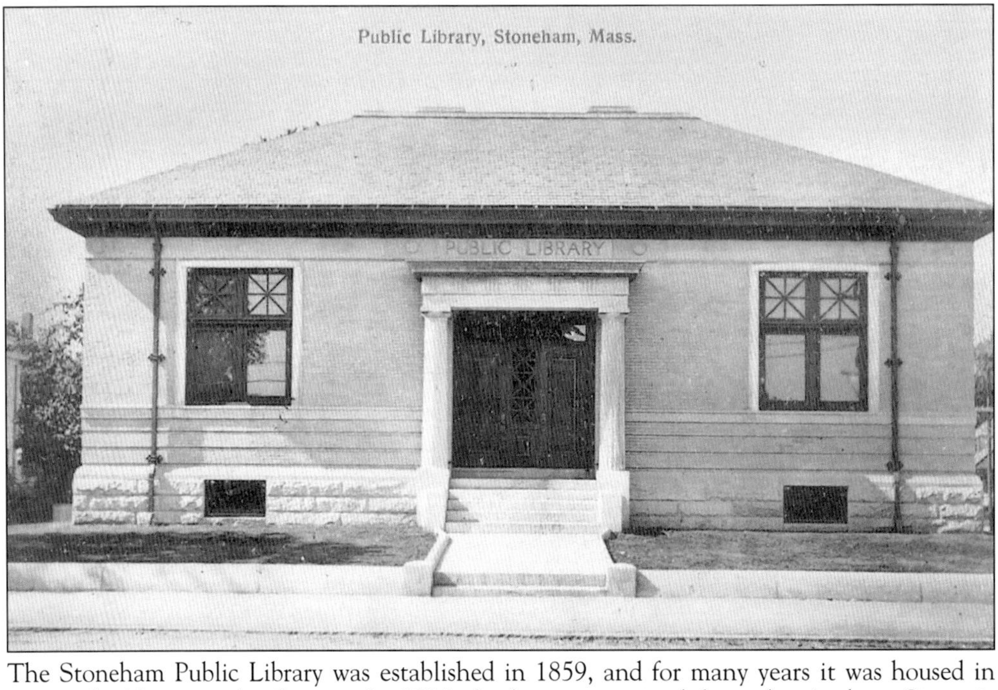

The Stoneham Public Library was established in 1859, and for many years it was housed in various buildings in the Square. In 1904, funds were received from the Andrew Carnegie Foundation to construct the original portion of today's building. Significant additions were made in 1931 and 1983. Those in 1931 were from the bequest of Miss Annie H. Brown.

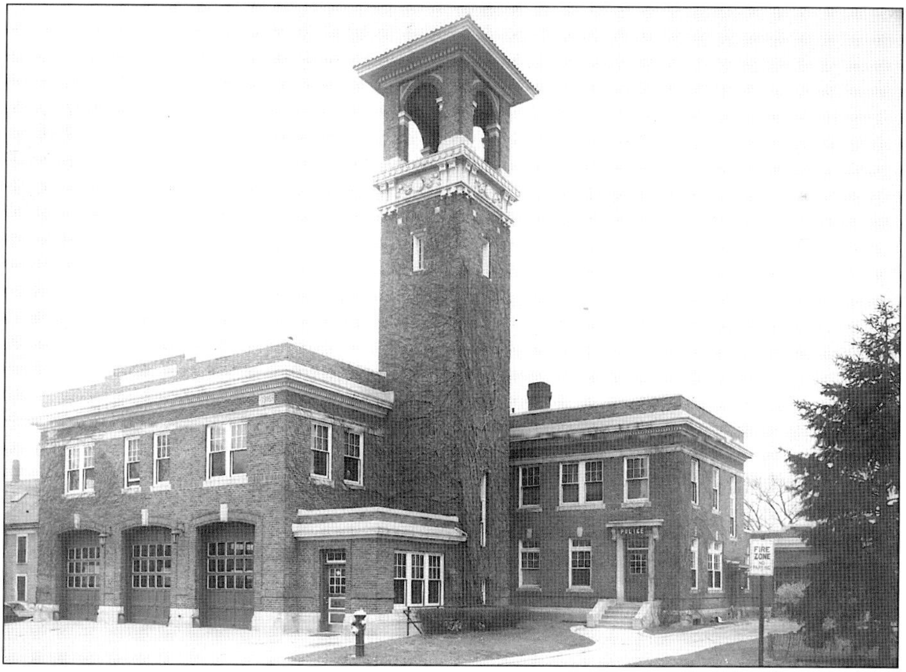

Construction of a combined fire and police station was begun in 1916, and the building was occupied in February of the following year. The total cost was just over $50,000, of which $7,000 was for the land. Ironically, the location chosen had been the site of a major fire on July 5, 1903. The fire department portion had a stable for its horses, which were still in use. Currently the building is occupied solely by the fire department and has recently been renovated to meet today's needs.

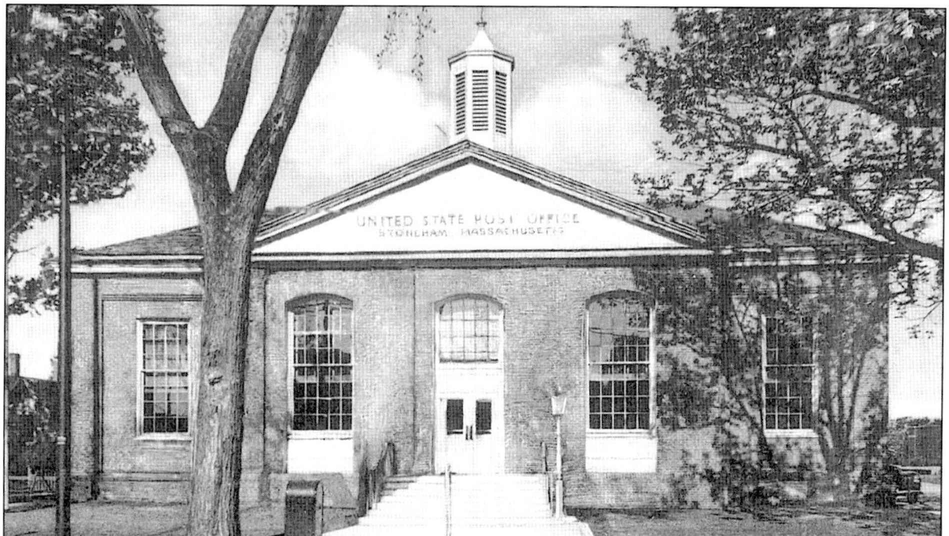

Stoneham's first postmaster was appointed in 1832, and for over 100 years, the post office was located in various stores in the Square. A separate building was not erected for the post office until 1941. The site chosen was that of the former Arad Gerry Mansion. The post office was extensively remodeled in 1997–1998.

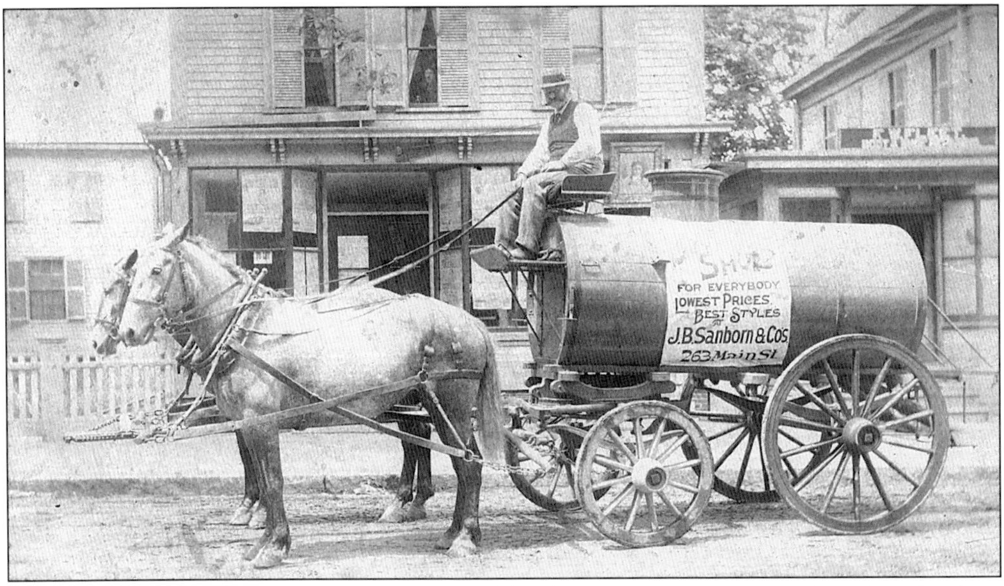

Before paving, streets were watered by a sprinkler during the summer months to lay the dust. Driver Jim Forrest's tank carries advertising for J.B. Sanborn and Co. In the background can be seen the shop of F.W. Fleet, a boot and shoemaker and repairer.

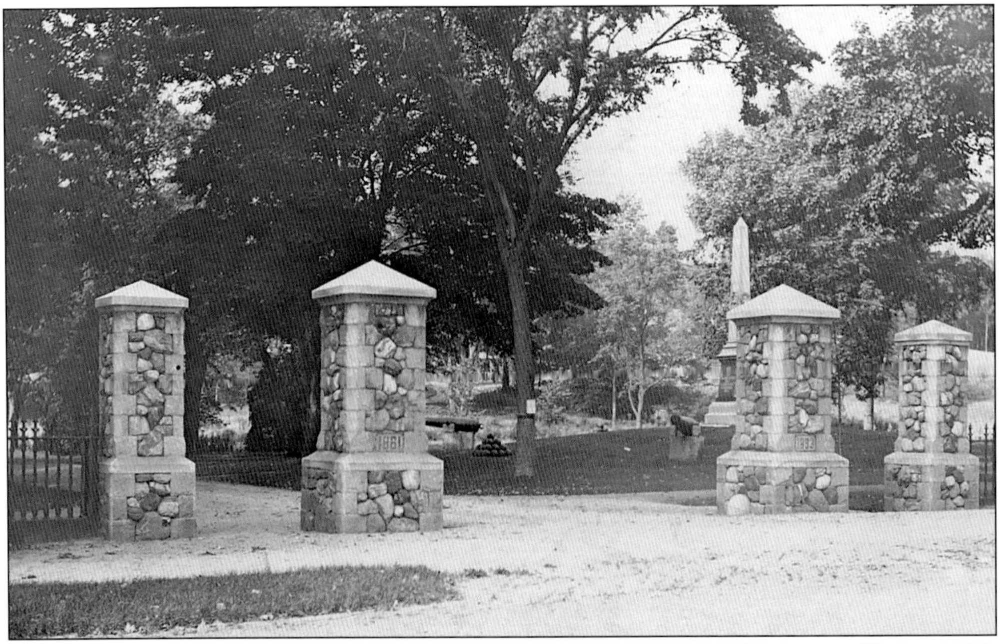

Lindenwood Cemetery was consecrated in May 1861, and the stone pillars were added in 1893. At the right of the entrance is the Soldiers' Monument, which was originally dedicated in 1869 and upgraded during 1898 and 1899. Many soldiers who have died in recent years have been buried at this spot.

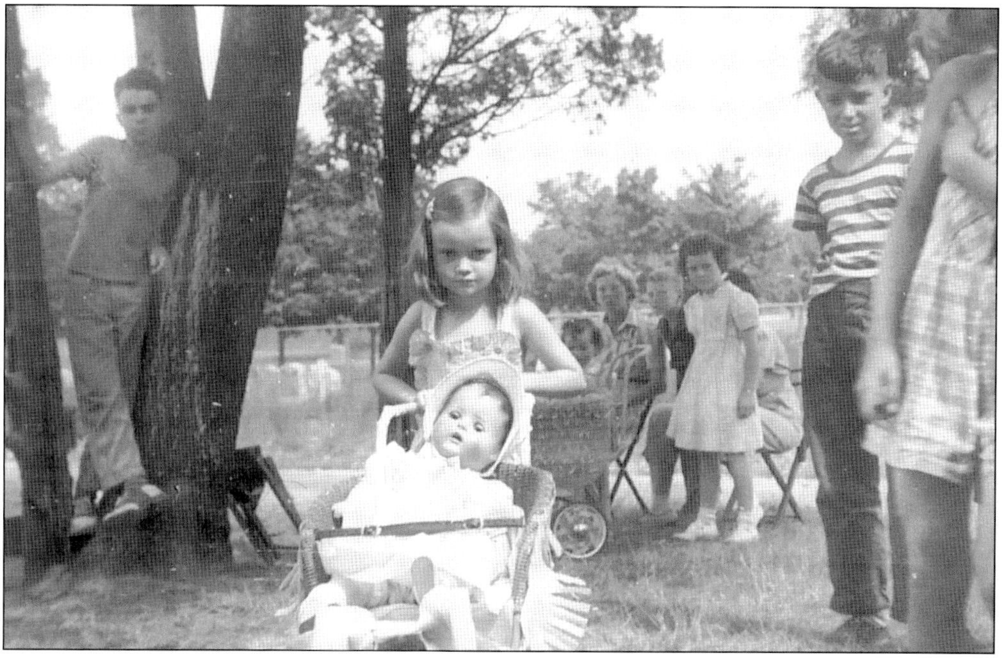

The A.P. Rounds Playground at the corner of Broadway and MacArthur Road was created on land donated to the town in 1929 by Albert P. Rounds, a local contractor and builder of "Land on Heights" Development. A field day closed each season's playground activities, and Dianne Burnham poses proudly after winning first prize for the "Best Dressed Doll" at the September 2, 1942 event.

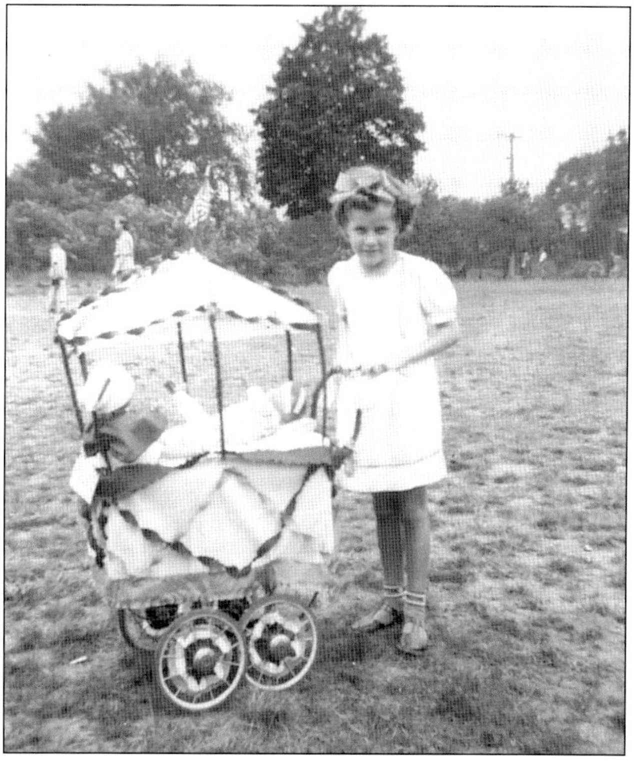

Another first prize winner at the 1942 field day at A.P. Rounds Playground was a Red Cross Ambulance, reflecting Stoneham's active participation in the war effort. Dorothy Cartwright is proud of her entry. Similar events were held at all the neighborhood parks and playgrounds in Stoneham. Mr. Rounds was interested in all of them, serving many years as a park commissioner.

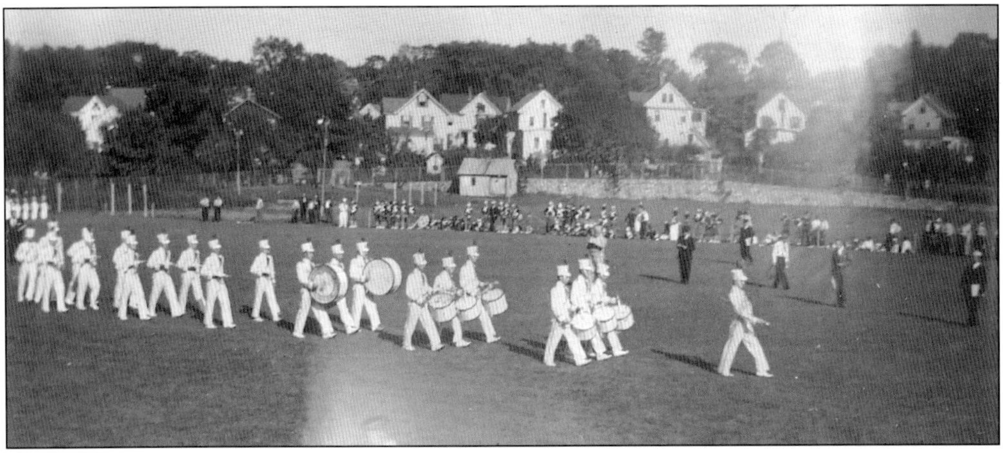

The transformation from Gould Meadow to Recreation Park began in 1925 and culminated in 1940. After the land was purchased, swampy areas were filled in and drainage problems were corrected. Much of the work was accomplished with funds supplied by the Federal Works Progress Administration. The park was formally dedicated on September 28, 1940, but World War II put future plans on hold. "Rec" Park continues to serve as one of Stoneham's prime recreation spaces.

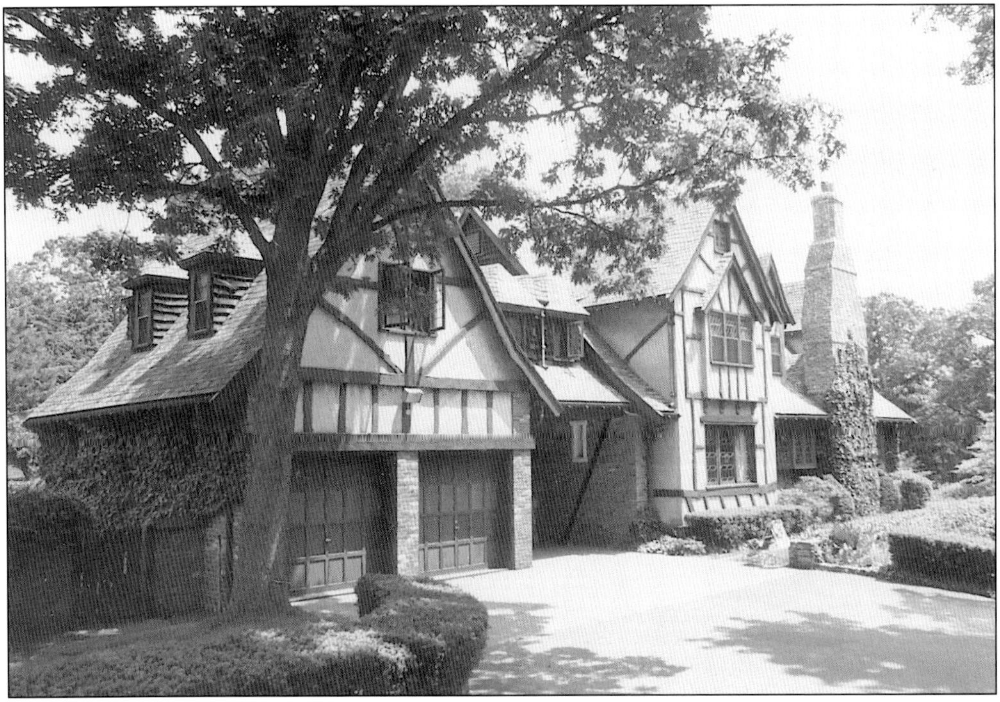

Whip Hill Park contains 30 acres of conservation area and this gracious English Tudor manor. The park was donated to the town of Stoneham by Mrs. Angie Crockett and is supervised by the Conservation Commission. Residents enjoy the area's trails, rhododendrons, azaleas, and frog pond.

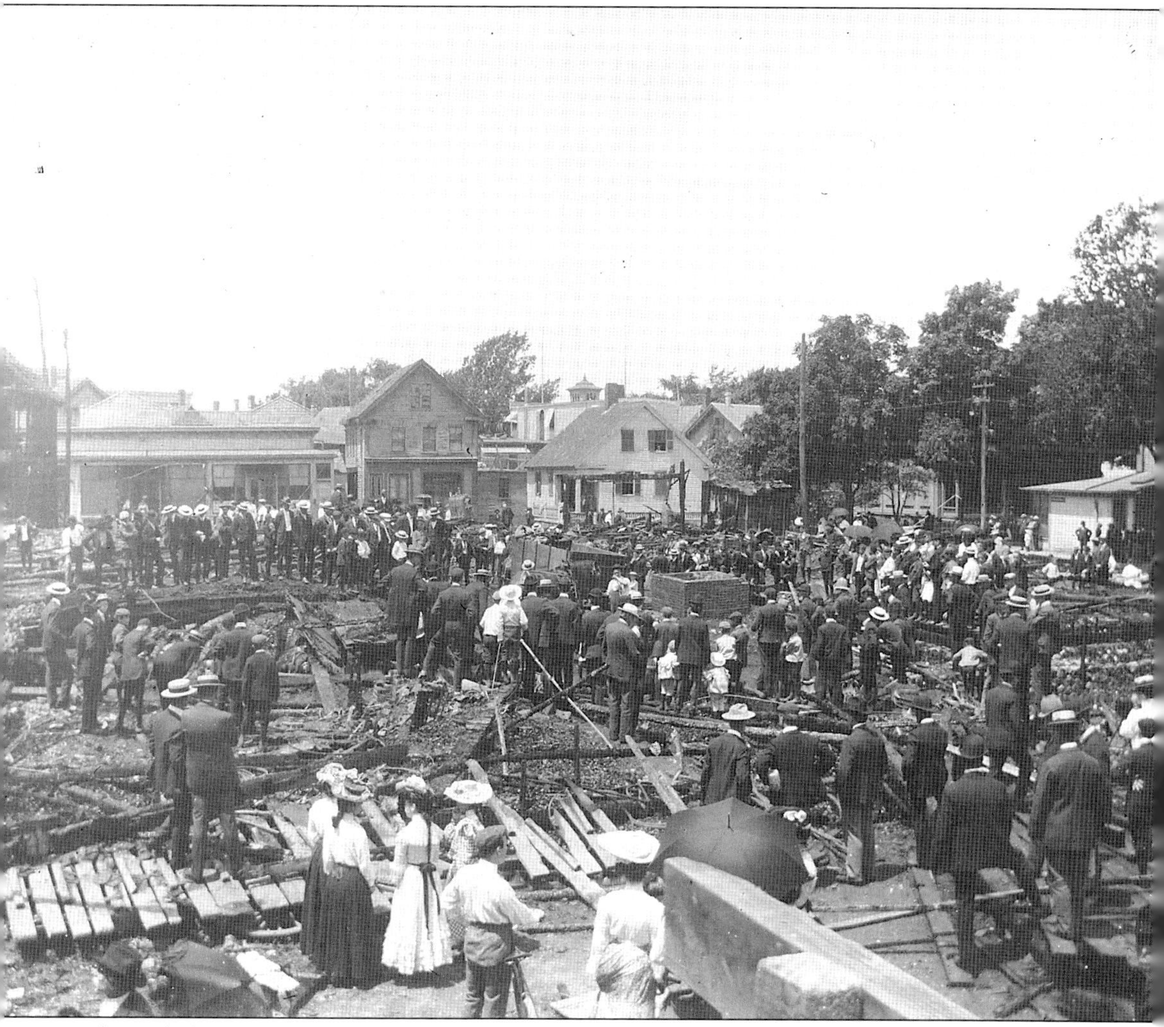

In the early hours of July 5, 1903, a fire originated in the Litch and Hayward Stable on Block Street. It also endangered Central, Fuller, and Emerson Streets as well as the entire Central Square area. Firemen concentrated on saving the T.H. Jones Factory on Franklin Street, the largest industrial establishment in town, since the back of this building was in danger. Successful in their fight, the firemen were able to save the jobs of 600 people, but 14 buildings, mostly small wooden structures, were lost. Eight horses perished in the stable, and many firemen had their hands badly burned. The date of the fire strongly suggests that fireworks may have been the cause.

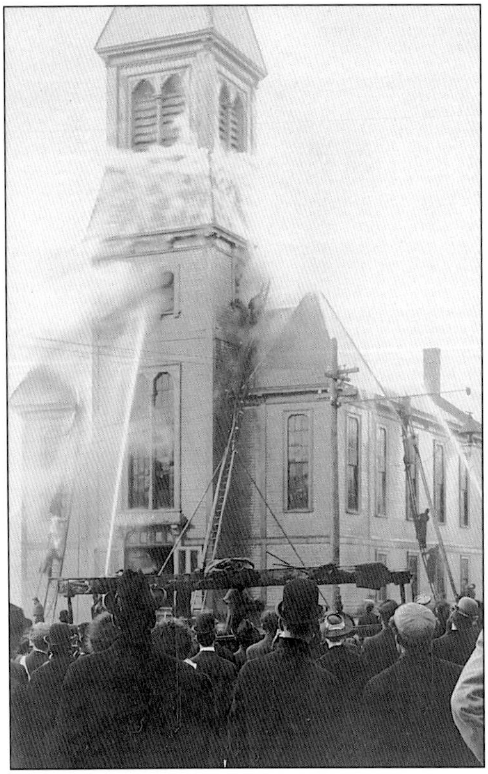

A fire in the original St. James Methodist Church on Common Street happened on March 24, 1909, and was considered of suspicious origin as it started in two spots and there had recently been church fires in Reading and Wakefield. The fire was confined to the tower, but much water damage was done to the lower level.

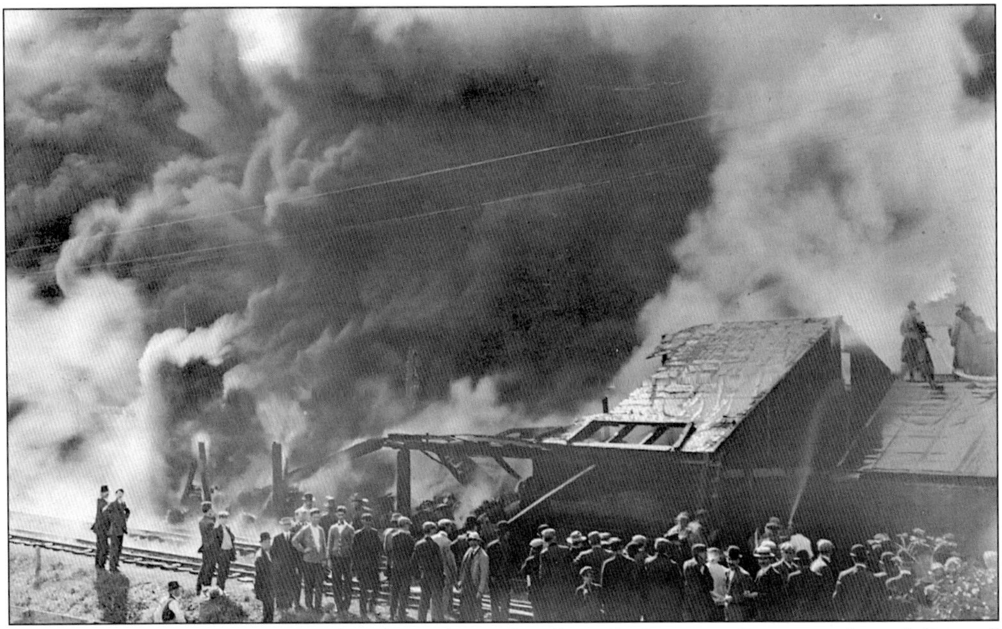

A very dangerous fire was fought along the railroad tracks between Pomeworth and Central Streets on September 22, 1910. The blaze began in a coal elevator used to store barrels of resin in a crude state, a substance used by Vera Chemical Co. in manufacturing paper sizing. A spark from a passing locomotive is believed to have started the blaze, which burned fiercely and gave off dense smoke. The site was more recently known as the George Mann Company.

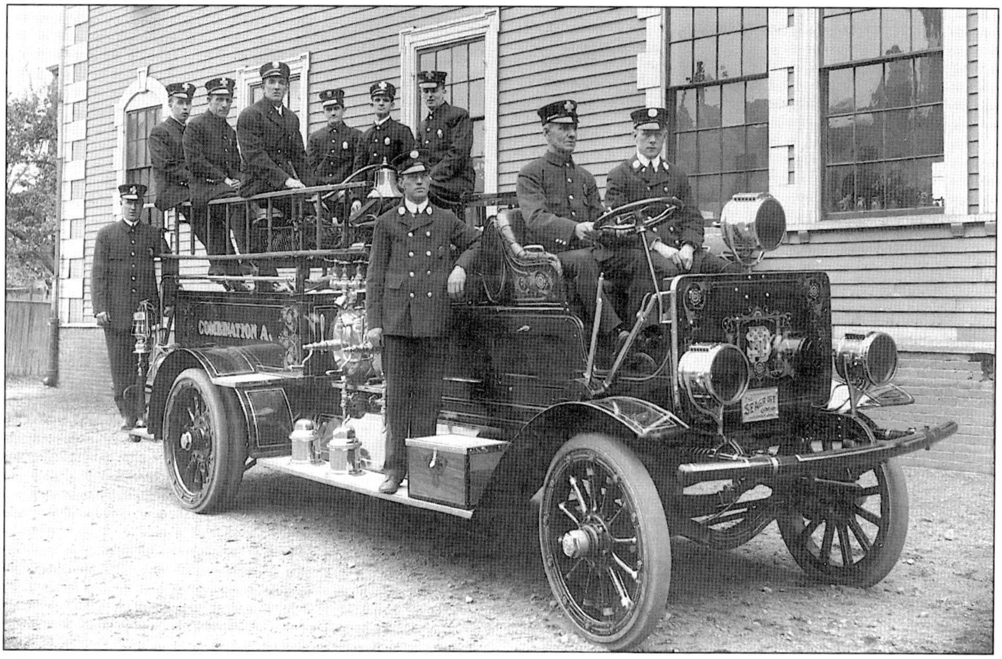

The first piece of motorized equipment owned by the Stoneham Fire Department was Combination A, a hose and chemical wagon. It was purchased in 1912 at a cost of $5,775 and was used in response to the great Salem fire on June 25, 1914. The men pictured, from left to right, are Harry Potter, William J. Plummer, Frank A. McDonald, John E. Finnegan, George E. Potter, Frank Flowers, Herbert E. Plummer, Lt. Louis M. Willett (on running board), driver Stillman Crouch, and Capt. William A. Brooks.

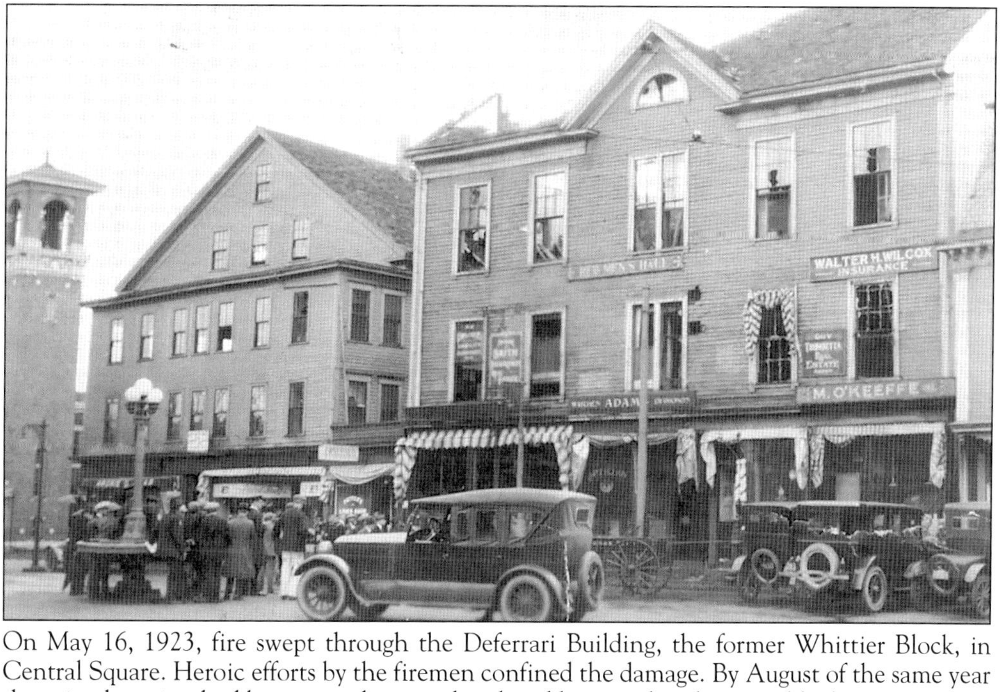

On May 16, 1923, fire swept through the Deferrari Building, the former Whittier Block, in Central Square. Heroic efforts by the firemen confined the damage. By August of the same year the ruined portion had been torn down and replaced by a modern business block.

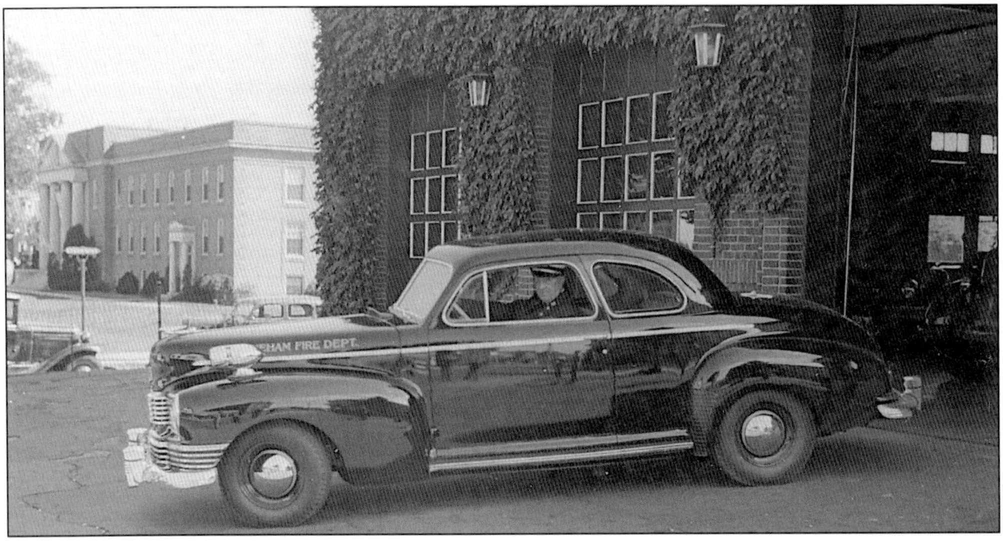

Chief William F. McCall poses proudly in his new chief's car. McCall was a call fireman from 1914 to 1924 and served as a permanent member of the Stoneham Fire Department from 1925 to 1948. He was appointed chief in 1927 and served until his retirement in 1948. There were several large fires on McCall's watch, including blazes at Wills' Block (1933) and the Bell Block (1940). In addition, the 1938 hurricane created many problems with the fire alarm system, requiring several months for necessary repairs.

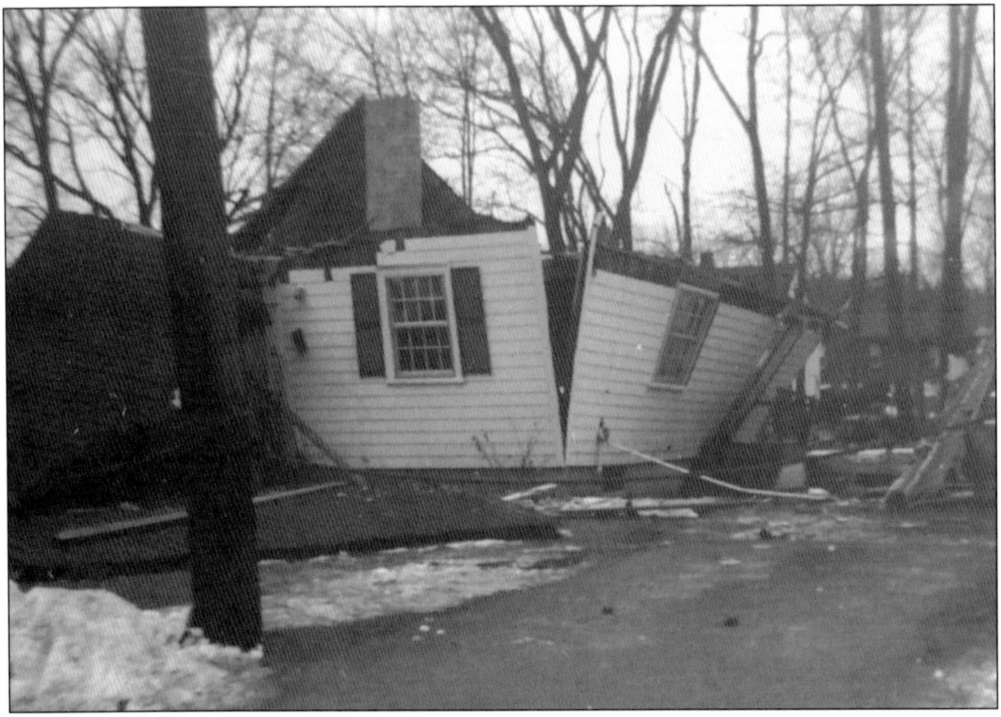

A gas explosion in a home at 40 West Street on January 21, 1954, resulted in the deaths of Patrolman Andrew Keane and his wife, Margaret. An investigation showed the cause of the fire to most likely be gas escaping from a broken gas main. This ignited when a cigarette was lit, lifting off the roof and blowing off one side of the house completely.

Patrolman Peter F. O'Toole, a member of the Stoneham Police Department for 15 years, was a popular figure on the streets of Stoneham in the 1920s and 1930s as he walked the beat. The name O'Toole has long been associated with law enforcement in this area.

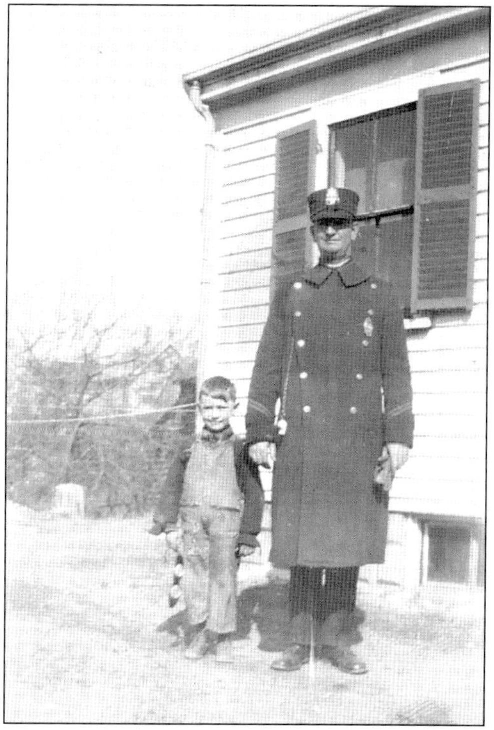

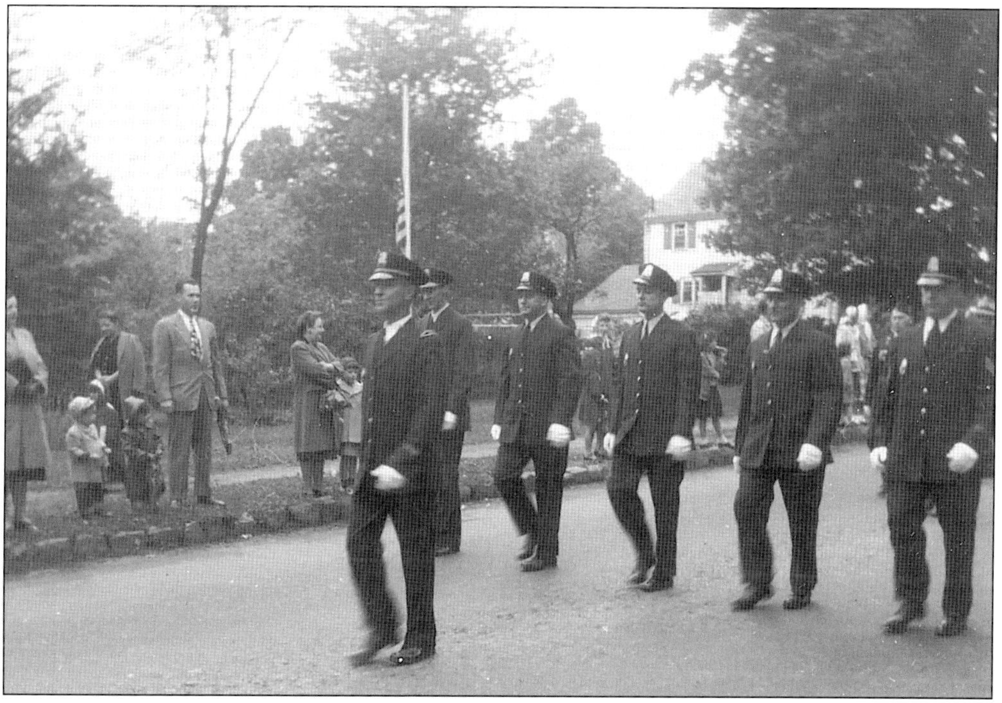

Lt. William H. O'Toole Sr. proudly leads a contingent of Stoneham's finest in the 1948 Memorial Day Parade. Behind him, from left to right, are Patrolmen Bernard C. Vacon, William H. O'Toole Jr., Andrew J. Tuney Jr., Warren H. Barnes, and Sgt. Dennis L. McKinnon. Lt. O'Toole joined the forced in 1924 and retired in 1963.

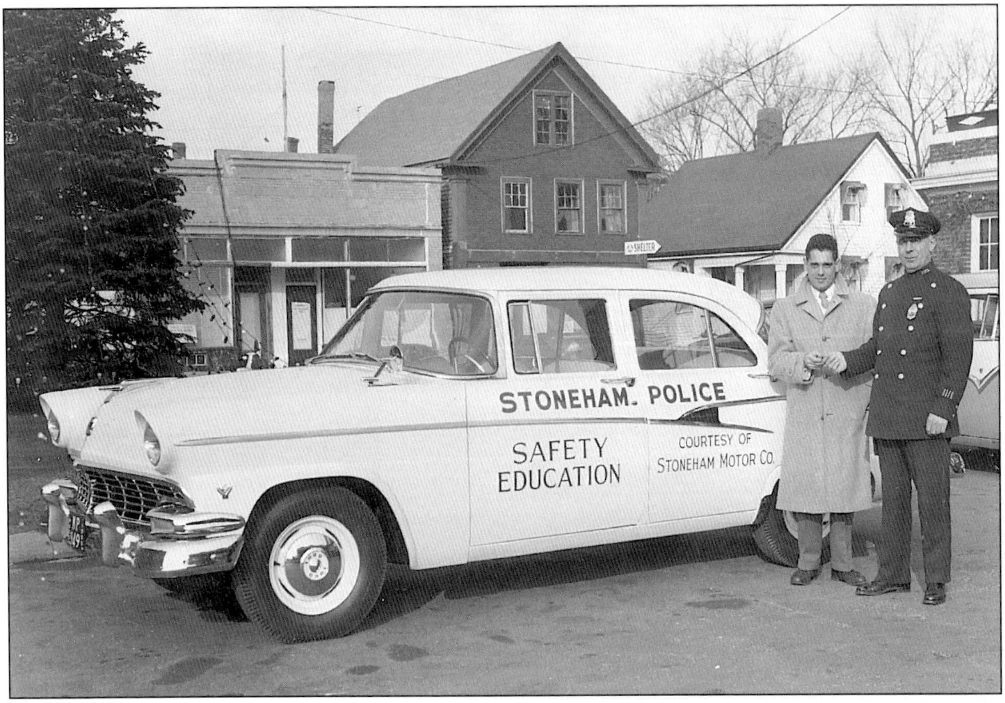

On December 10, 1955, the police department received a 1956 Ford Sedan for one dollar through the courtesy of the Stoneham Motor Company. This car was to be used in the Safety Education Program. John Melkonian is shown presenting the keys to Safety Officer George J. McDonough.

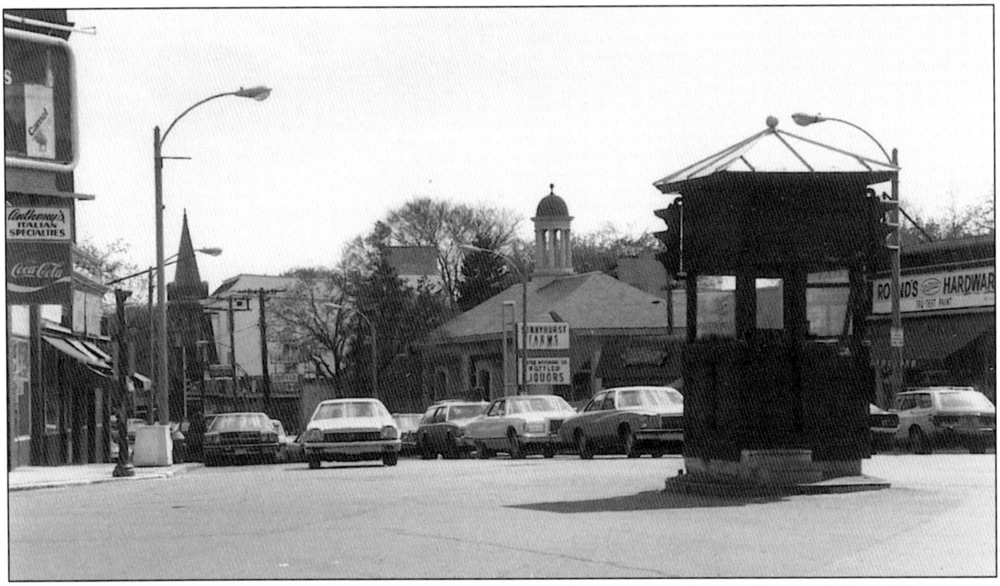

For the vast majority of "Townies" the Square is not the same without the cop's box. Longtime residents know it was green and recall it decorated for the Christmas holidays. The box survived several collisions with vehicular traffic and even a town meeting article in 1963 that sought its removal. In August 1983, the box was badly damaged in an accident. Although repaired and returned, it was not the same, and in September 1996, it was removed from the Square.

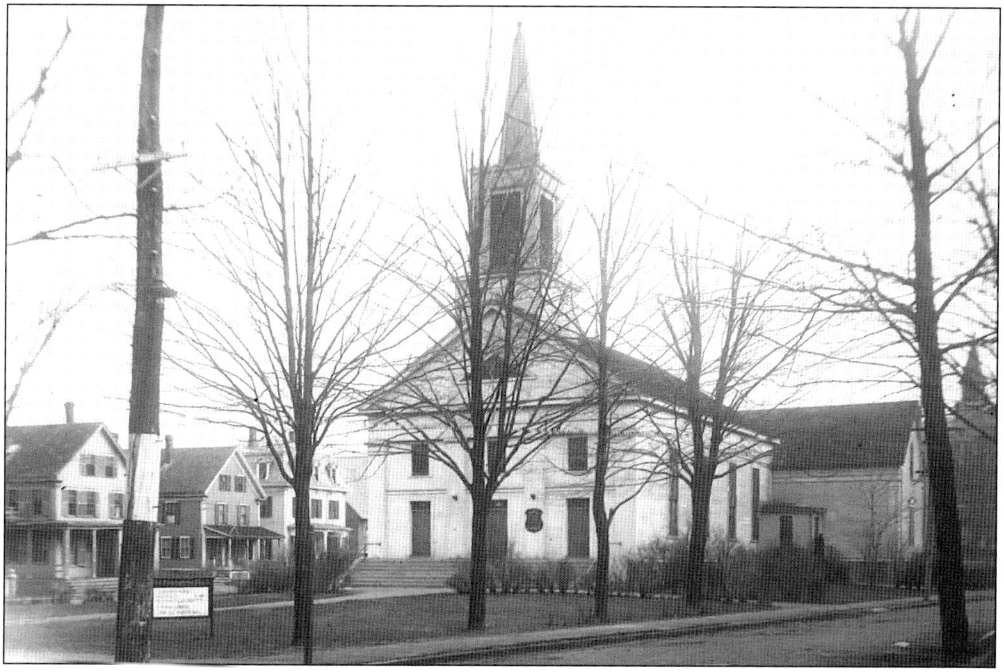

In 1840, when a fire destroyed the First Congregational Church's 1803 building on Spring Street, members decided to rebuild, but this time along the Medford to Andover Turnpike. When first built, the church was surrounded by much open space that was often used for community functions. In time, it became necessary to use this land for building purposes. The creation of the Town Common nearby will no doubt recreate the earlier appearance of a church and its adjacent common.

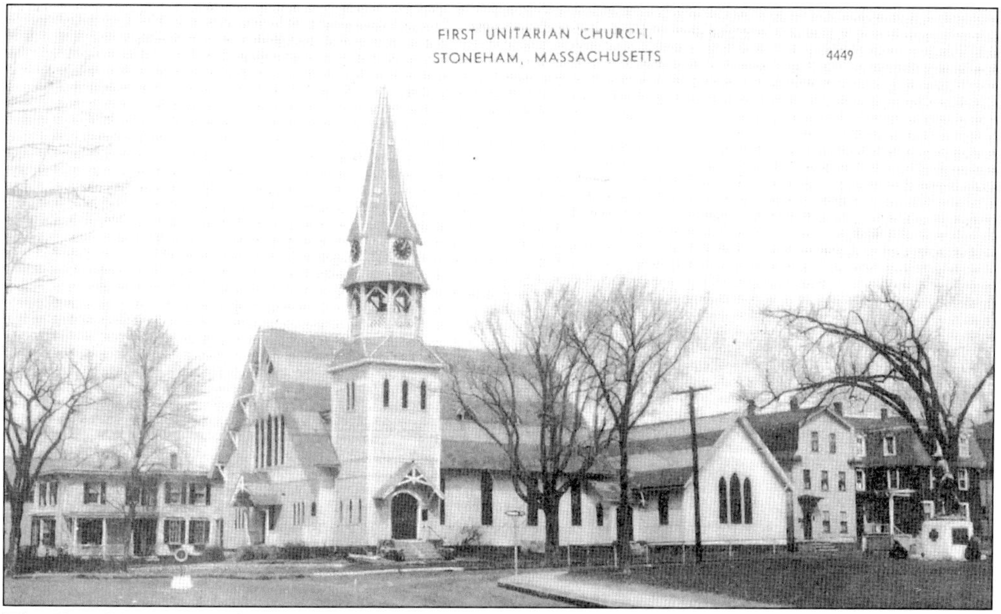

The First Unitarian Church was erected in 1868 and dedicated on January 1, 1869. Its steeple, removed during March 1986, at one time housed the "Town Clock" and a bell that now rests on the lawn. The church closed during the summer of 1995.

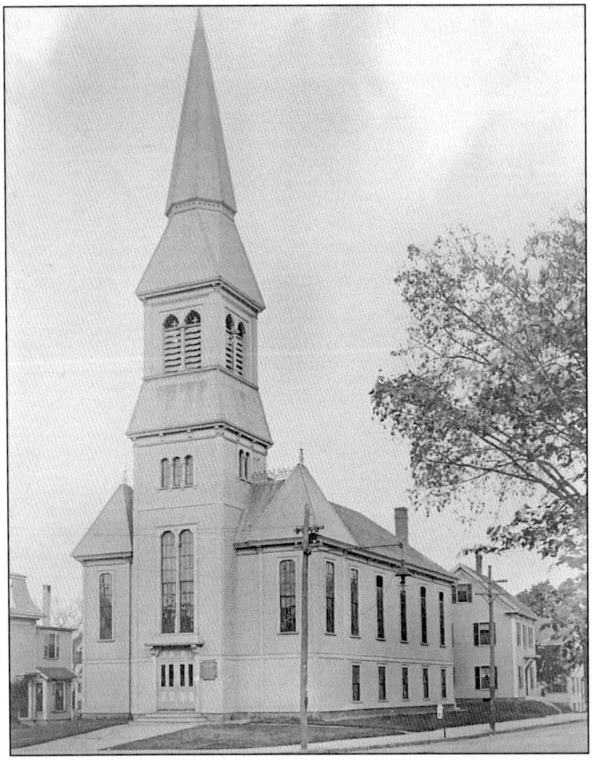

Methodists began to meet in Stoneham in the fall of 1855 and began working toward having their own place of worship. St. James United Methodist Church laid the cornerstone for a building on Common Street in July 1868, and the building was dedicated in December 1870. Unfortunately, this church burned on March 24, 1909. When insurance would cover only about half of the cost of repair, the decision was made to construct a new building.

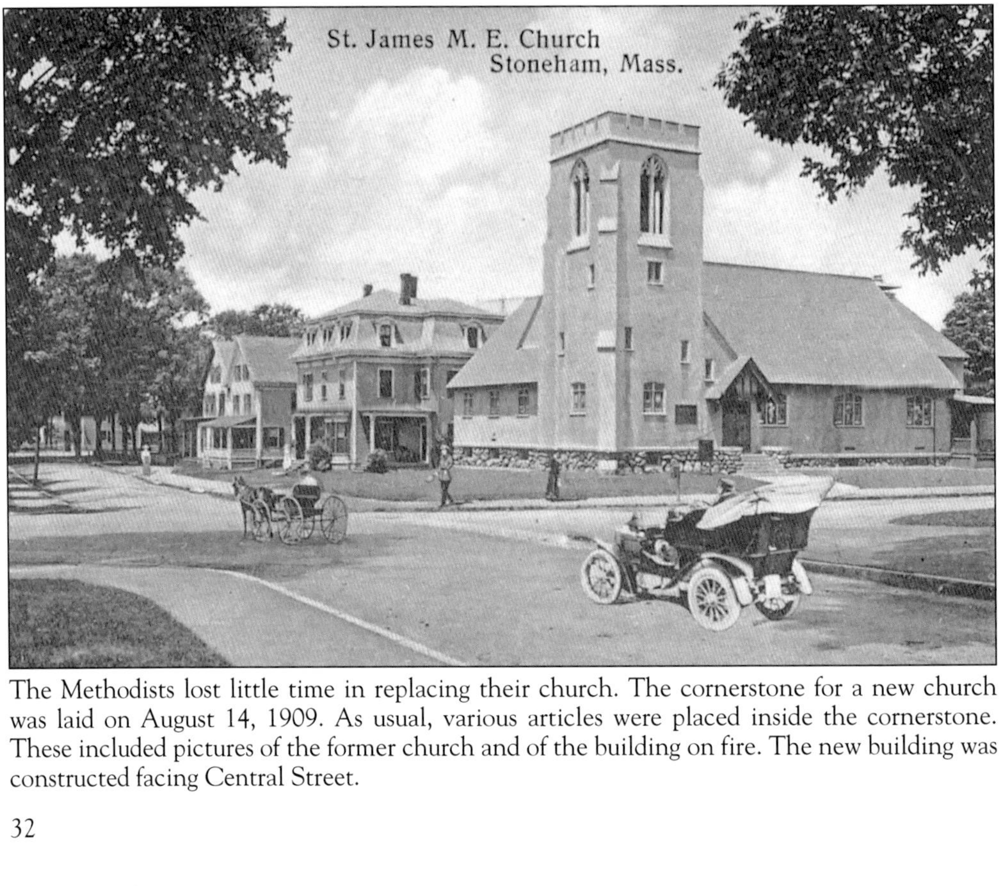

The Methodists lost little time in replacing their church. The cornerstone for a new church was laid on August 14, 1909. As usual, various articles were placed inside the cornerstone. These included pictures of the former church and of the building on fire. The new building was constructed facing Central Street.

The cornerstone for St. Patrick's Church was laid in 1887, and the building was completed in 1888. On March 15, 1987, the capsule in the 1887 cornerstone was opened and its contents revealed. On September 25, 1987, these artifacts plus current ones were placed in the capsule, which is to be opened again in 2087.

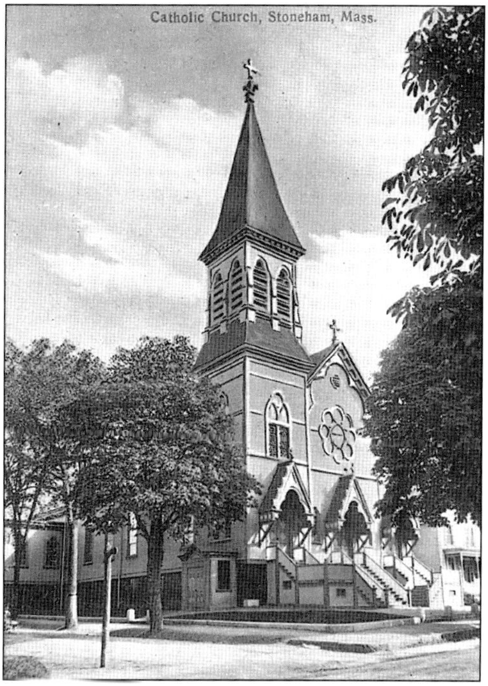

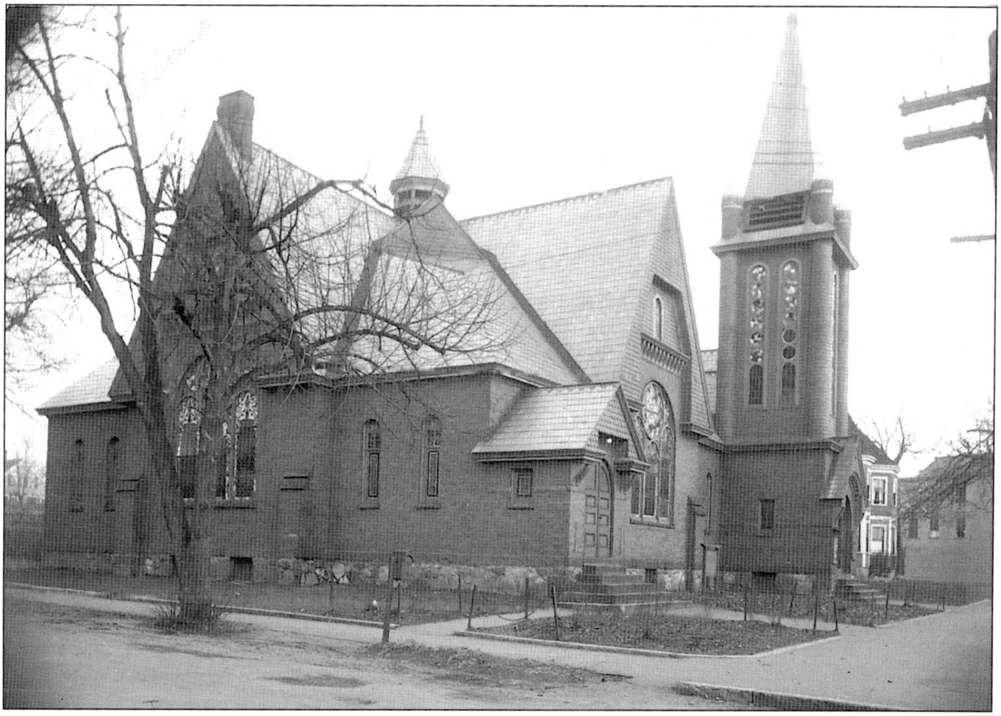

Baptists began to meet in Stoneham *c.* 1868 and formally organized in February 1870. A chapel was built and dedicated in 1871 near the corner of Common and Pine Streets, and this was the Baptists' place of worship for 22 years. That building is now the property of the American Legion. In 1892, the Baptists dedicated their new church at the corner of Main and Hancock Streets.

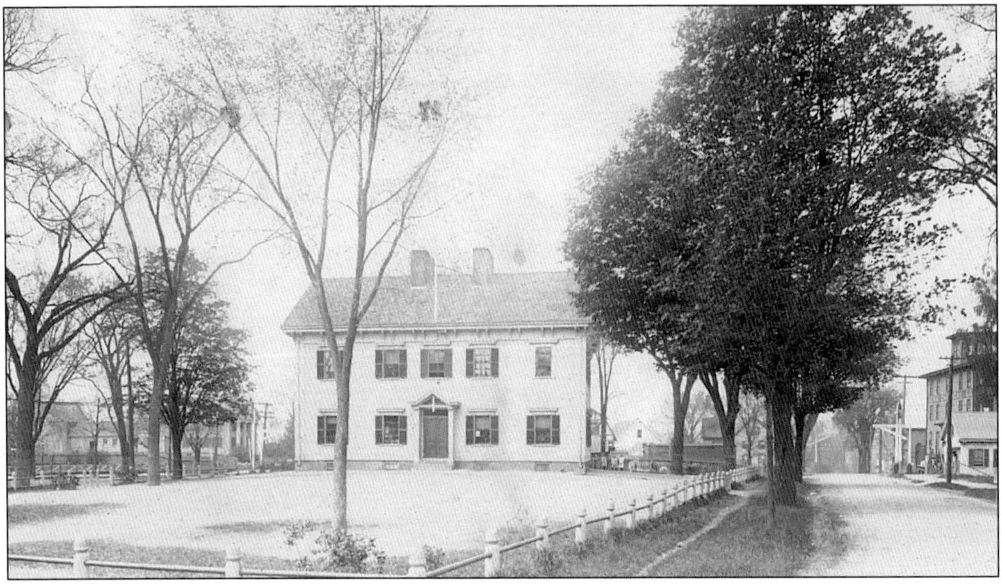

The "Old" North School stood at the intersection of Central, William, and Main Streets. It opened in October 1851 and closed in June 1939. In 1941, the building was demolished and the lot was sold. Later, the site became a popular one with teenagers with the construction of the "DQ" or Dairy Queen.

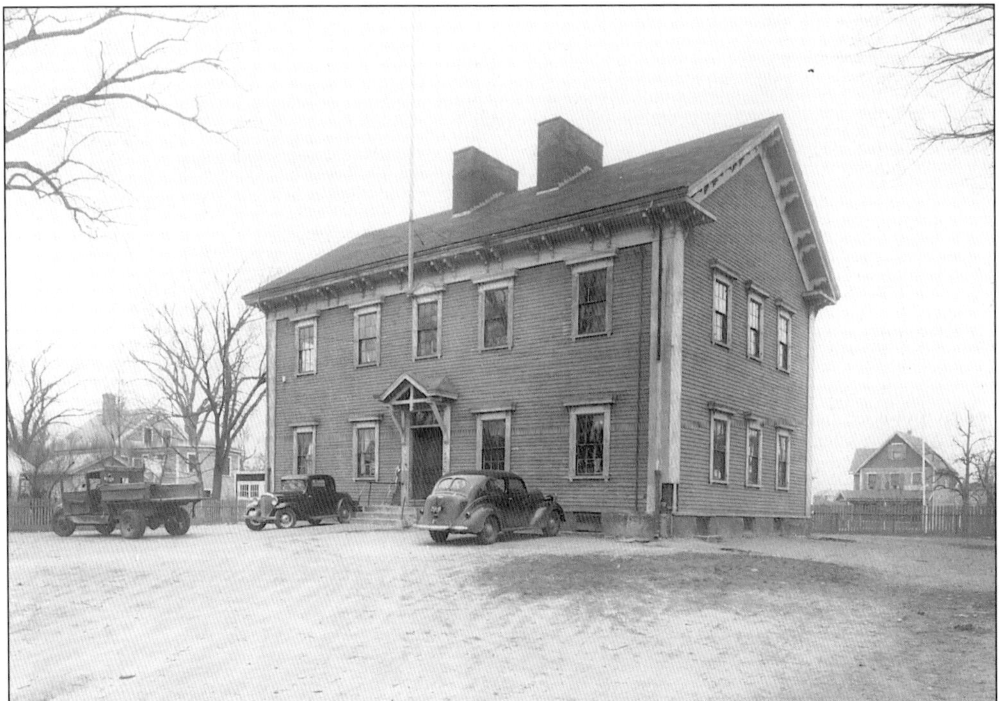

The "Old" South School was built on Gerry Street in 1851. It was closed in 1938 and sold in 1944 to the Seventh-Day Adventist Church of Stoneham. It is now operated as the Dorcas Society, providing community services and clothing distribution to those in need.

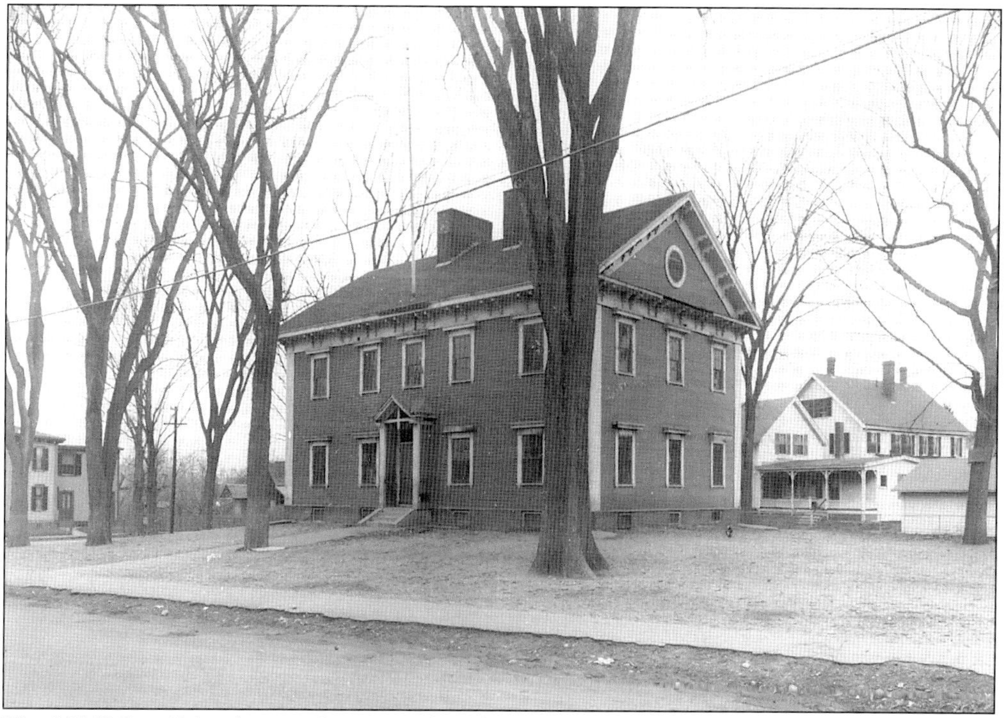

The "Old" East School is another example of how buildings can be recycled. Built in 1851 and closed in 1939, this structure was sold in 1940 to St. Patrick's Parish, which operated it as a high school in the 1940s. Later, the Knights of Columbus used it as their meeting place, and more recently it became the Boston Korean Seventh-Day Adventist Church.

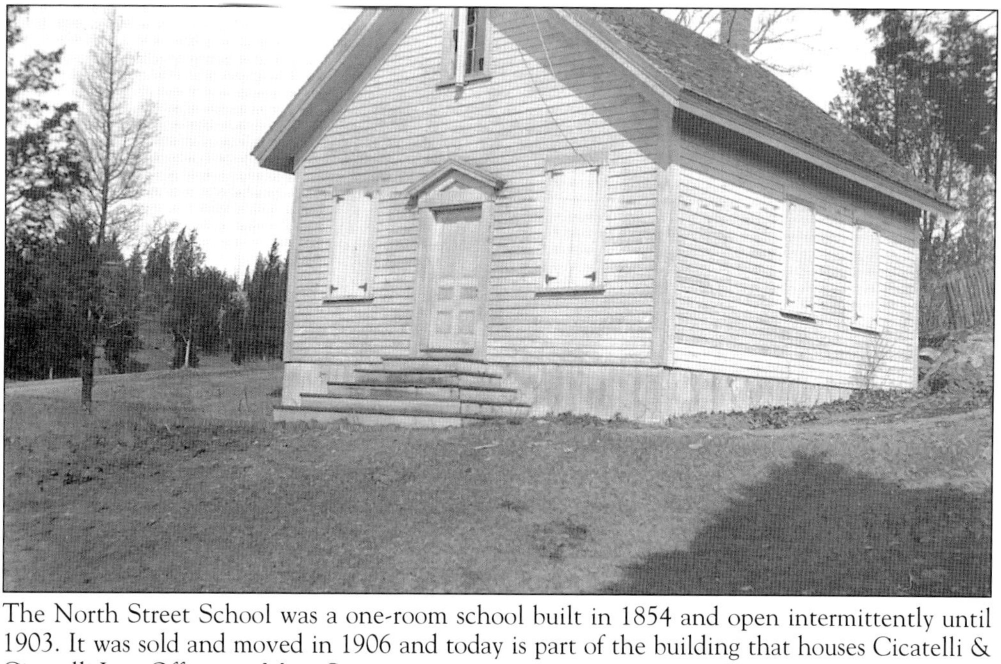

The North Street School was a one-room school built in 1854 and open intermittently until 1903. It was sold and moved in 1906 and today is part of the building that houses Cicatelli & Cicatelli Law Offices on Main Street.

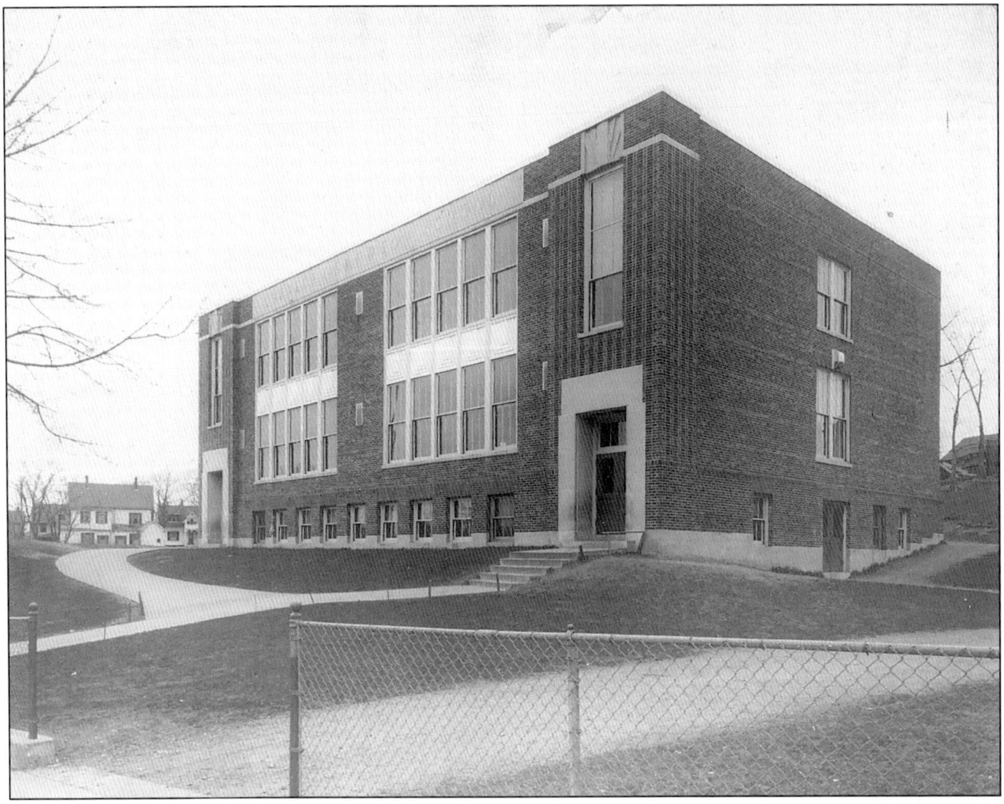

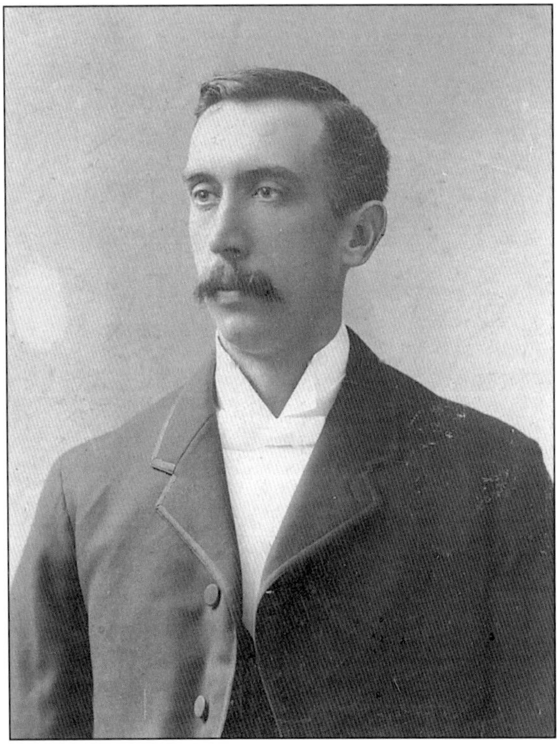

The Charles J. Emerson School on Wright Street was opened on December 1, 1930. It contained eight classrooms plus auxiliary rooms and was fireproof throughout. The cost of the building was $110,000. Closed in June 1979 and later sold, the building is today known as Emerson Condominiums.

Charles J. Emerson came to Stoneham in September 1895 and served as the principal of Stoneham High School until June 1926. He was much beloved by students and fellow teachers and made such a profound impression that the first school building constructed after his retirement was named for him. Emerson is the only school official ever to be so honored.

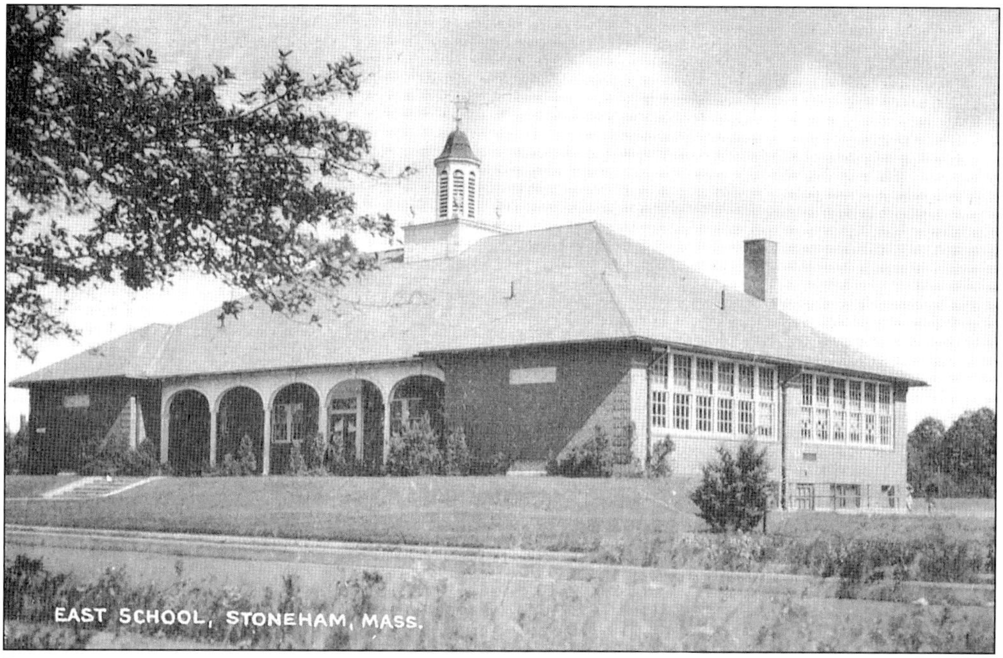

This neighborhood school was built on Beacon Street in 1938. It replaced the "Old" East School on Spring Street, and so was referred to by townspeople as the "New" East School. Some federal funds were used in its construction. The school was closed in 1981 and has since been a rental property.

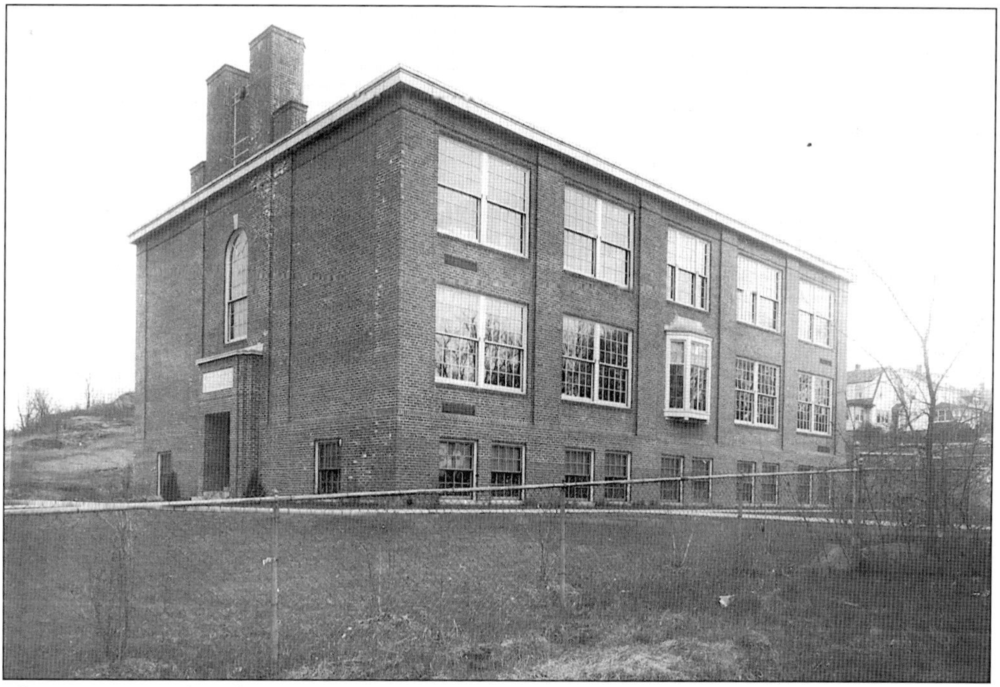

The "New" South School was built on Summer Street in 1938. It was closed in 1998 and demolished the following year to make way for a "Newer" South School, being built as phase one of Stoneham's school building program.

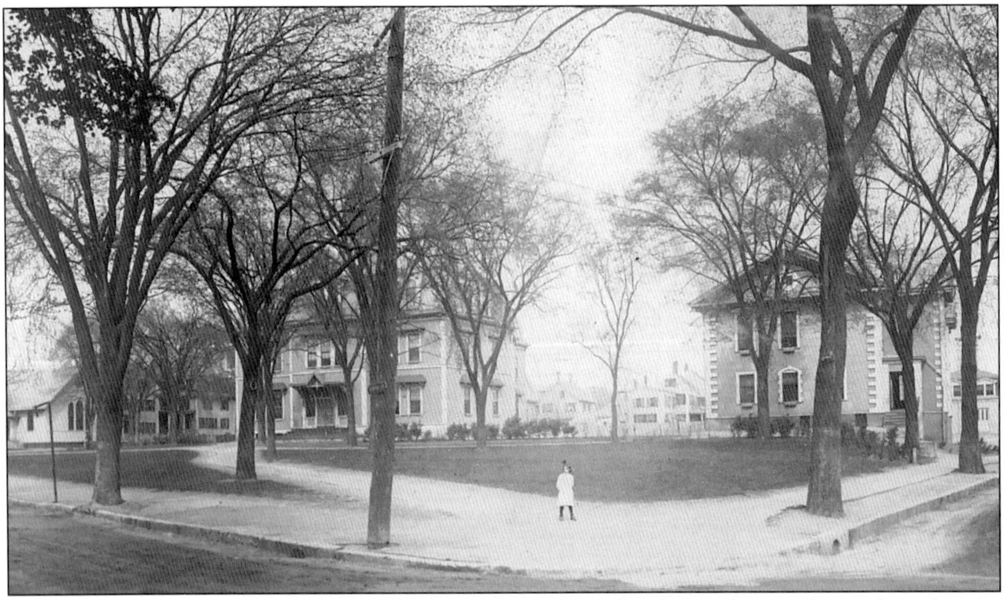

The building at the left, constructed as Stoneham High School in 1871, was located on the site of the present police station. The high school was later renamed to honor Town Clerk Silas Dean. Beside it is Center School, built as the town hall in 1847.

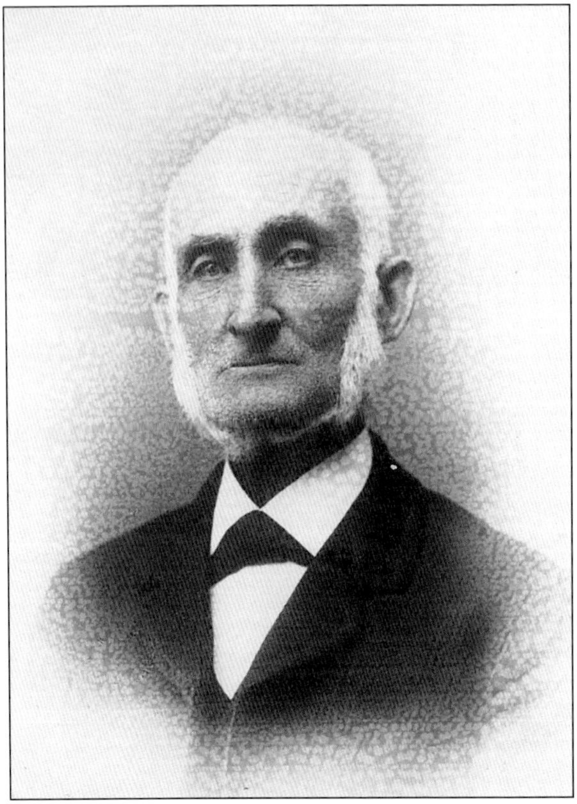

Silas Dean served as town clerk for 39 years, and he wrote a history of Stoneham that was first published in 1843. The Town Clerk's Office was in his home on Pine Street, where at one time he also kept a private school. In his early life, Dean was a shoemaker; in later life, he became an auctioneer.

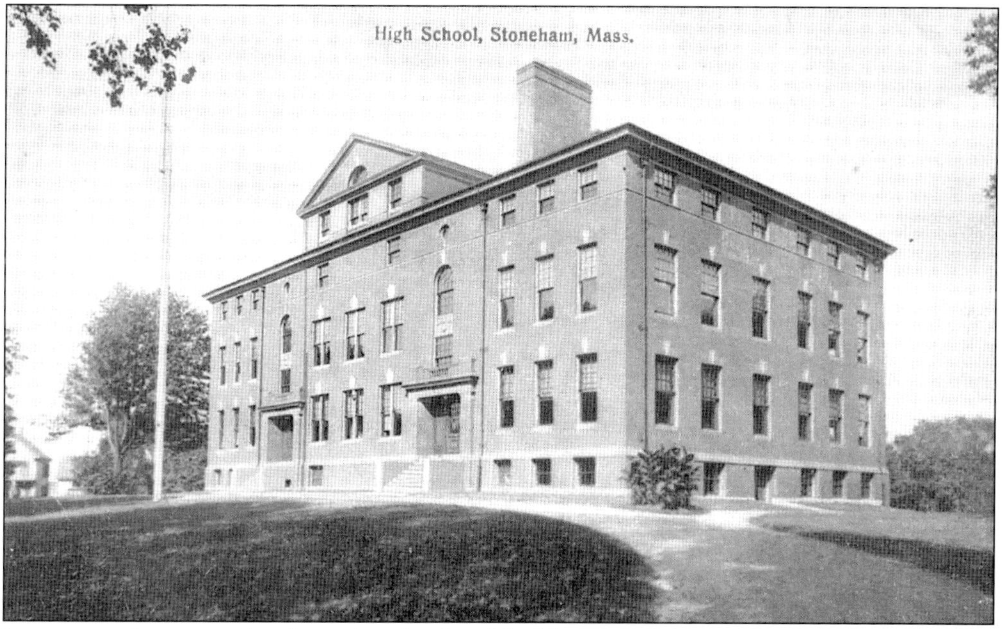

Here is another example of recycling land and buildings. This location was originally the site of the William Street Cemetery from 1844 to 1899. At the turn of the century, bodies were removed and construction began for a building that opened in 1901 as Stoneham High School and served in that capacity until 1955.

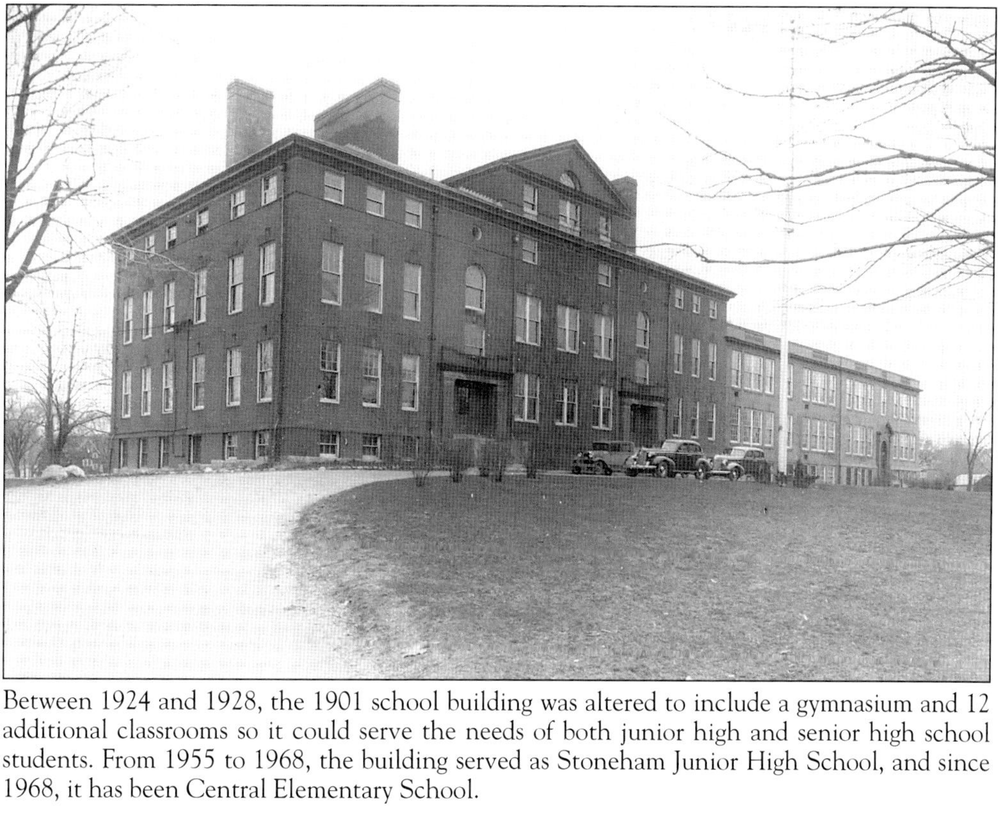

Between 1924 and 1928, the 1901 school building was altered to include a gymnasium and 12 additional classrooms so it could serve the needs of both junior high and senior high school students. From 1955 to 1968, the building served as Stoneham Junior High School, and since 1968, it has been Central Elementary School.

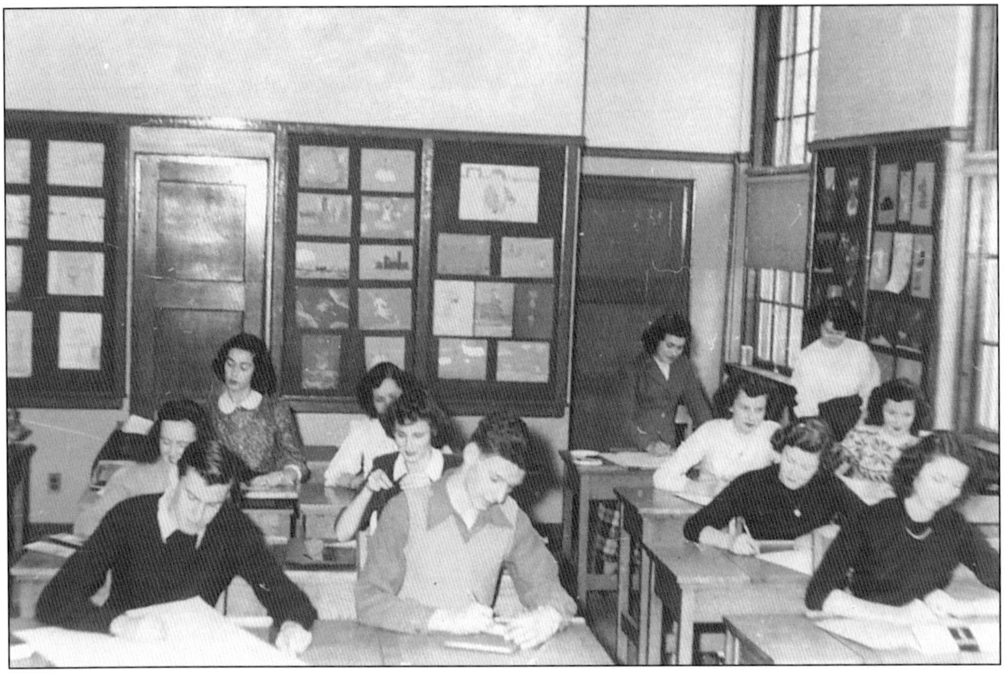

For about 70 years, the carnival ball has been a highlight of the year at Stoneham High School. Students participate in skits and perform musical numbers. Others, such as these in a 1949 art class, design the sets, which are always spectacular. The 1949 theme was Moon Valley.

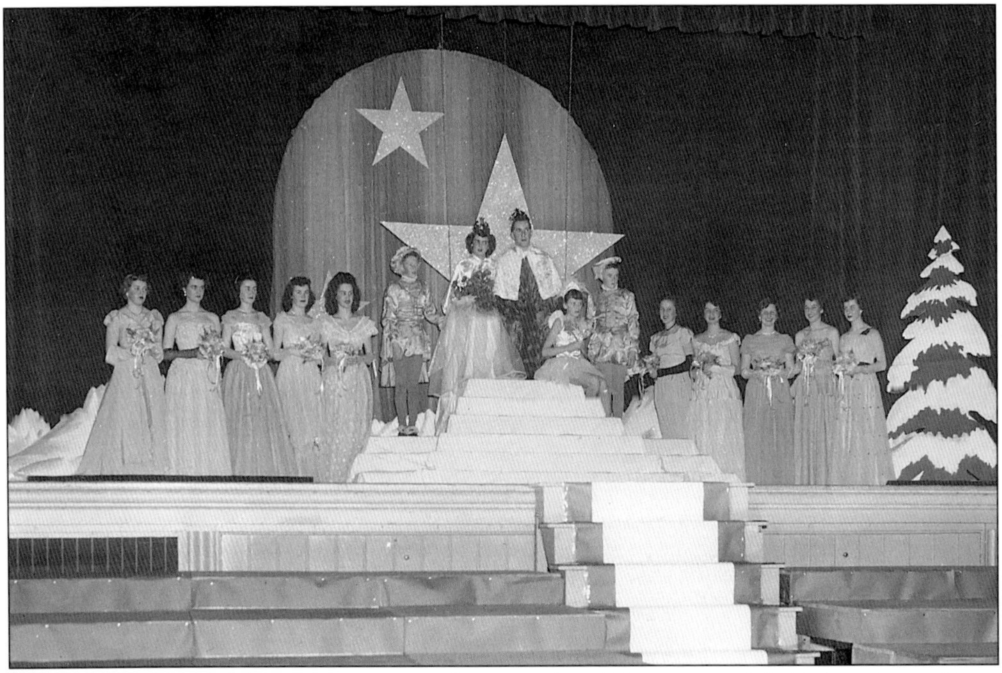

The king, queen, and royal court preside over the 1950 Carnival Ball festivities. Here, King Paul Norden, Queen Joan Christie, and their attendants, pages, and the Crowning Star greet a capacity audience at the town hall. With her wand, the Crowning Star carried out the coronation.

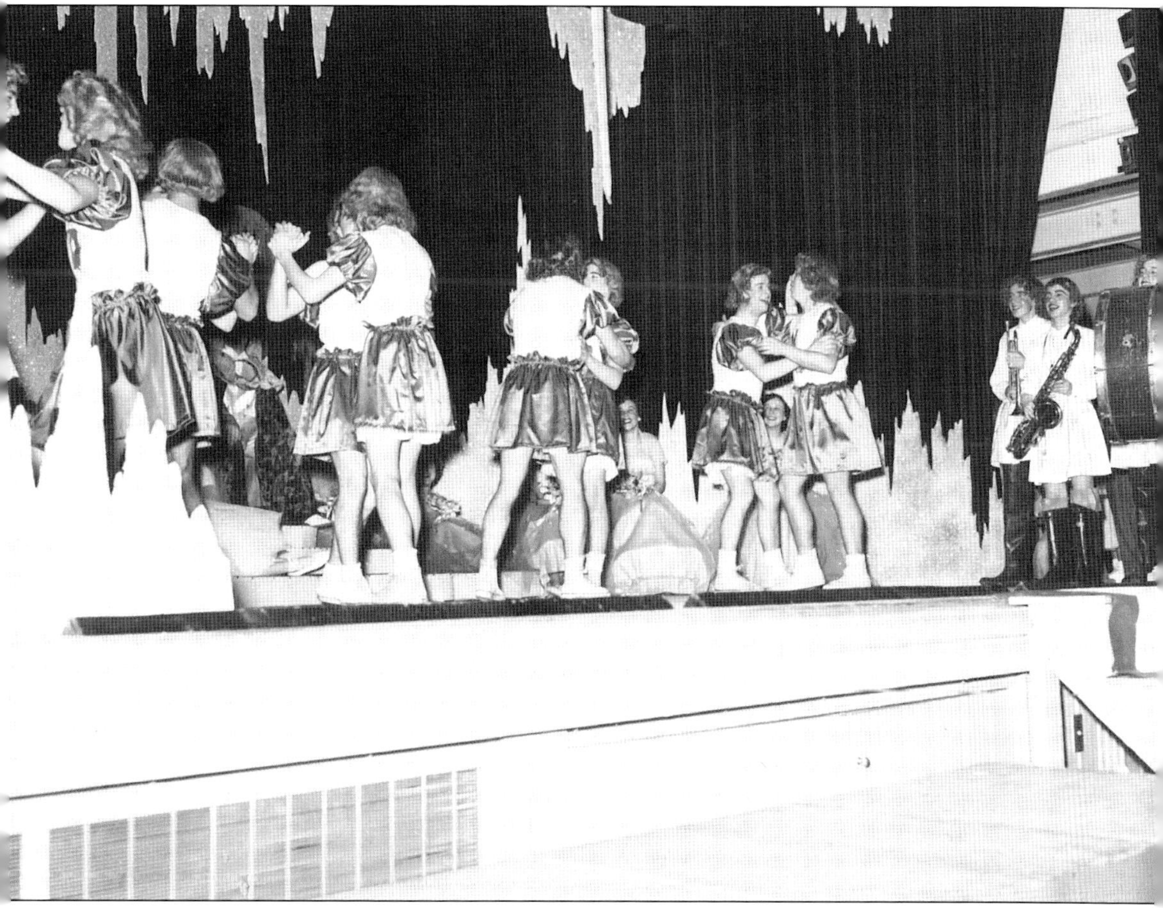

Throughout the years, all has not been pomp and circumstance at the annual carnival ball. The biggest laugh at the 1952 Carnival Ball came when the football team danced onto the stage in cheerleading outfits. Their skirts may have been short, but the laughs they brought were long. After a set of cheers for King John Welch and Queen Dorothy Jardine, the team raised their leader high. The "girls" in this cheering squad include "Harriet" Malonson, "Francine" Picano, "Wilhemina" Canavan, "Claire" McCarthy, "Pinky" Whitney, "Alberta" Fallavolita, "Loretta" Scammon, "Francine" Odlum, "Janet" Kenney, and "Lenora" Fiske.

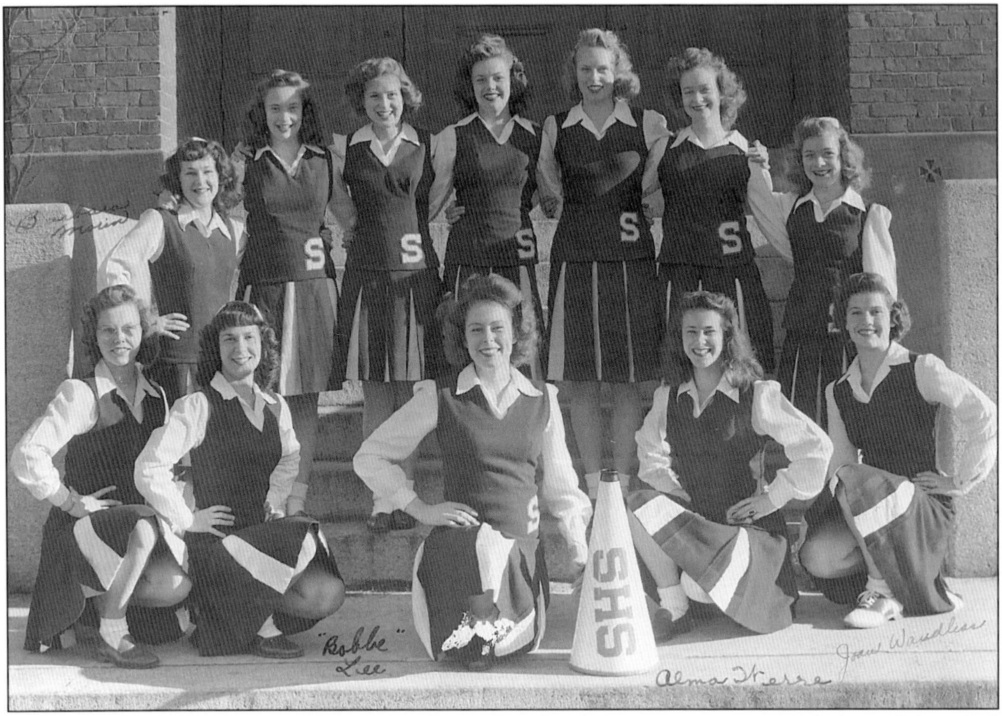

Who wouldn't try a little harder when cheered on by these attractive young ladies of the 1945 cheering squad? They are, from left to right, as follows: (front row) Barbara Court, Virginia Morin, Marjorie Picot, Ruth Morin, and Joan Wandless; (back row) Barbara Morin, Barbara McGilveary, Roberta Lee, Shirley Martin, Marilyn Jelley, Alma Werre, and Patricia Nelles.

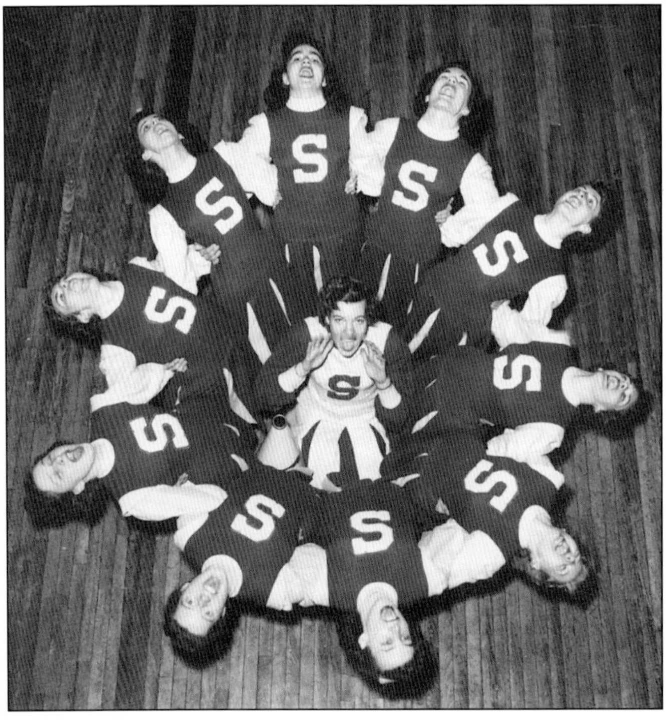

Give a yell! Surrounding Captain Gail Anderson (Wright) are the 1951–1952 cheerleaders doing their best to bring victory to Stoneham High School. They are, clockwise from the top, Dorothy McCall, Judy Bryant, Terry Corkum, Dorothy Jardine, Carolyn Dike, Marjorie Whiles, Judy Ranlett, Carolyn Zaltman, Beverley Goudey, and Jane Shaw.

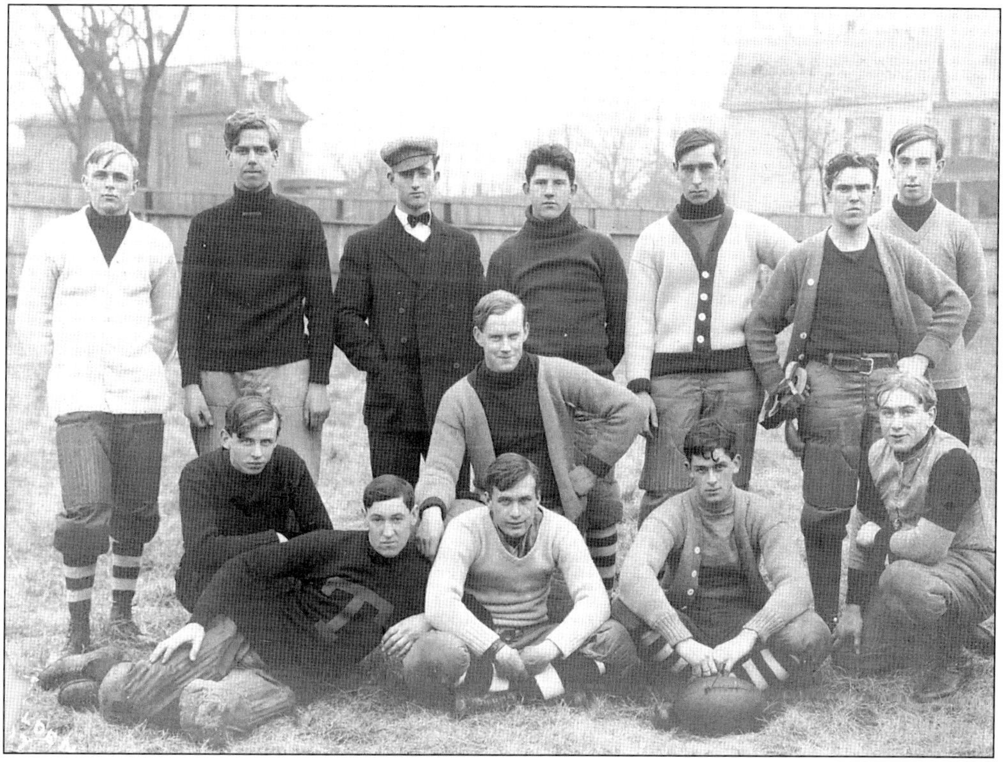

In the earliest days of football at Stoneham High School, there often were not enough boys for a team. As a result, alumni were allowed to be team members. Shown here is the 1907 team comprised of the following, from left to right: (front row) Donald Munro, Lester Tarbett, Sidney Patchett, Warren Sleeper, and Roy Hovey; (middle) Russell Ervin; (back row) Ira Bumpus, Albert Symmes, Marty McHale, Bill McHale, Peter Hay, Warren ?, and Frank Cogan.

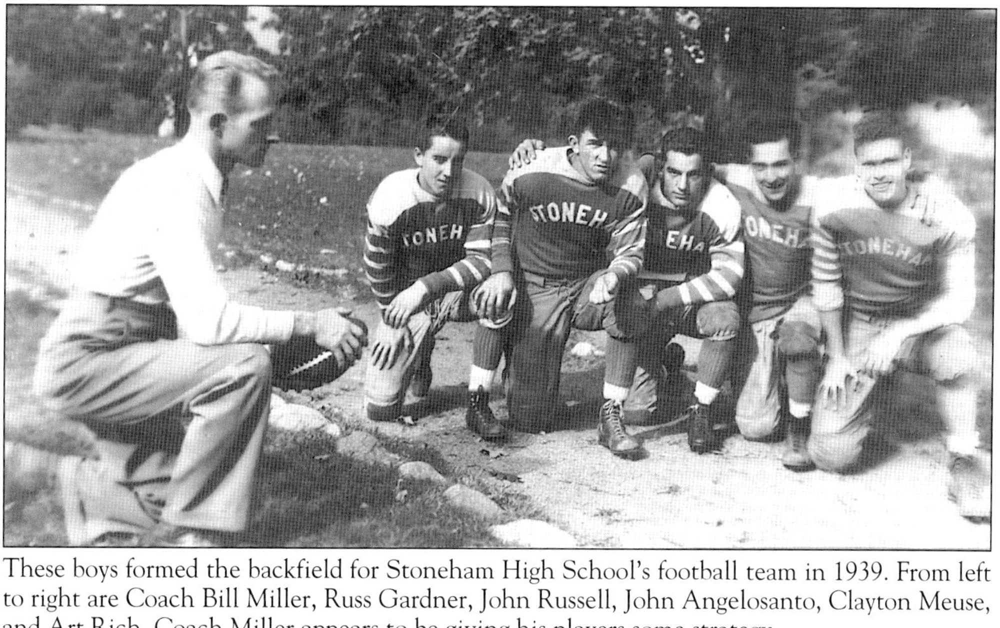

These boys formed the backfield for Stoneham High School's football team in 1939. From left to right are Coach Bill Miller, Russ Gardner, John Russell, John Angelosanto, Clayton Meuse, and Art Rich. Coach Miller appears to be giving his players some strategy.

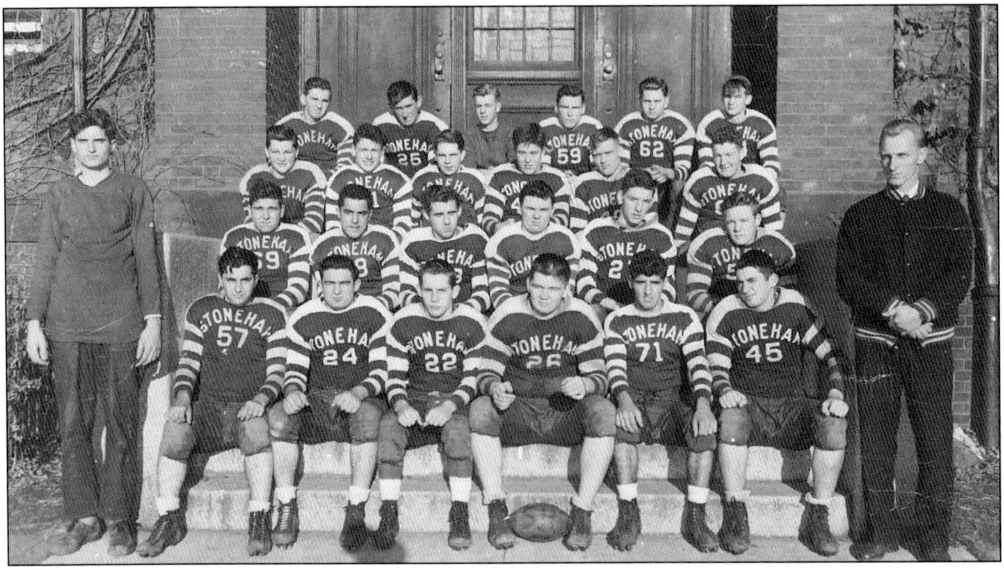

A determined looking 1948–1949 squad is posed on the high school steps. They are, from left to right, as follows: (front row) Manager Bob Corkum, John Geragosian, Americo Fionda, Ken Leland, Captain Joe Beane, Don Moreira, Henry Knight, and Coach William E. Miller; (second row) Dick Crowe, Rudy Minghella, Frank Sousa, Jack Foley, Charles Bamberg, and Mitch Corbett; (third row) Art Beane, Larry Murphy, Dick Hersam, Andy Crowther, Arthur Roy, and Carmelo DiFuria; (back row) Irving Rohrbacher, William Jordan, Manager Dave Burton, John Burns, Dick Burns, and Dick Wetzler.

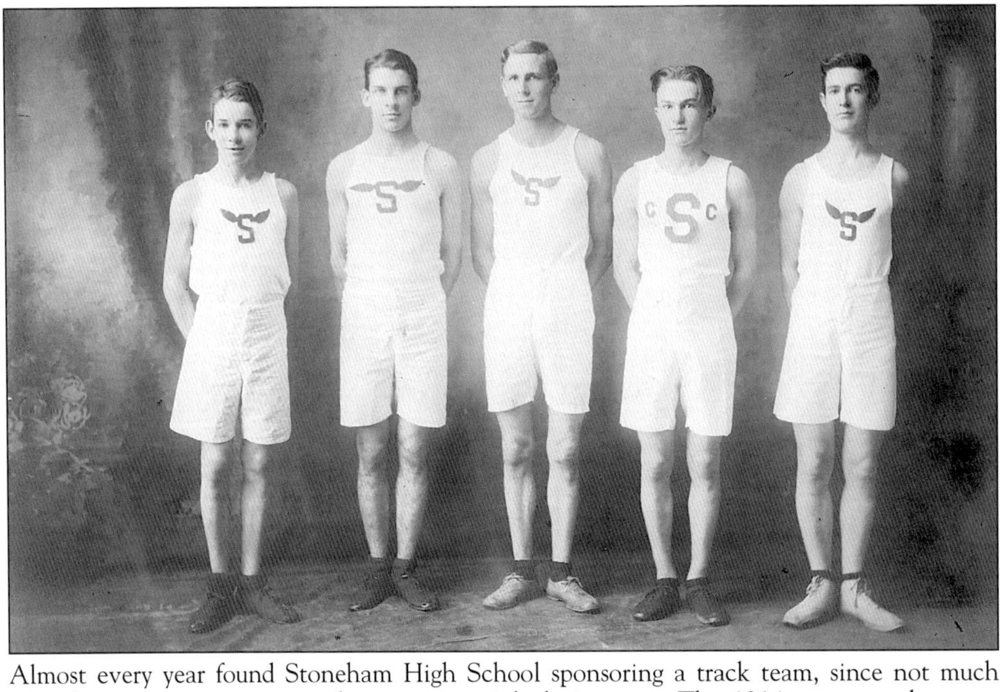

Almost every year found Stoneham High School sponsoring a track team, since not much special equipment was required nor any special playing area. The 1914 team members are, from left to right, George McDermott, Tom McDermott, Stanley Kinsley, Wesley Fisher, and Lawrence Worthen.

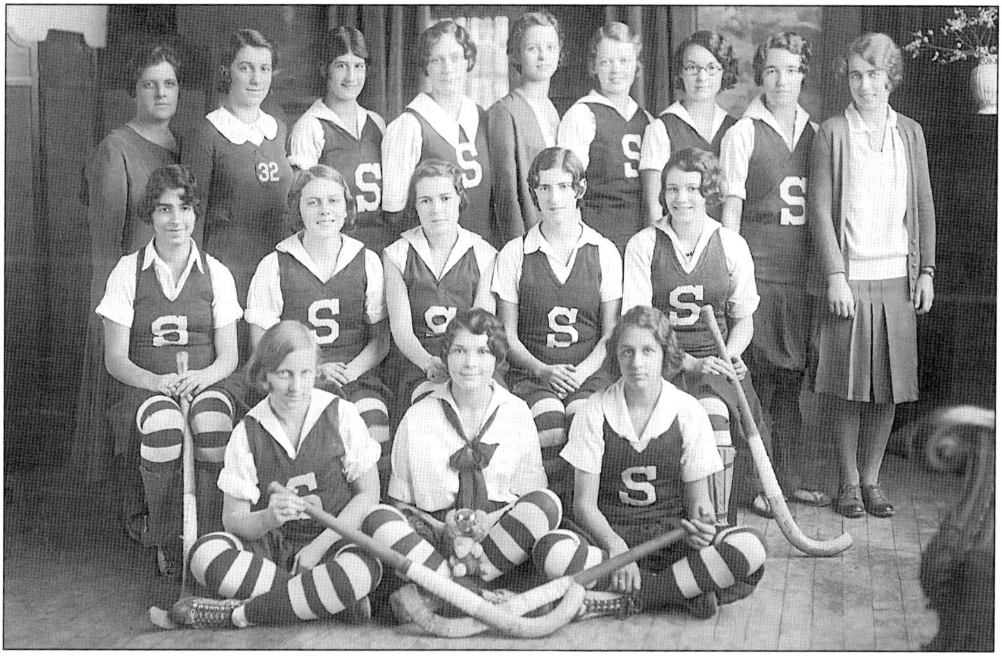

There were few athletic activities for girls in the 1930s, but field hockey was one of them. The 1930–1931 team consisted of the following, from left to right: (front row) Virginia Tolman, Evelyn Lamb, and Ethel Duff; (middle row) Marion Baduvakis, Helen Frederickson, Cynthia Smart, Dot Corcoran, and Bernice Blaisdell; (back row) Coach Vera Lawson, Jane Tilden, Nora Bagdikian, Ruth Blockel, Pauline Miller, Mary Patch, Adelaide True, Doris Trainor, and Miss Cook.

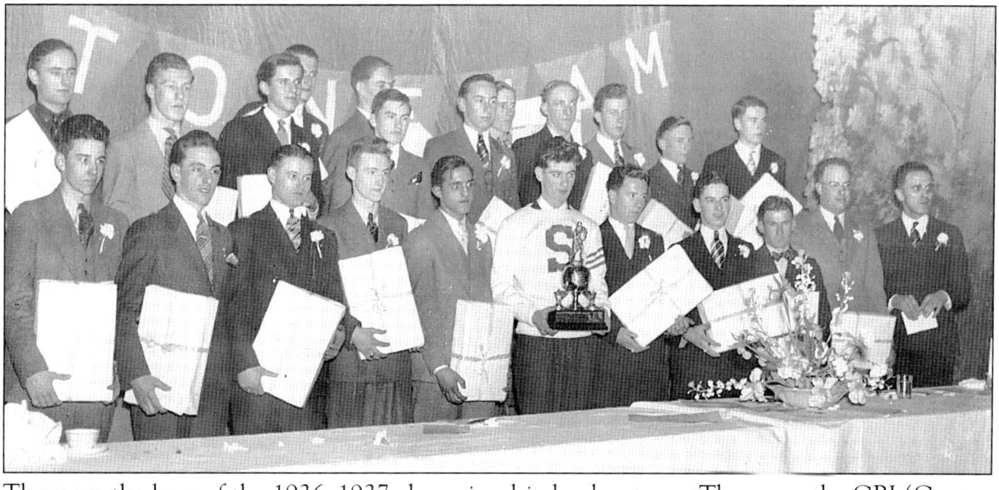

These are the boys of the 1936–1937 championship hockey team. They won the GBI (Greater Boston Interscholastic) League for the second year in a row and were given a testimonial dinner at the Old Armory Hall. From left to right are as follows: (front row) Dean Morrison, Rico Eramo, Bob Gray, Larry Hurley, Larry Petroni, Cliff Thompson, Bill Dowd, Art Donaghey, Joe Tole, Coach Howard "Doc" Gordon, and William M. Nadeau (vice principal and faculty manager); (back row) Gerald Mahoney, Warren Richards, Doug Surette, Bill McLaughlin, unidentified, James Huff, Eddie Bruce, Bill Truesdale, Francis Mahoney, Brad Leach, Richard Rush, and Joe Conley.

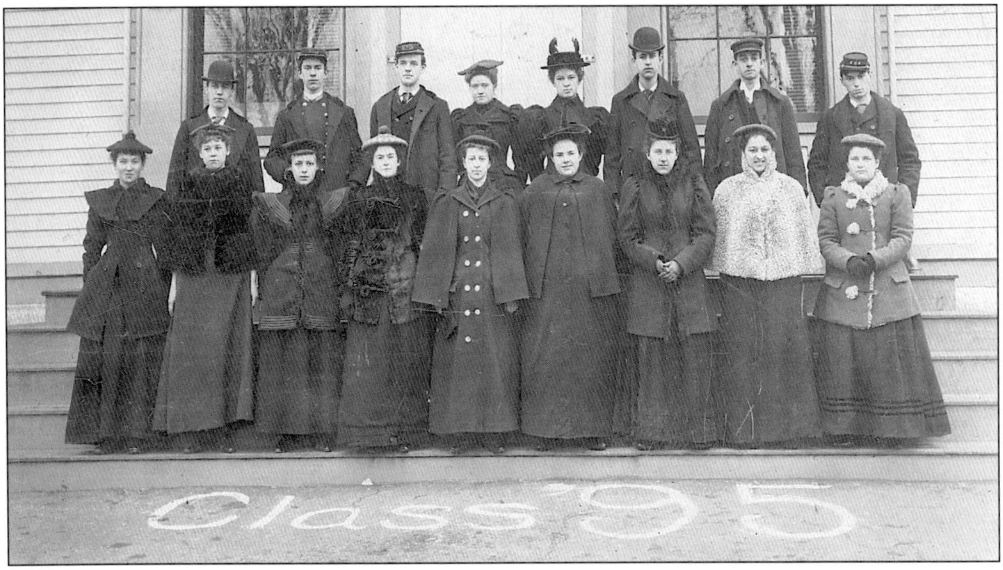

On Friday afternoon, March 15, 1895, these hopeful young ladies and gents said goodbye to Stoneham High School. They are, from left to right, as follows: (front row) Evelyn Doucette, Florence Lewis, Mary Yeaton, Harriet McEchern, Emma Theobald, Mary Emerson, Alice Smith, Helen Stevens, and Bessie Glidden; (back row) Morton A. Sturtevant, Herbert Richardson, James A. Patch, Mertie Newton, Zetta Moody, Henry Forgette, Warren Holden, and Frank Fisher.

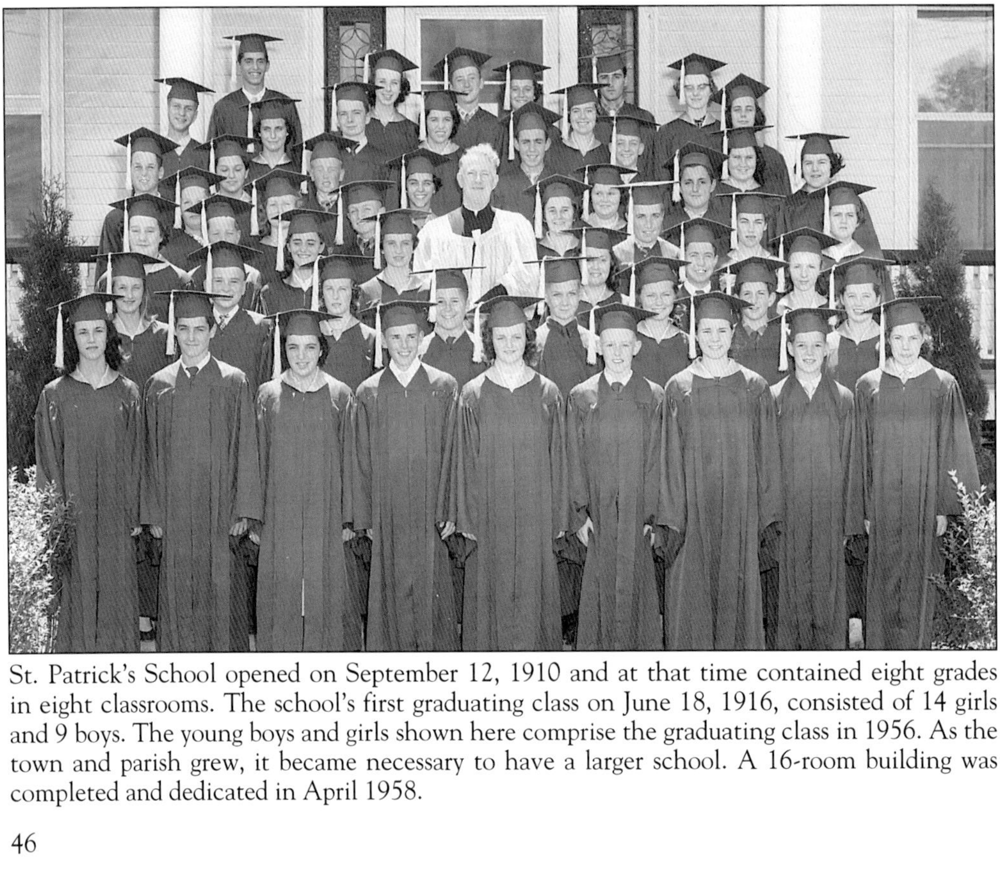

St. Patrick's School opened on September 12, 1910 and at that time contained eight grades in eight classrooms. The school's first graduating class on June 18, 1916, consisted of 14 girls and 9 boys. The young boys and girls shown here comprise the graduating class in 1956. As the town and parish grew, it became necessary to have a larger school. A 16-room building was completed and dedicated in April 1958.

Three

Beneath These Rooftrees

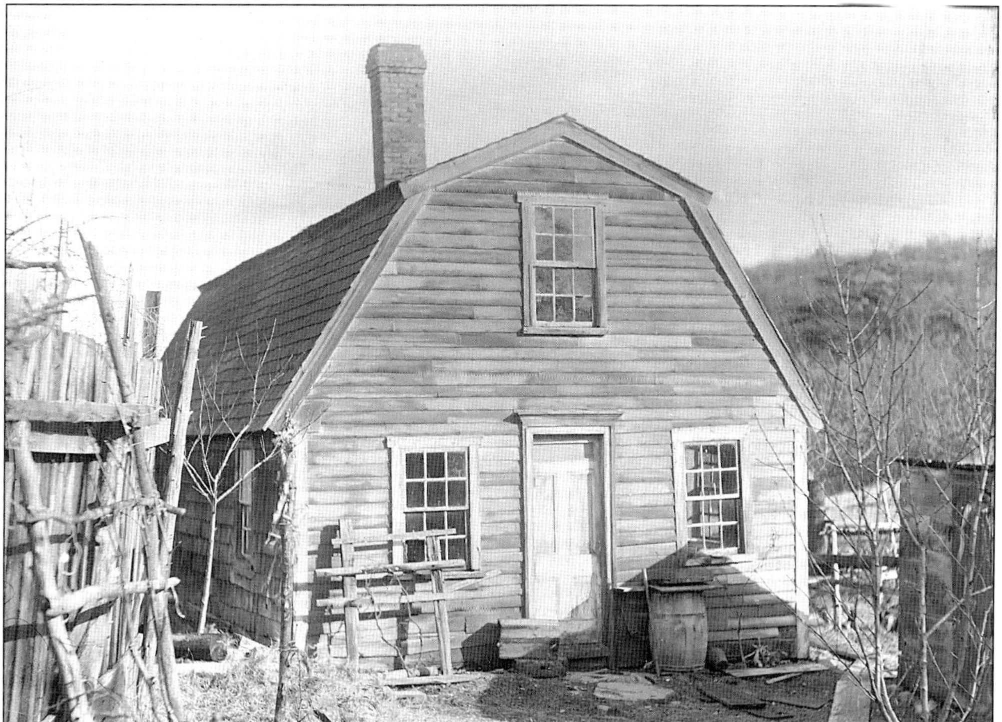

The Knight/Hadley/Butler House was located off Pond Street. This early dwelling is said to have been built *c.* 1712 by Ebenezer Knight. Prior to being razed *c.* 1925, it was used as the headquarters for the Wayside Bicycle Club.

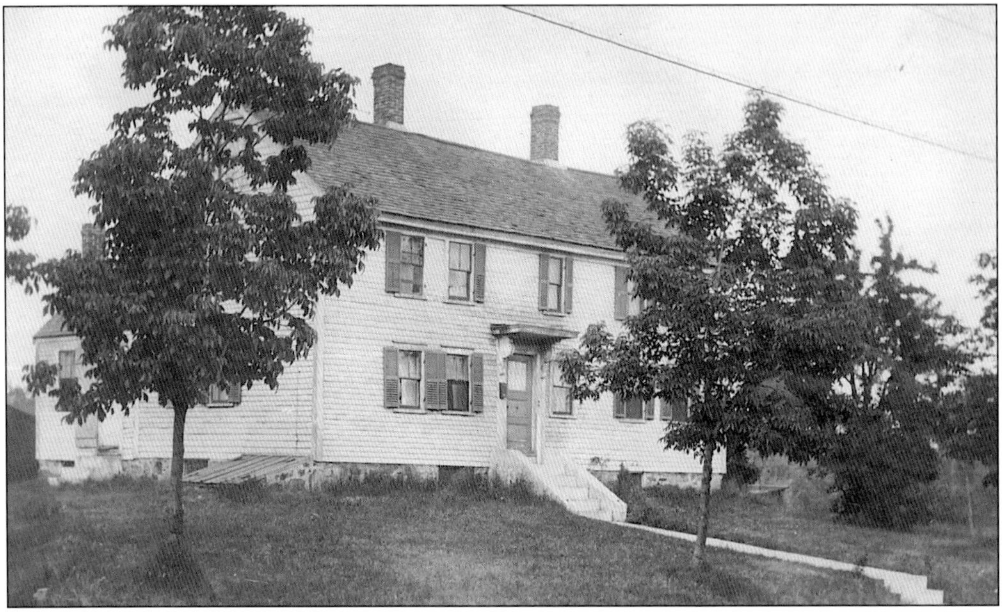

This is the only remaining 18th-century farm and is the sole intact example of Stoneham's agricultural origins. The structure is believed to have been erected *c.* 1747 by Elisha Knight. Today known as Weiss Farms, Inc., it has been operated by four generations of the Weiss family since *c.* 1928.

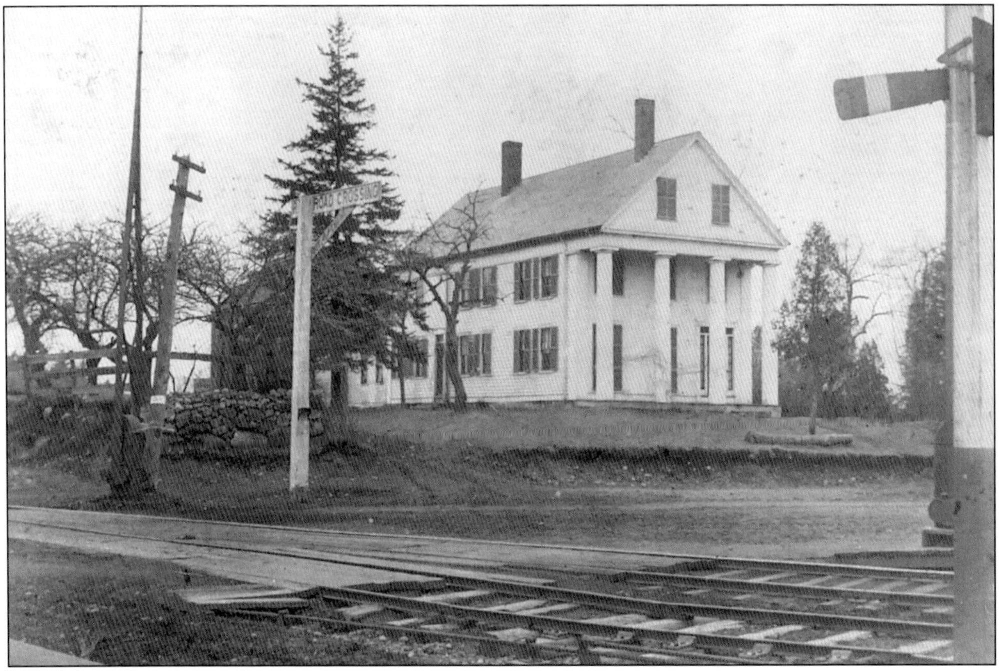

The David H. Burnham House was located on the west side of Main Street opposite the Farm Hill Railroad Station. This large Green Revival home stood on 3 acres and contained 16 rooms plus a stable. In the 1865 state census, David refers to himself as a "Farmer" and his son, David T.H. Burnham, as a "Station Agent," no doubt at the Farm Hill Station. This house was razed *c.* 1945.

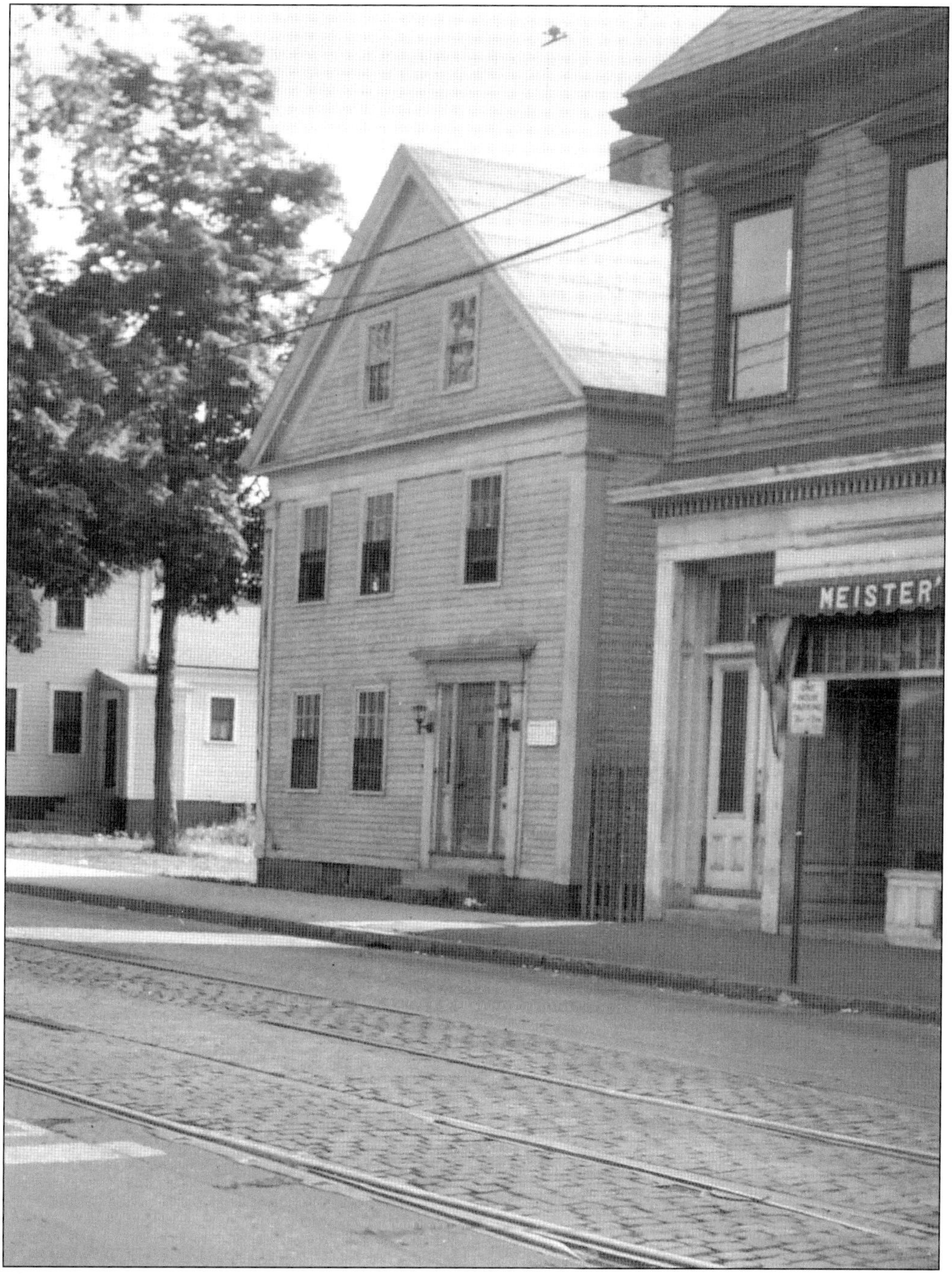

The Underground Railroad House was located on Main Street near the present site of the Trodella Building. Probably erected c. 1840, it was the home of Deacon Abijah Bryant, an active abolitionist. Deacon Bryant's ancestors had at one time been slave owners, but they eventually freed their slaves. This house operated as a stop on the Underground Railroad, which helped fugitive slaves escape to Canada from the South. Fugitives were brought into the house under the cover of darkness and kept in the cellar until another "station" was notified and prepared to receive them. The house was razed in June 1953.

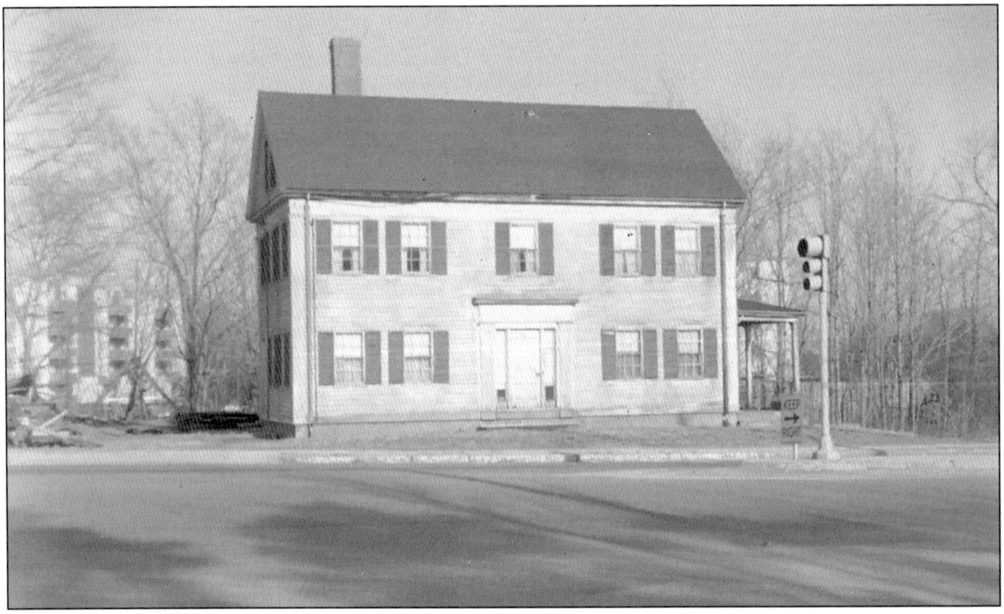

The Steele family home was built in 1842. It was located at the corner of Main and North Streets, long known as Steele's Corner. The Steele family made shoes, kept a dairy herd, and built several buildings in various parts of town. Atop the hill opposite their home was a beautiful cedar grove called Steele's Grove that was used for outings. The Steele home was razed in June 1979 and is now the site of Seville Condominiums.

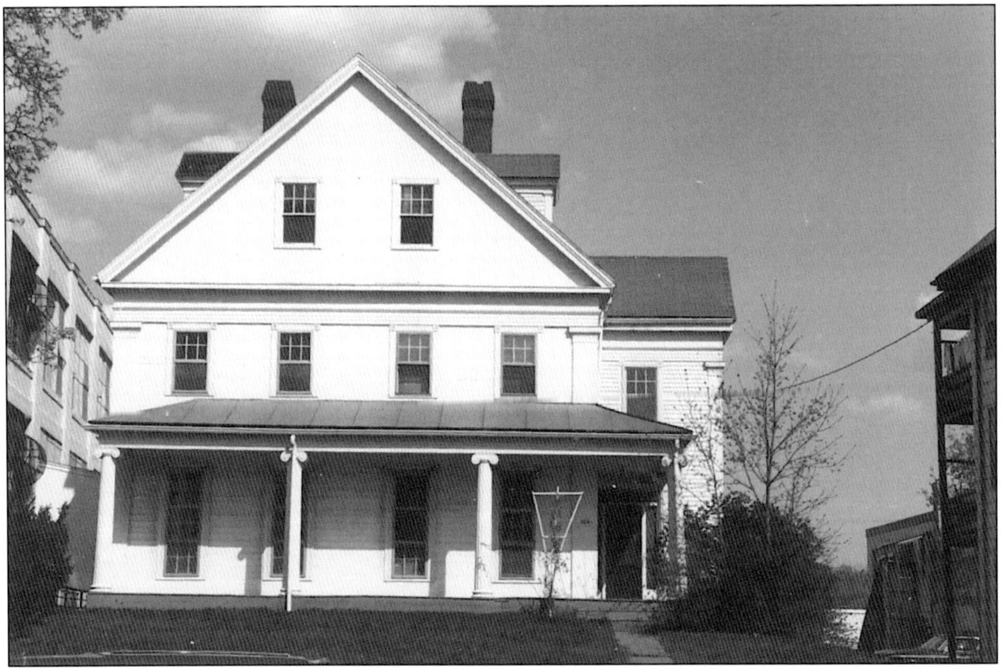

This Greek Revival home was built c. 1842 for Warren Sweetser, an early shoe manufacturer, storekeeper, and Stoneham's second (and fourth) postmaster. Sweetser's store/factory was located on the site where the Chase Block is today. Mr. Sweetser is considered a "father" of the Stoneham shoe industry. His is a fine older home waiting to be recycled.

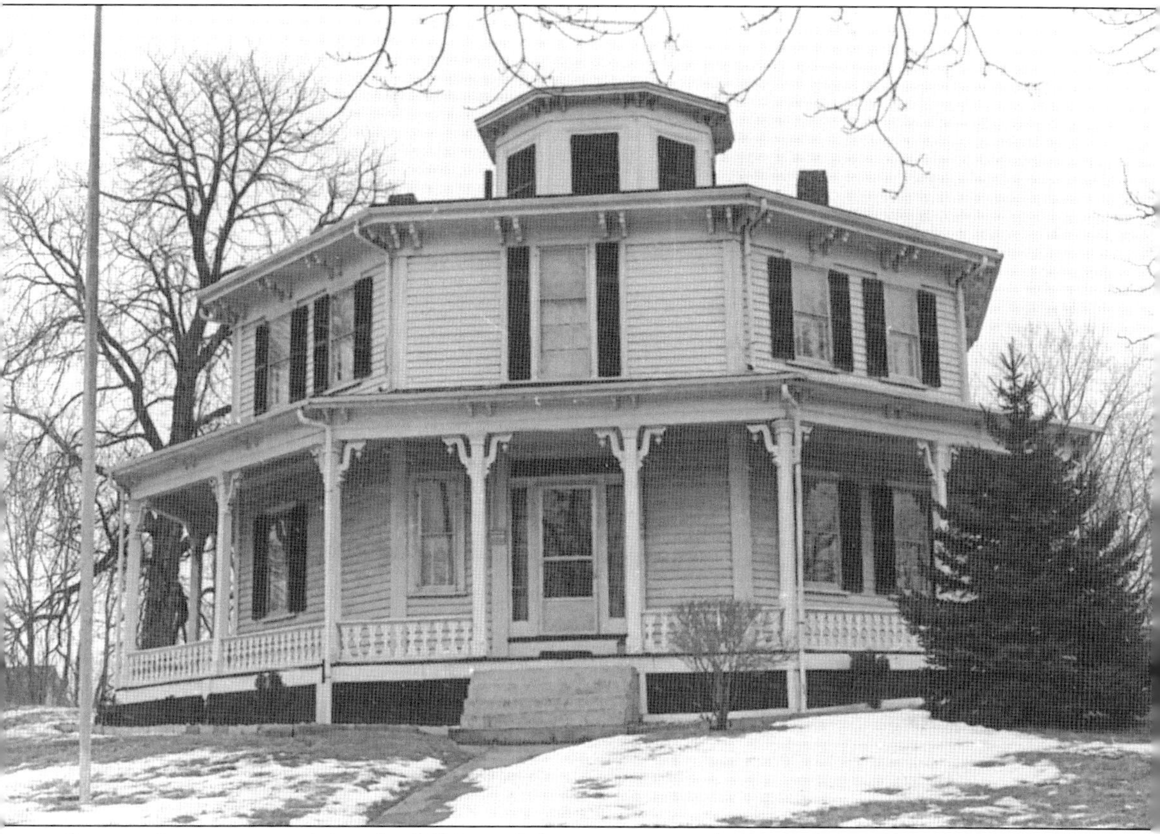

Octagon houses were a fad in the 1850s, and three were erected in Stoneham. This one, located on Pine Street, is thought to have been the first, and was built for Enoch Fuller and his family c. 1850. Mr. Fuller was a currier and died shortly after the house was finished. Originally the house contained a fireplace in every room, and a spiral staircase ascends from the first floor to the third-floor cupola. At one time the structure was used as a lodging house; in recent years, it became a two-family residence. Stoneham's other octagon homes are located on Spring and Summer Streets.

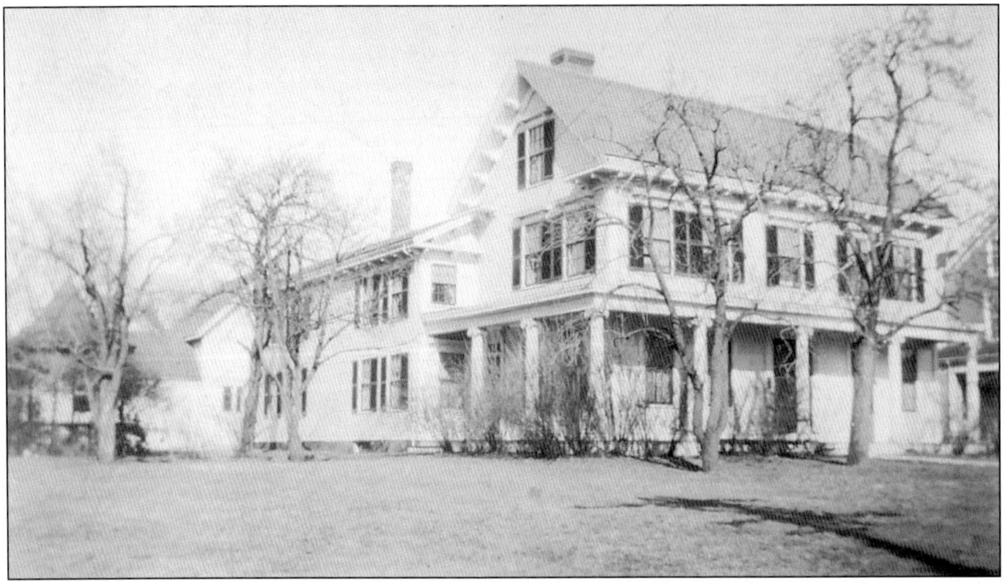

This home was constructed *c.* 1850 for William G. Fuller and his family. Mr. Fuller was in the leather business and in real estate, and he served as the representative to the General Court in 1840. Today, the property serves as a retirement home known as Fuller House.

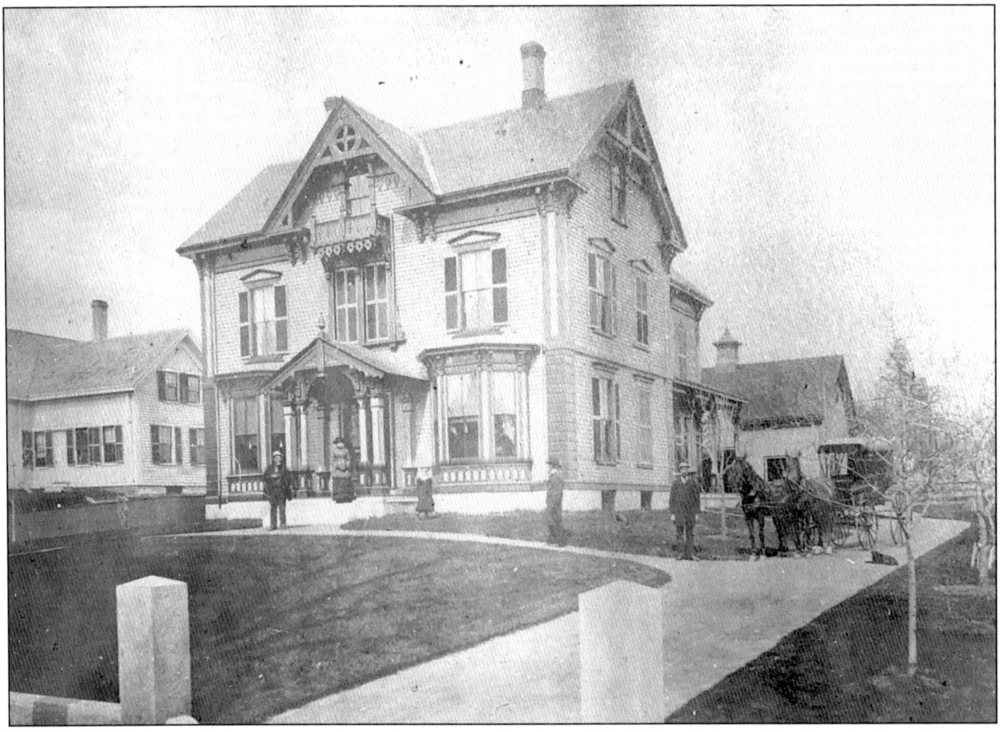

This Italianate-style home on Pine Street was built in 1865 for Robert P. Turnbull, a leather manufacturer associated with William Tidd and Co. The building is known as the Hay House, having been sold to Peter Hay in 1881 and occupied by his son Winthrop until 1932. The Hays were descended from one of Stoneham's earliest settlers.

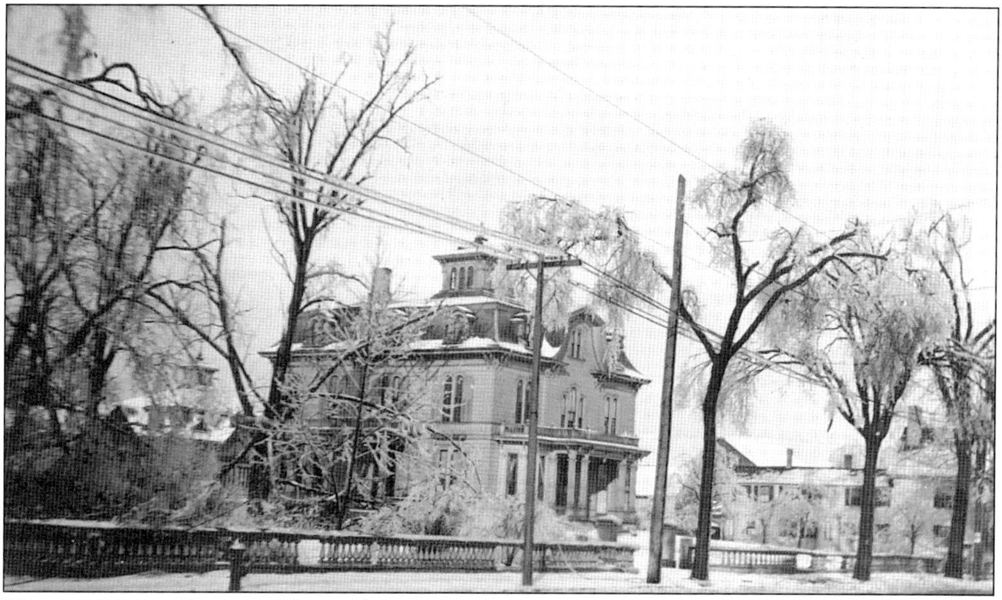

The Arad Gerry Estate was located at the corner of Main and Hersam Streets. Built in 1867, it contained 14 rooms plus a ballroom and a reception room on the third floor. In 1928, the town considered purchasing the property for use as a town office building. The house was razed in 1941, and the post office was constructed on this site.

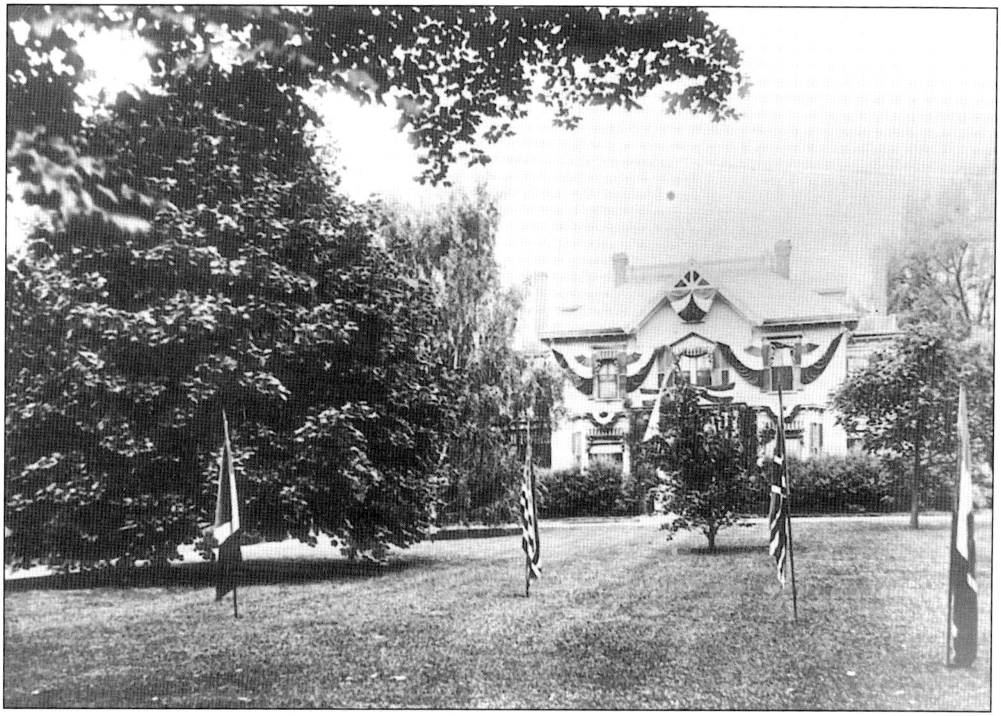

The William B. Stevens home is shown decorated for the town's 200th anniversary in 1925. This home was built at the corner of Main and William Streets in 1871–1872 for Dr. William F. Stevens and was later occupied by his son. It was razed in 1952 to make way for a new First National Store.

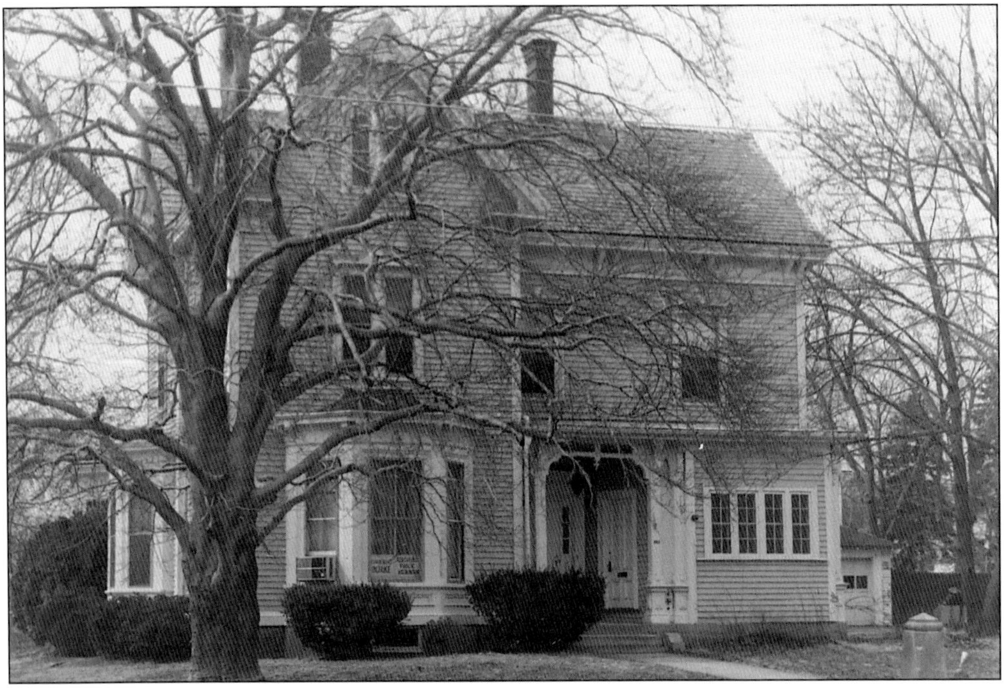

Carpenter Charles A. Libby built this Main Street home at a cost of $6,000 during the summer of 1875 for Edward Buswell, a shoe manufacturer and partner in Drew & Buswell. Although Buswell died within a few years, the home was retained by his widow Clara and family. It is an excellent example of Italianate style and one of the few surviving period houses on Main Street.

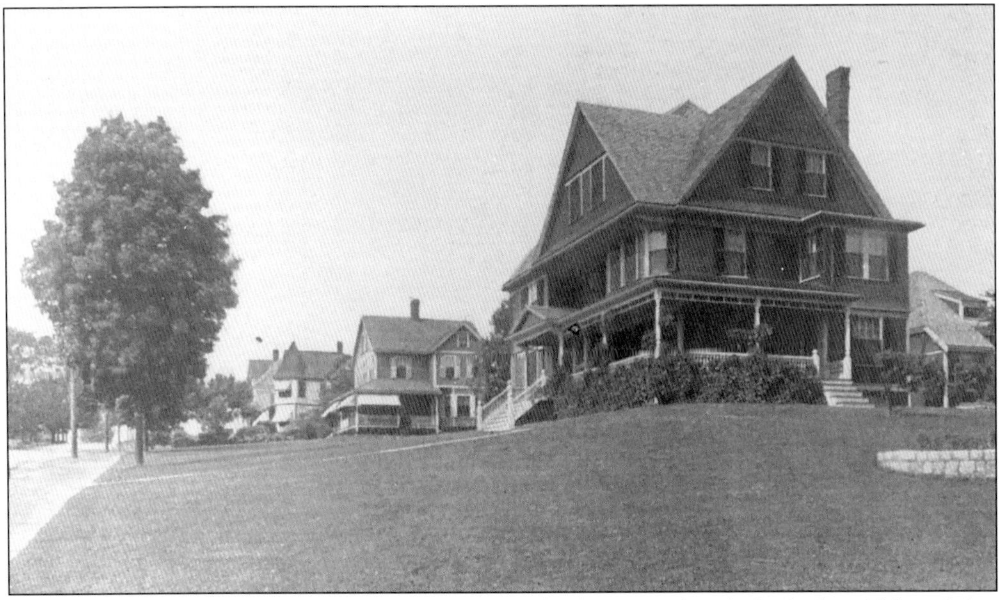

This fine High Street home was built c. 1892 for Charles F. Buck, a hide dealer. Although his business was located in Boston, Buck was always active in Stoneham's civic affairs. He served on the school committee, the finance and advisory board, the planning board, and as a public library trustee. He held offices in the local banks and at the Home for Aged People, now known as Fuller House.

Four

Of Relaxation and Recreation

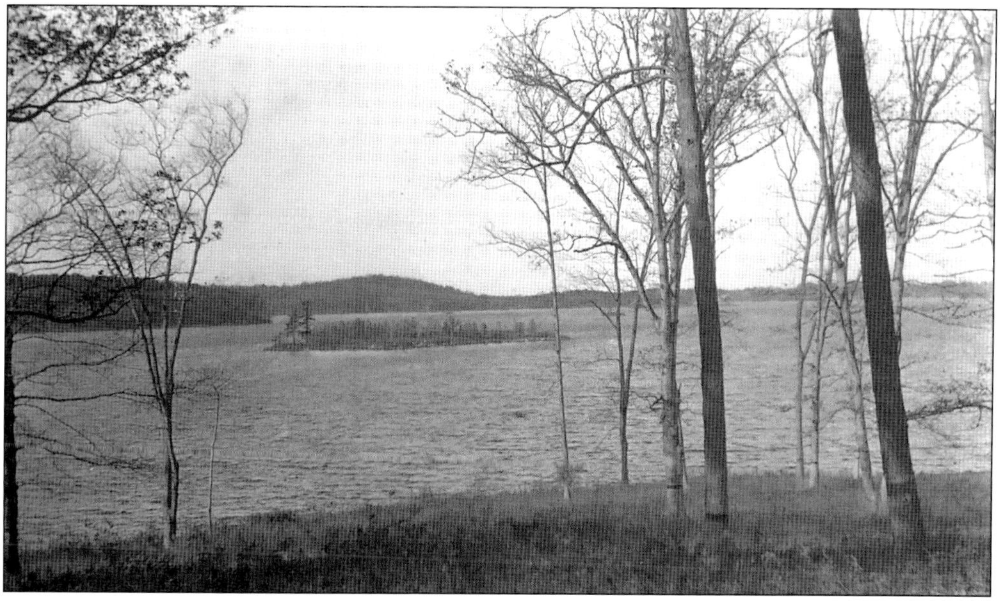

Great Island lies at the southerly end of Spot Pond. Before the water level was raised a century ago, the island was about four times as large. Most people think of the island as the site of boxing matches in the 1850s and 1860s and wonder about Shute's marker (who he was, and when and why he fell).

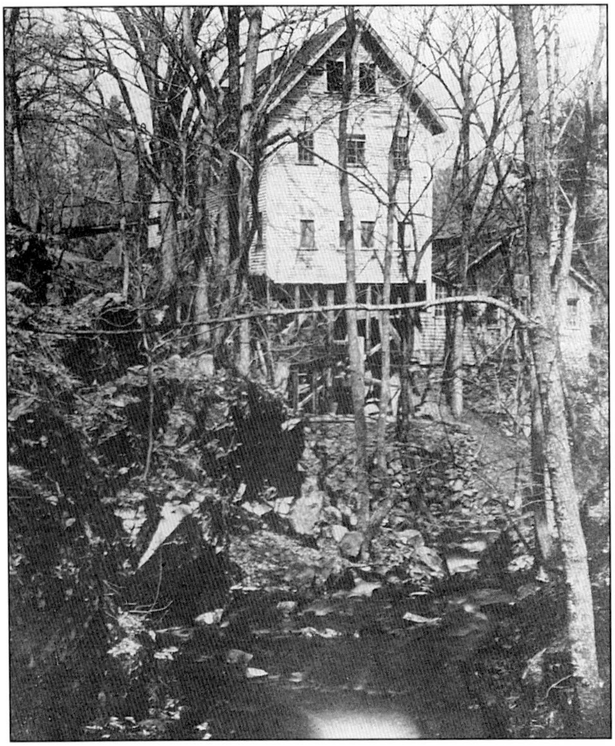

This mill is believed to have been built on Spot Pond Brook c. 1812 for the grinding of spices such as cinnamon and ginger. In addition, the mill ground and pulverized drugs for wholesale druggists in the Boston vicinity. In 1850, Converse and Robson operated the mill and employed 14 men.

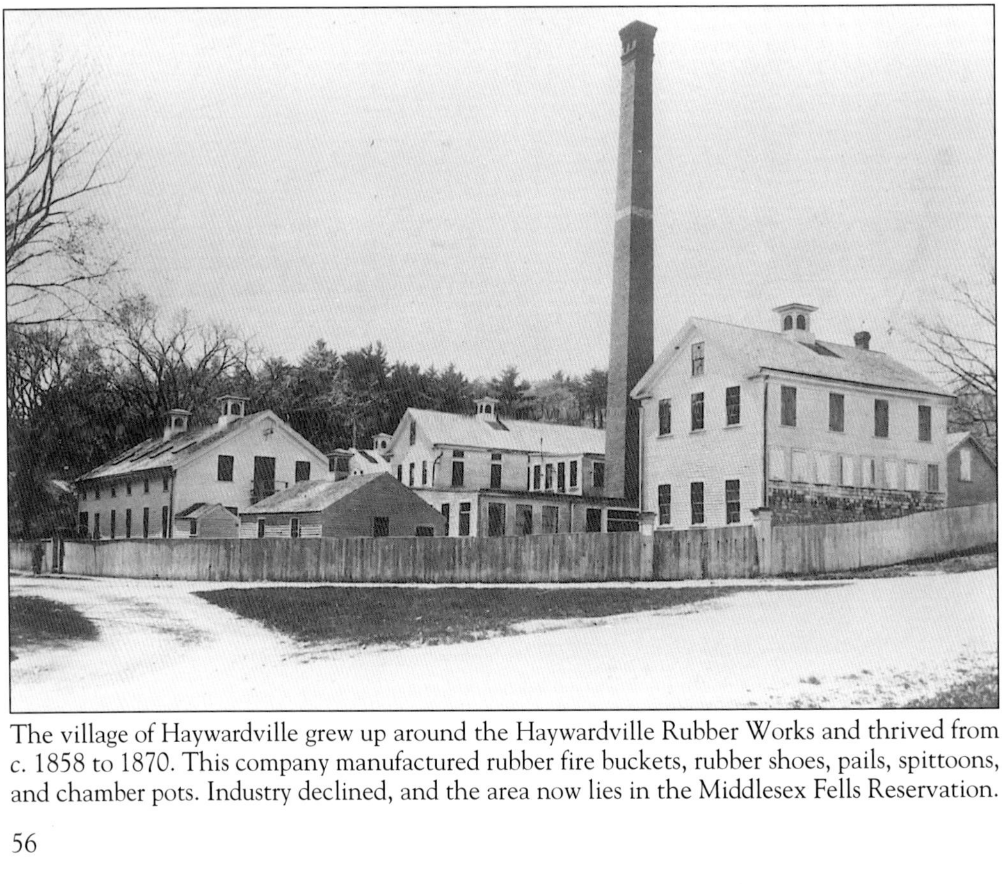

The village of Haywardville grew up around the Haywardville Rubber Works and thrived from c. 1858 to 1870. This company manufactured rubber fire buckets, rubber shoes, pails, spittoons, and chamber pots. Industry declined, and the area now lies in the Middlesex Fells Reservation.

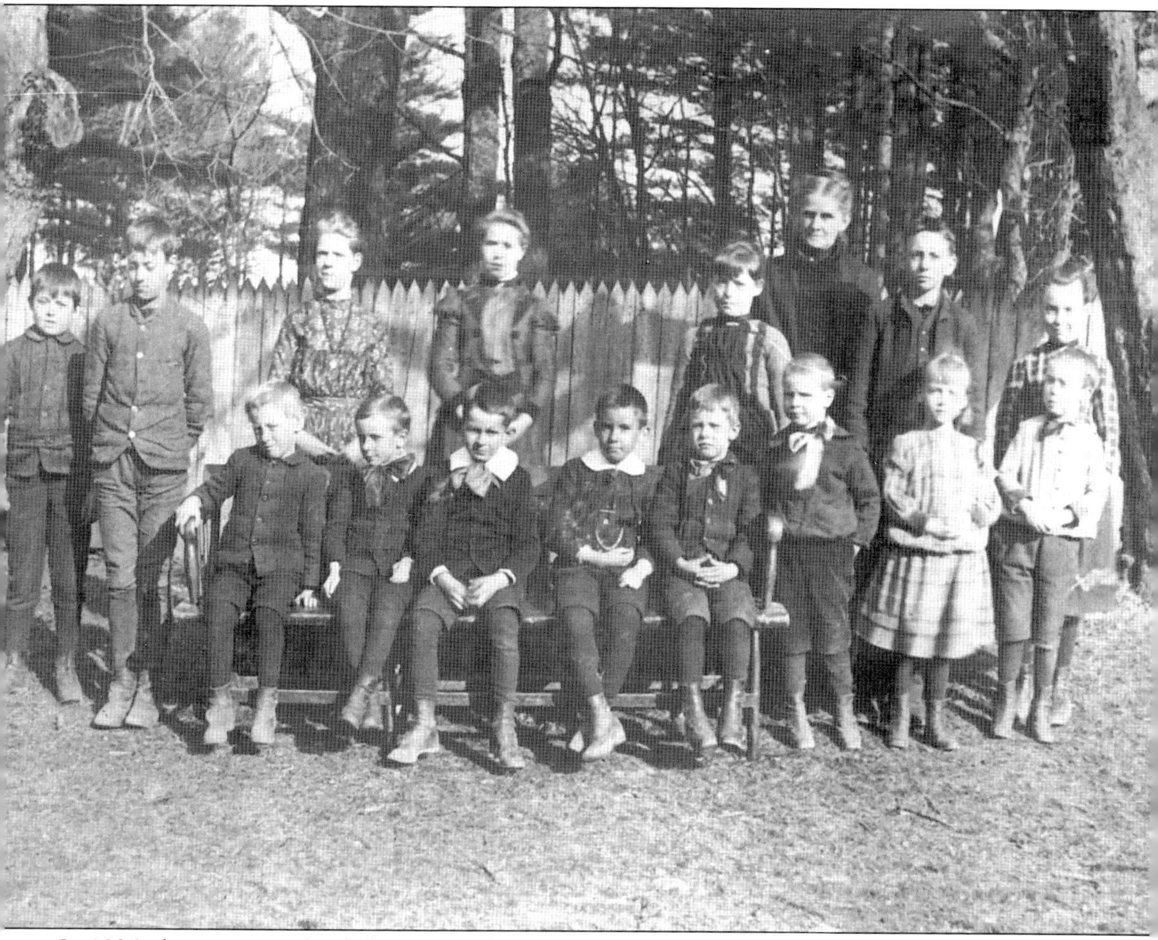

In 1836, the town was divided into six school districts. The area near Spot Pond was marked as District 4, but was more familiarly known as Wyoming. In 1851, a new building was erected on the south side of Pond Street to educate the children who lived in the Spot Pond/Haywardville area, and this one-room school was in operation from 1851 to 1899. Enrollment began to decline by 1870 as industry declined in the nearby Haywardville area. Shown here is longtime teacher Susanna (Dean) Richardson with her pupils. Mrs. Richardson taught at this school from April 1863 until it closed in April 1899 with the exception of the fall and winter terms of 1882–1883, when her son was born.

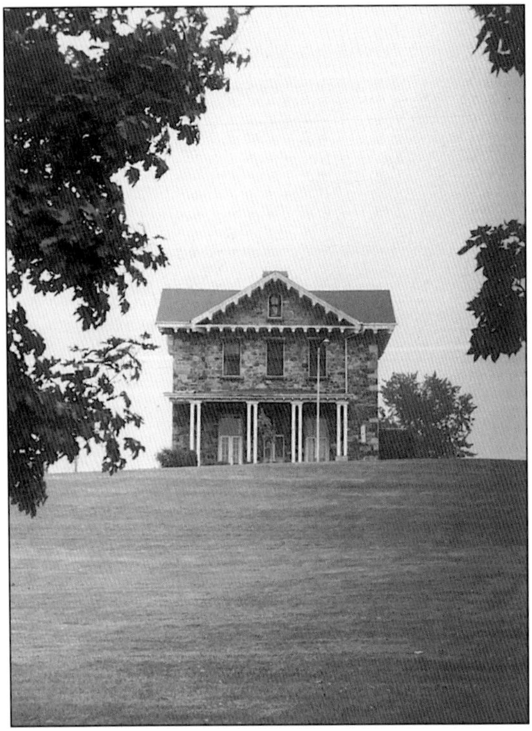

Langwood Hall was built near Spot Pond *c.* 1847 by William Bailey Lang, a Boston iron and steel dealer and one of three Boston businessmen involved in developing the Wyoming area. Lang was an amateur architect and designed his own home. He chose to build on the east side of Woodland Road on a slight knoll, perhaps offering a better view of Spot Pond. Langwood Hall was later part of the Hotel Langwood and the New England Memorial Hospital. It was demolished in 1986.

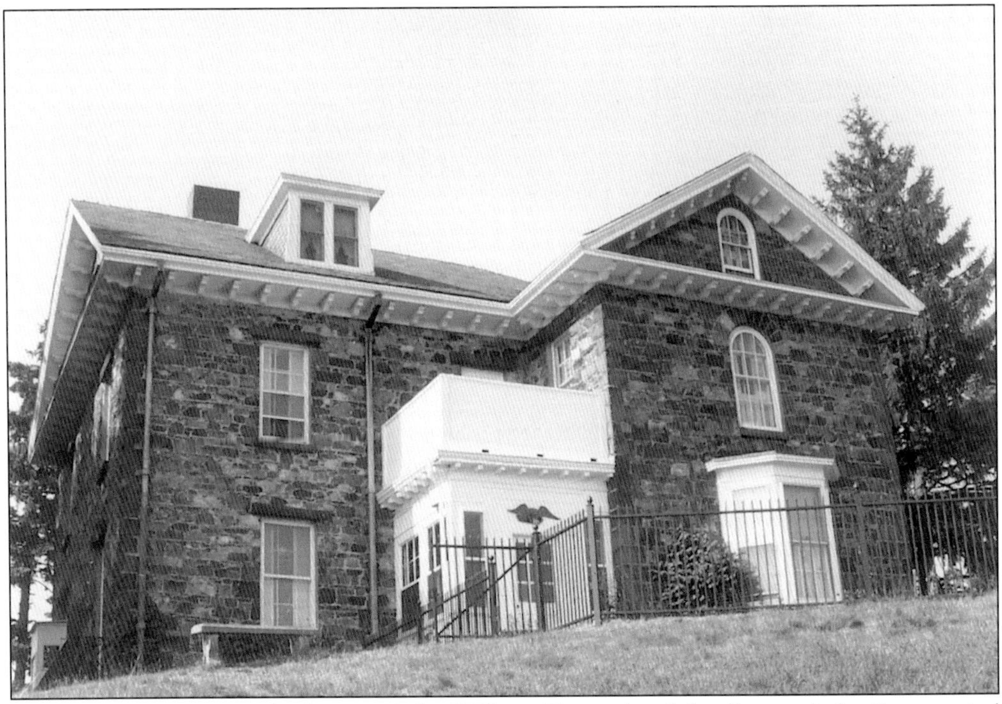

The Botume House was built *c.* 1848 for William Foster, but John Botume's family occupied it from 1855 to 1898. Botume served in the state legislature from 1867 to 1869 representing Melrose, Stoneham, and Winchester. The Metropolitan District Commission now uses this mansion for its headquarters.

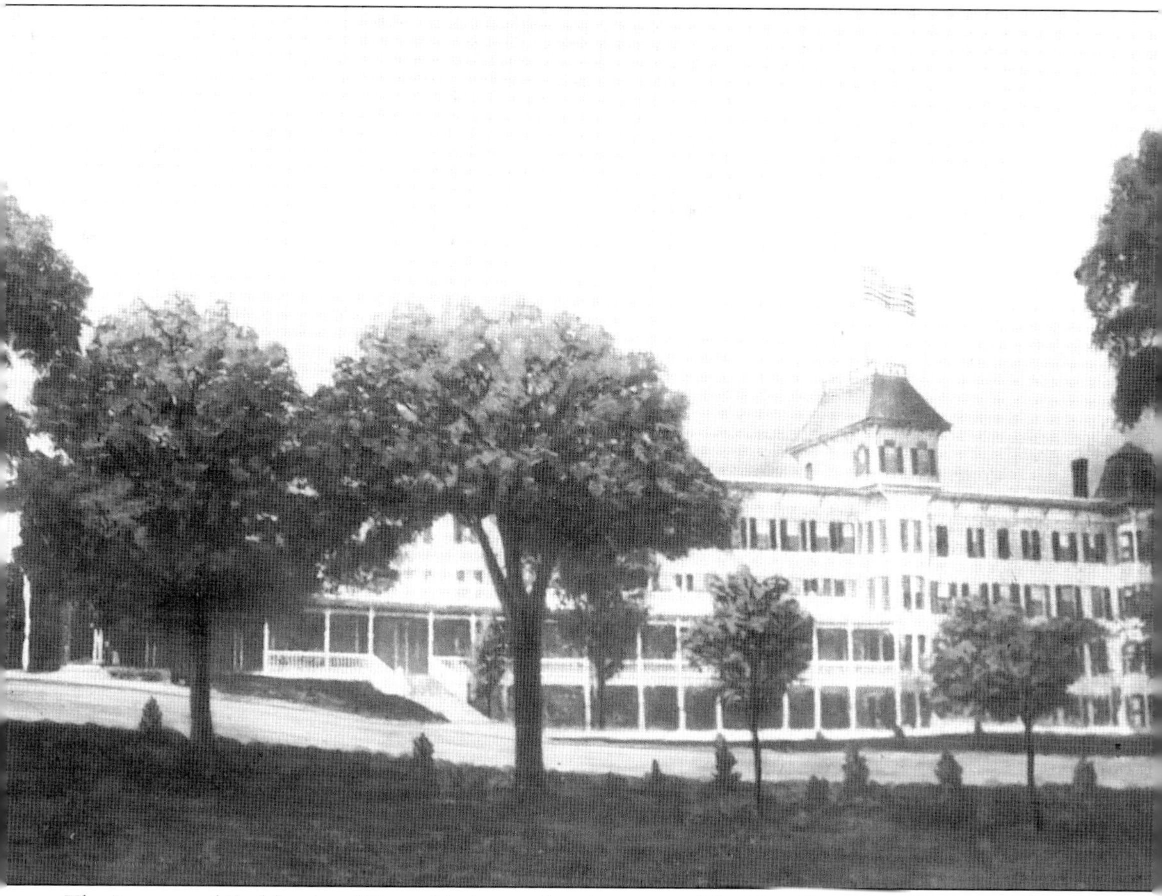

The Langwood Parkland and Trust Co. began development of the Hotel Langwood c. 1890. This view is from a painting and shows the annex, which was constructed to the north of Langwood Hall. Open year round and with rates from $2.50 to $5 per day, the hotel contained 150 rooms on four floors, and the views of Spot Pond from the veranda were spectacular. In addition, there were cottages such as Maple Cottage and Summit Cottage, and another building, known as the Wigwam, served as a social center and amusement hall. A garden provided fresh vegetables in season, and cows and chickens were kept to provide the freshest milk and eggs. It is said that cockfighting was held in a pit in the cellar, and that gambling took place in a hidden room reached by a narrow, secret staircase. After a fire on April 1, 1902, the owners sold the building to the Seventh-Day Adventist General Conference.

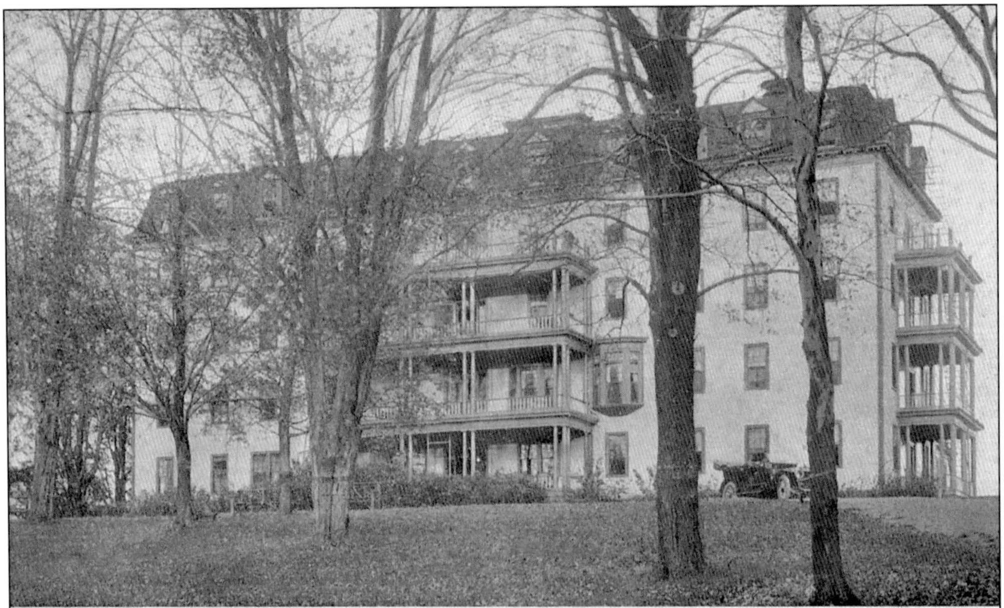

The New England Sanitarium, Stoneham, Mass.

The Seventh-Day Adventists purchased the Hotel Langwood and surrounding land as a site on which to relocate their South Lancaster Sanitarium. This new main building was constructed in 1906. The "San" became New England Memorial Hospital in 1967 and later the Boston Regional Medical Center.

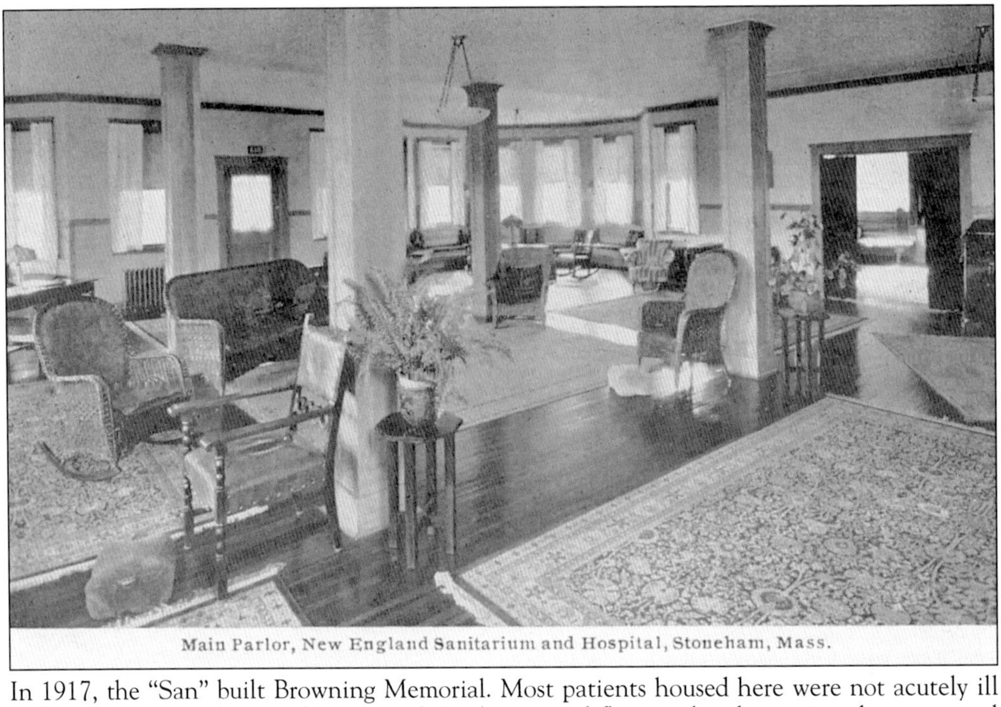

Main Parlor, New England Sanitarium and Hospital, Stoneham, Mass.

In 1917, the "San" built Browning Memorial. Most patients housed here were not acutely ill and could come and go as they pleased. In this second-floor parlor they enjoyed many social events, musicals, and lectures.

Bear Hill Observatory was built in 1910 and replaced an earlier wooden tower that was built by the Appalachian Mountain Club. The view is not only of the Middlesex Fells and Boston, but on a clear day includes the Blue Hill Range, Temple Mountain, and Mount Monadnock.

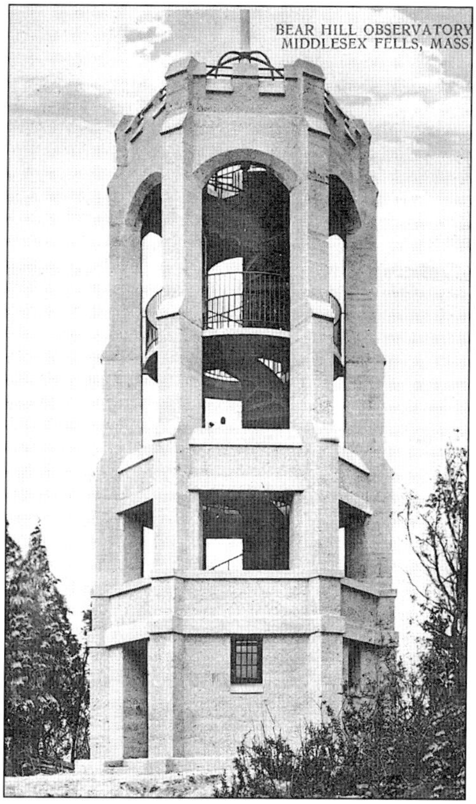

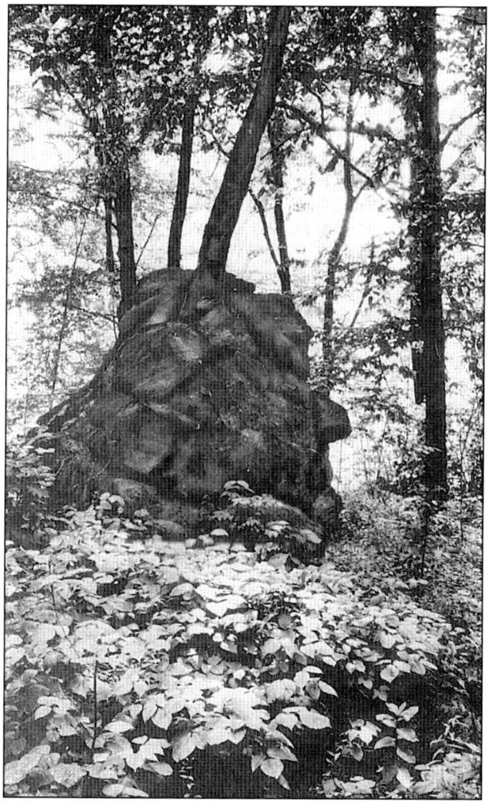

The Old Man of the Fells was a rock formation in the Middlesex Fells. Standing on a high ridge near Pine Hill, the rock overlooked Forest Street in Medford. Many compared it to a similar profile in New Hampshire. The construction of Route 93 destroyed this rocky profile.

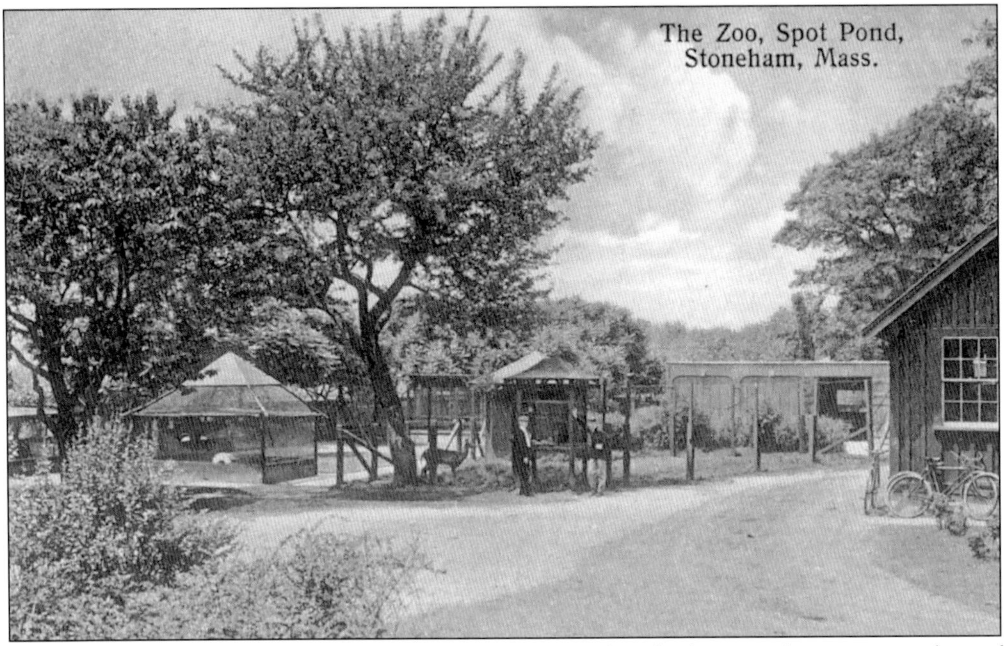

Charles Price began a small collection of local animals when he became the superintendent of the Middlesex Fells Reservation. His collection grew through the years, as did the number of people who came to visit it. Eventually, the Metropolitan Parks Commission began to help with the costs of feeding the animals and building their cages. This postcard was mailed on June 10, 1912, and its message says, in part, "In memory of the day we visited this place."

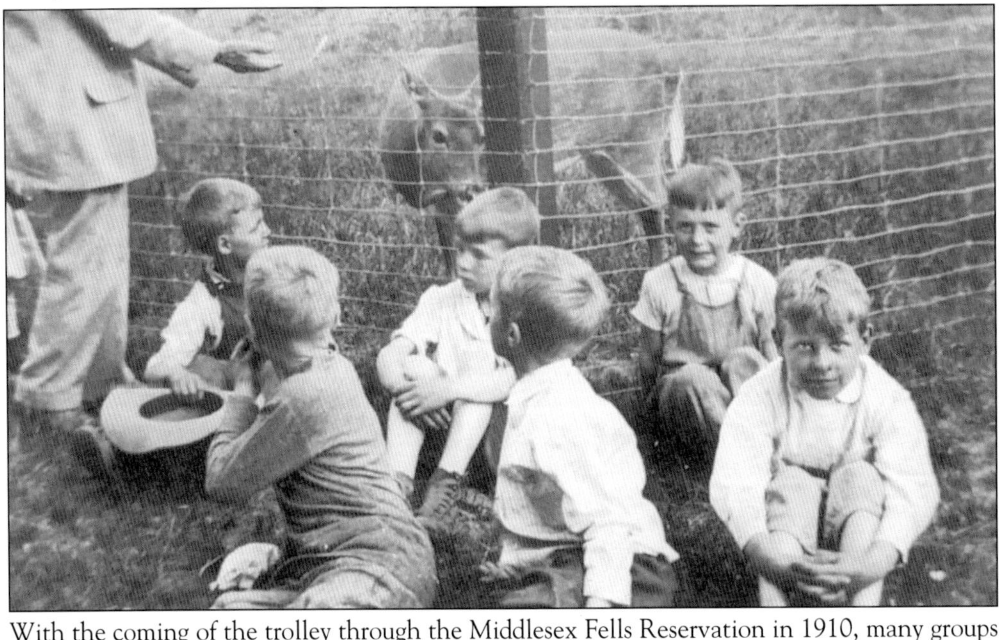

With the coming of the trolley through the Middlesex Fells Reservation in 1910, many groups of inner city youngsters were treated to a day in the suburbs, where they could enjoy the fresh air and countryside. This project was referred to as "Fresh Air Children," and churches and various social agencies acted as hosts. These children are part of a group of Fresh Air Children admiring a deer at the zoo c. 1915.

American elk or wapiti lived at the Middlesex Fells Zoo for many years. These animals are quite rare in the United States. They often weigh up to 800 pounds and are second in size only to the moose in North America.

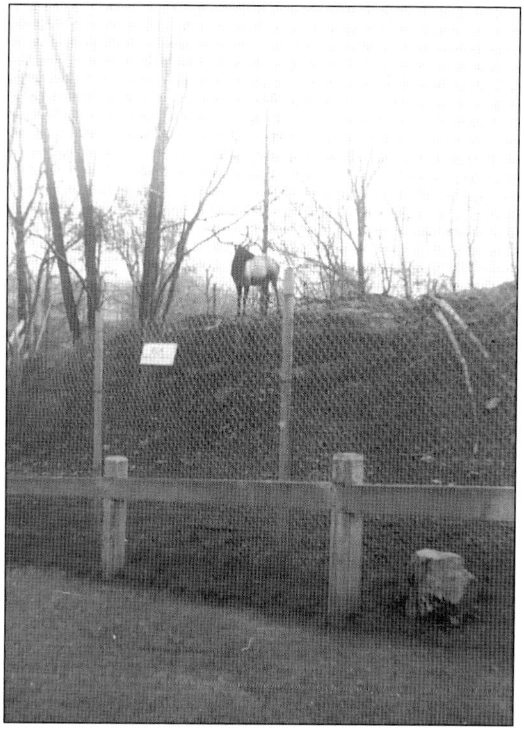

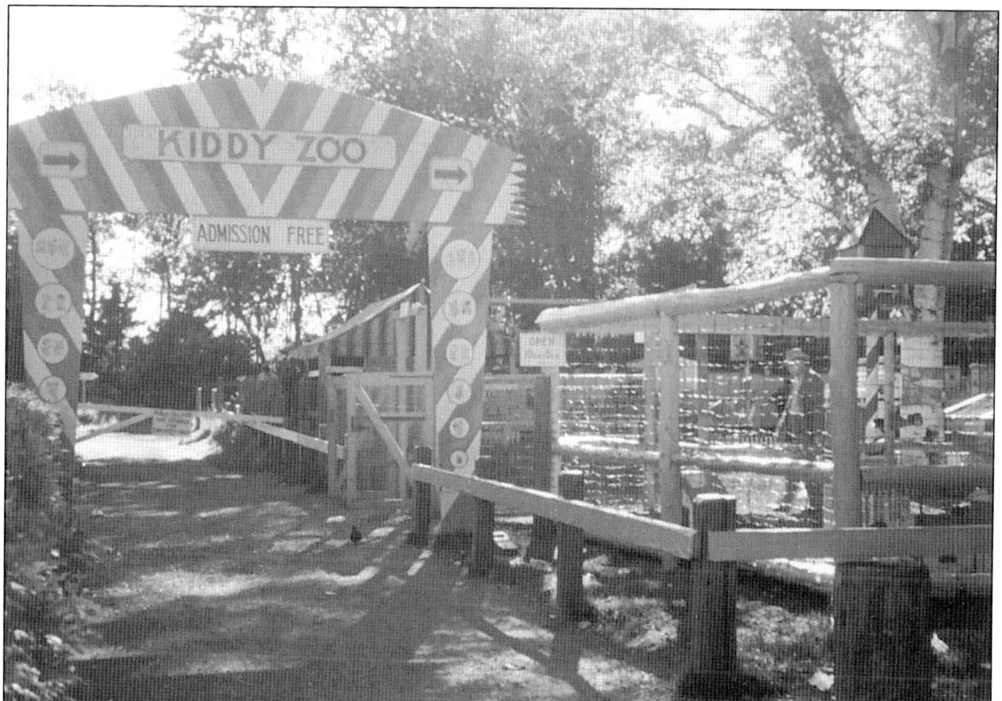

In the 1950s, the zoo had a popular feature known as the Kiddy Zoo. Among the exhibits it housed were a skunk (Petunia, admission one scent), three little kittens (who washed their mittens), Mary and her lamb, and sheep (Whitey and the Ink Spots).

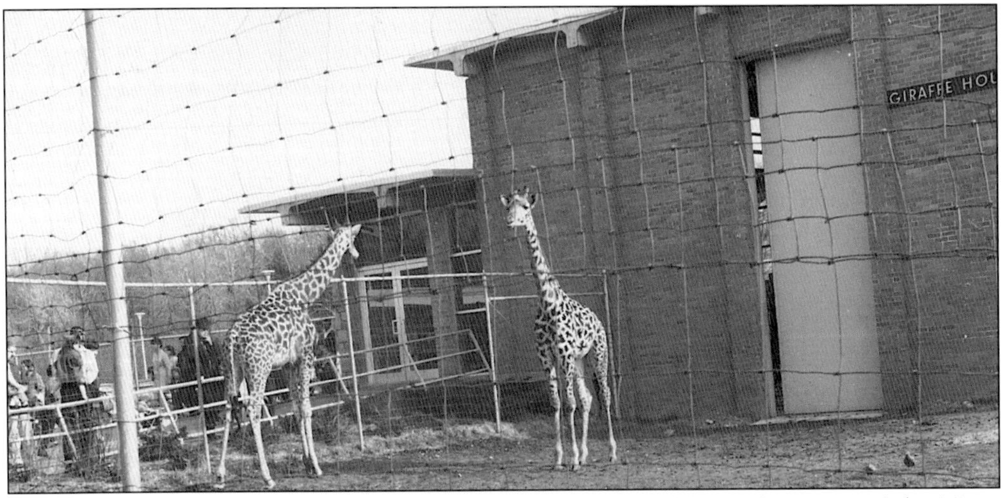

The arrival of giraffes at the Middlesex Fells Zoo posed a problem. They were of the Masai variety (the tallest of the species!). Now, where can a one-year-old animal already 11 feet tall live? The answer was to build a Giraffe House 20 feet high.

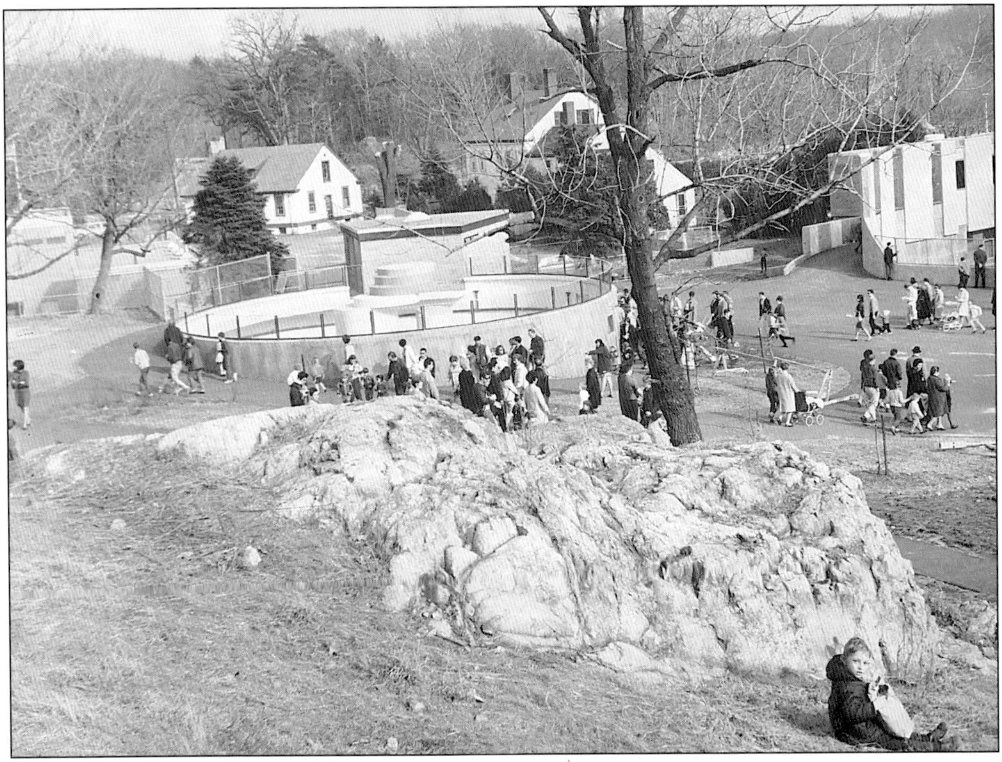

This is a 1960s view of the Middlesex Fells Zoo. Admission was free, and from early spring until fall, visitors came by the thousands, especially on weekends. Cars were often parked for a quarter of a mile on either side of the entrance, which is shown in the background of this photograph. Beside the zoo is the old Gould Homestead; the house's last residents before its demolition were members of the Walter D. Stone family. Mr. Stone became the first professional Middlesex Fells Zoo director in 1959, and after his untimely death, the zoo was renamed for him in 1969.

Peanuts was an African elephant whose antics delighted children at Stone Zoo in the 1970s and early 1980s. She enjoyed her daily walk or "safari" through the grounds. In 1982, Peanuts left Stone Zoo for a new home at the North Carolina Zoological Park in Asheboro.

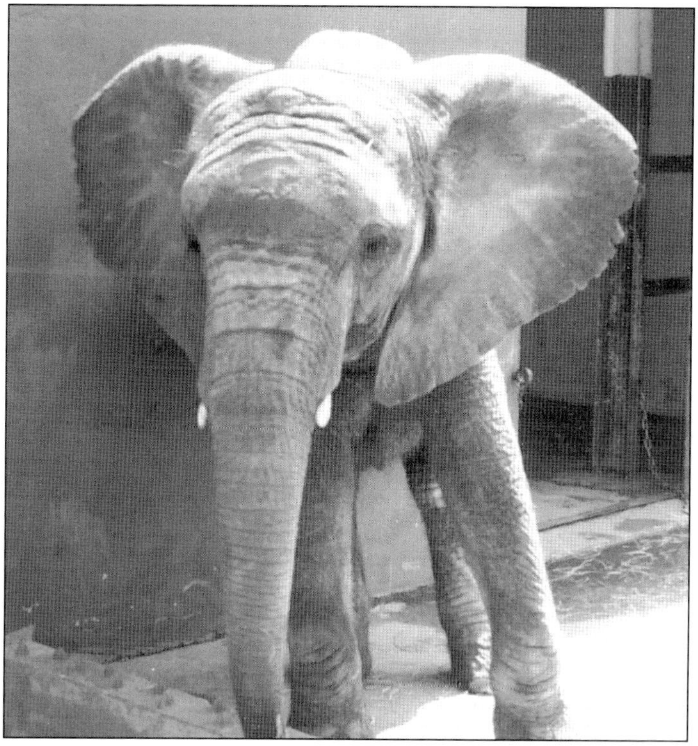

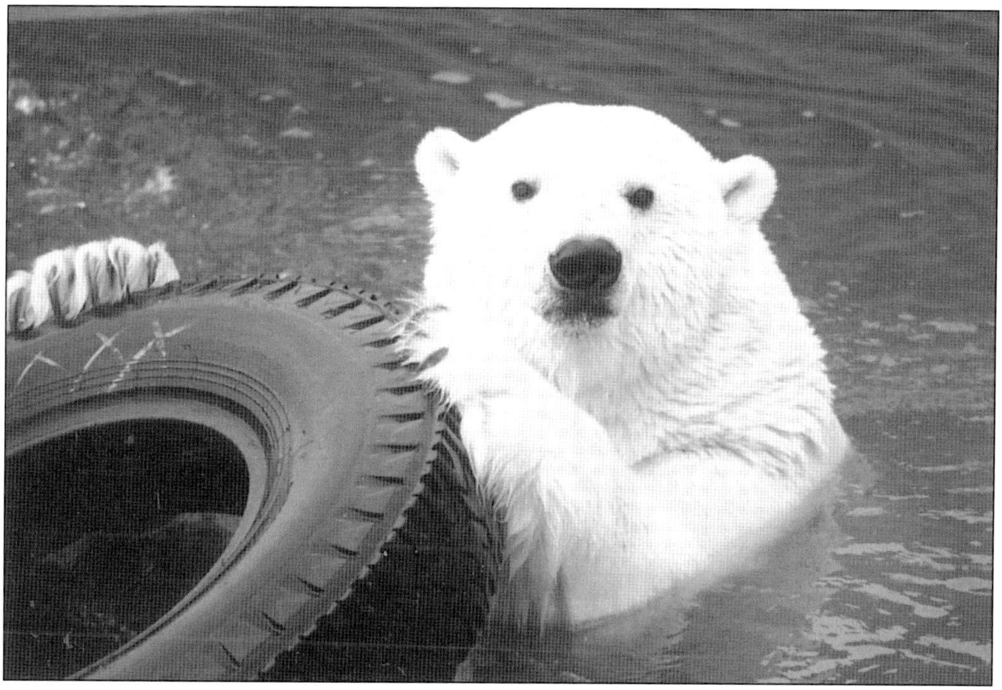

Major, Stone Zoo's polar bear, was 13 years old when he arrived in Stoneham on July 1, 1979. He came to Stoneham from the Worcester Science Center but is originally from Siberia. Major is treated to an annual birthday party each January. Though perhaps not as playful now, he is still a prime attraction.

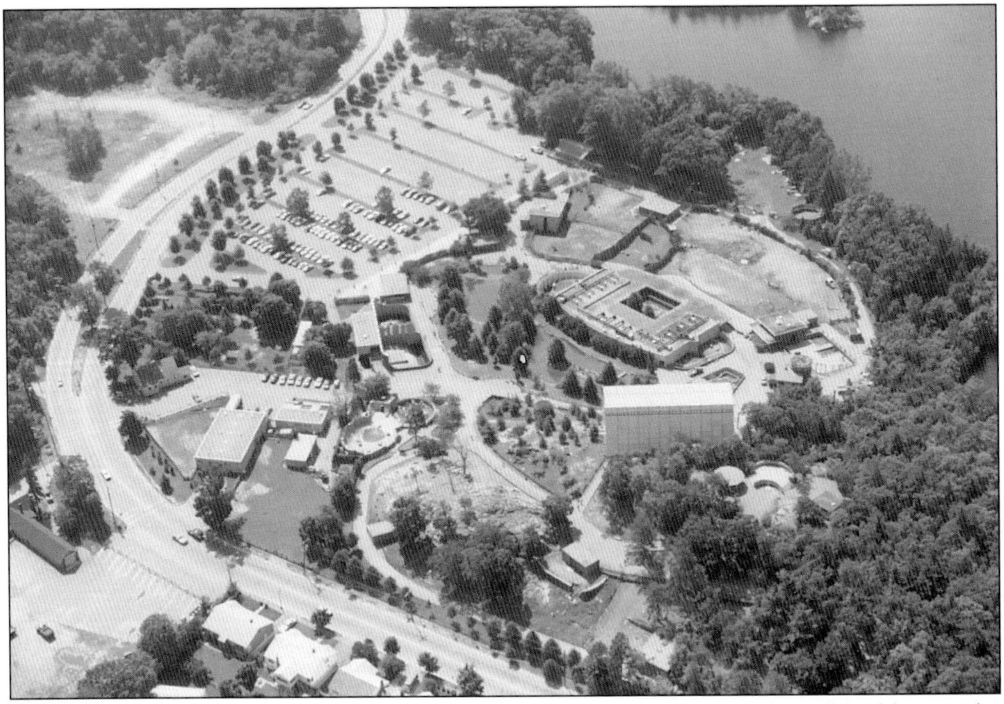

This aerial view of Stone Zoo was taken during the summer of 1980. The tall building at the right is the aviary, which was opened the previous year. At that time, it was the largest free-flight indoor aviary.

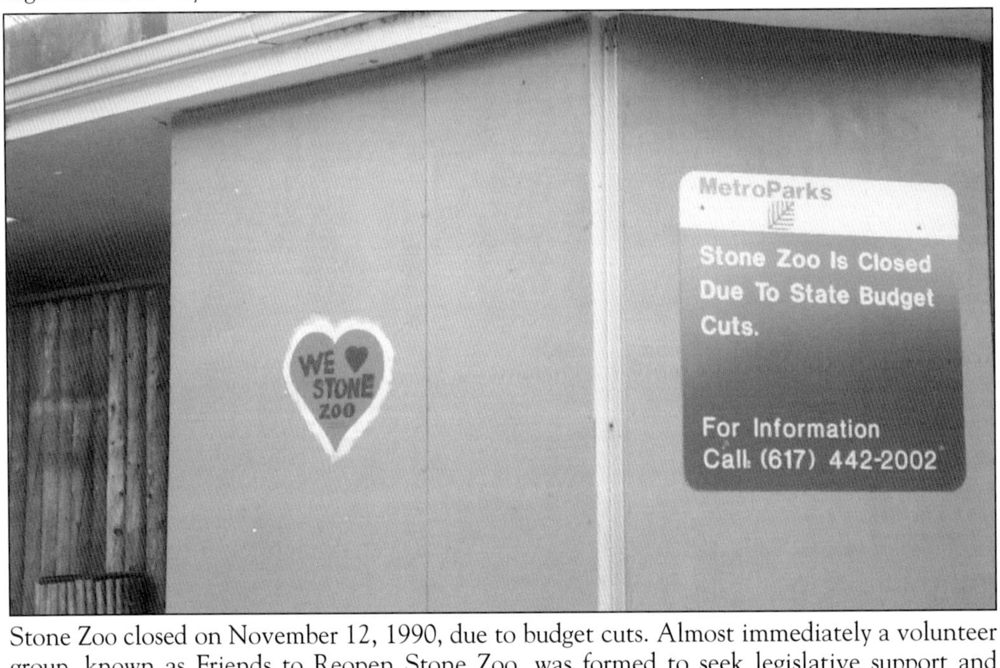

Stone Zoo closed on November 12, 1990, due to budget cuts. Almost immediately a volunteer group, known as Friends to Reopen Stone Zoo, was formed to seek legislative support and heighten community interest. The untiring efforts of this group, along with the persistence of our legislators, culminated in the reopening of the zoo on June 6, 1992. At present, the zoo is being renovated to create an earth park with a keystone animal in each section.

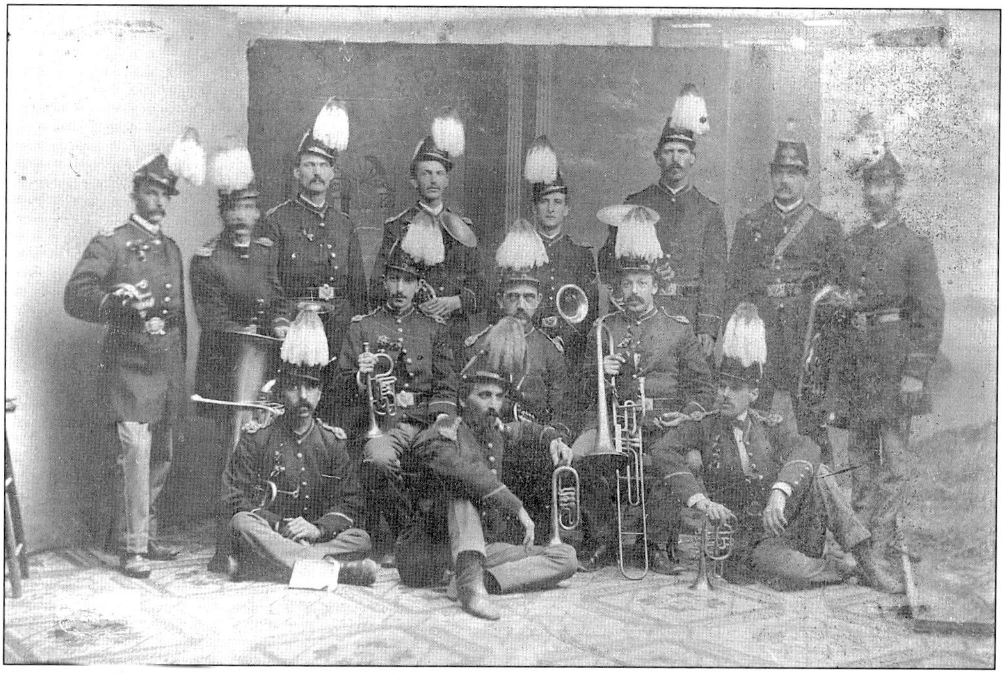

Every small town had a brass band from the close of the Civil War to the turn of the 20th century. Pictured here is the Stoneham Brigade Band, which was organized in May 1877. This 1878 tintype was taken in Lowell.

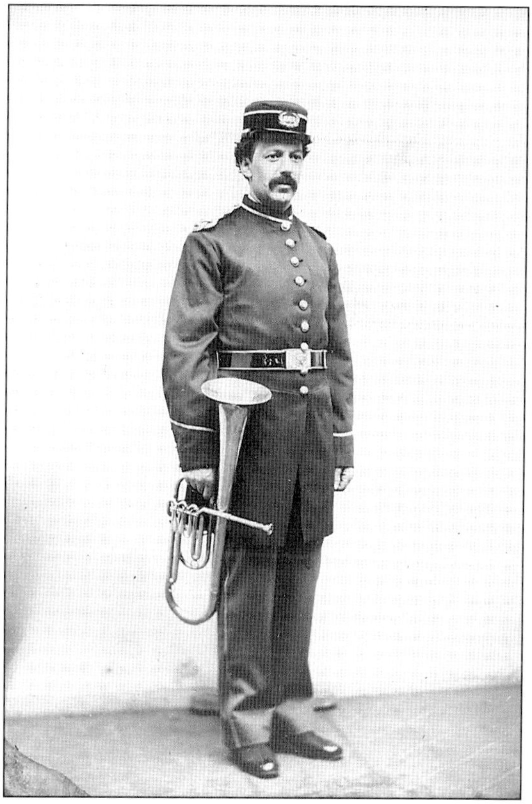

The young man with a horn is Alfred W. Theobald, a member of the Stoneham Brass Band in the 1890s. Theobald worked as a box maker, but spent most of his leisure time during the winter months practicing with the band. In spring came performances on Patriot's Day, Memorial Day, and the Fourth of July, as well as frequent outdoor concerts.

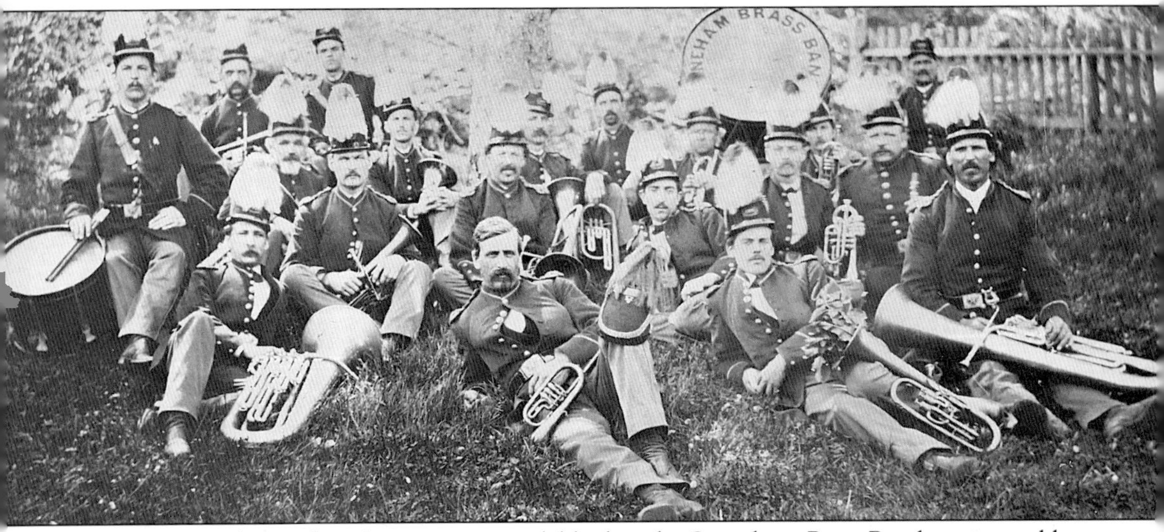

Unfortunately no identifications are available, but the Stoneham Brass Band as pictured here seems to have been typical. Such bands were usually composed of about 25 musicians of varying ages. In many instances, older member had participated in regimental bands during the Civil War. C. Emery Gilbert, for example, served as a musician in a Maine regiment, moving to Stoneham after the Civil War. He was the band's leader for about ten years. Another military musician was Caleb Noble, who played with the 19th Massachusetts Regiment. Through the years there were often father/son combinations, such as Joseph and Alfred Theobald and Joseph and Fred Nickerson. Wearing such natty uniforms with gold buttons and braid and topped by shakos, it is no wonder brass bands captured attention.

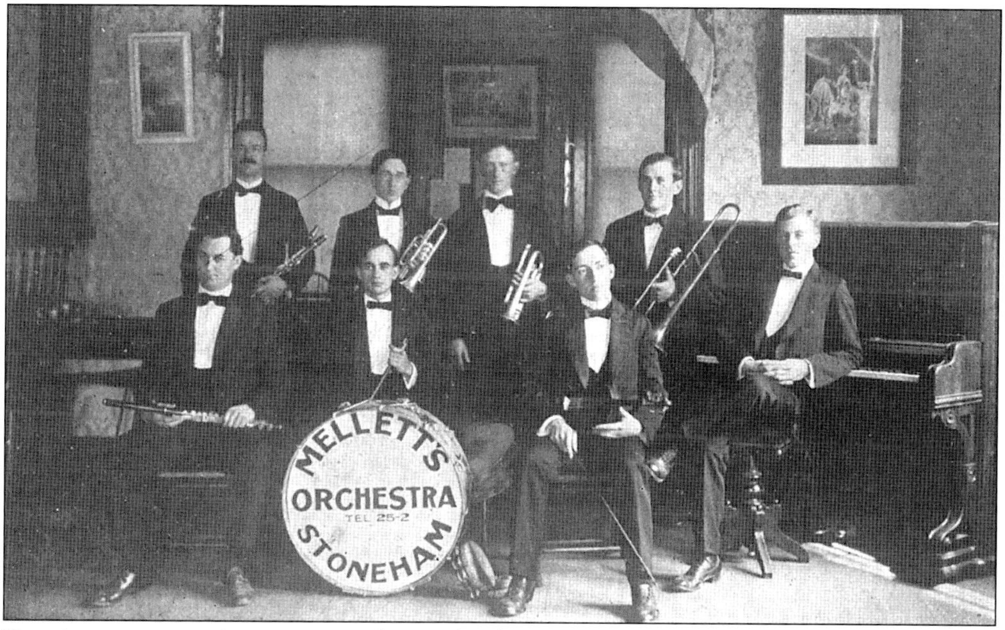

Dancing was a popular recreation during the first part of the 20th century, and dance bands such as Mellett's Orchestra were in great demand. Led by Harry Mellett, the band's lively tunes kept pace with the latest dance crazes. Everyone did the two-step, the turkey trot, and the fox trot, while the more daring in later years did the black bottom, the Charleston, and the Lindy.

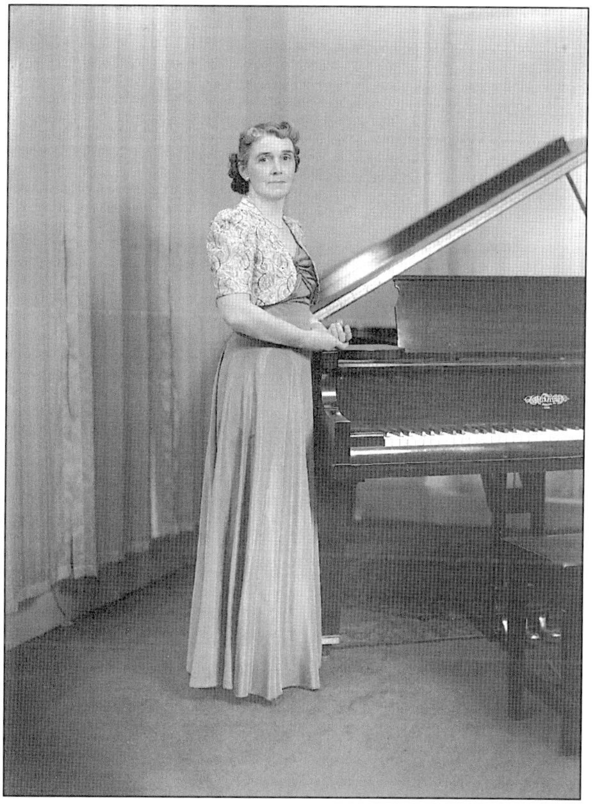

Kathryn B. English will long be remembered for her many community activities. Her passion for music was passed on to all with whom she came in touch. She was an active participant in the Home Front Trust and an organizer of community concerts; she also held elected offices on the school committee and was a public library trustee. Singing and working with the Christian Doctrine program were among her many contributions to St. Patrick's Church.

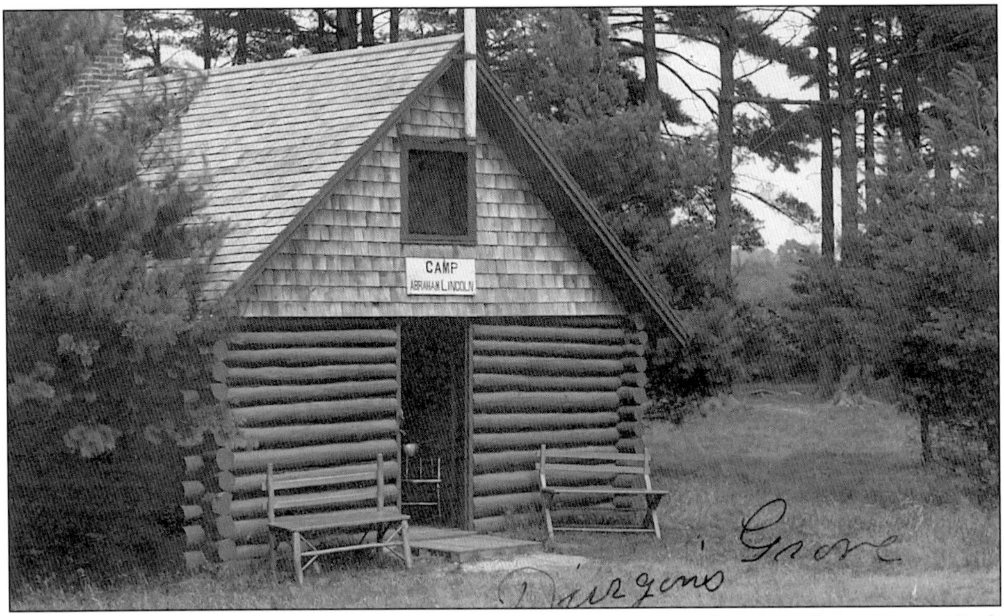

Picnic groves were popular in the late 1800s, and there were several in Stoneham. Durgin Park on Green Street contained about 17 acres and was operated by Erastus A. Durgin. This grove was also known as Abe Lincoln's Park and the Beechwood Farm Picnic Grove.

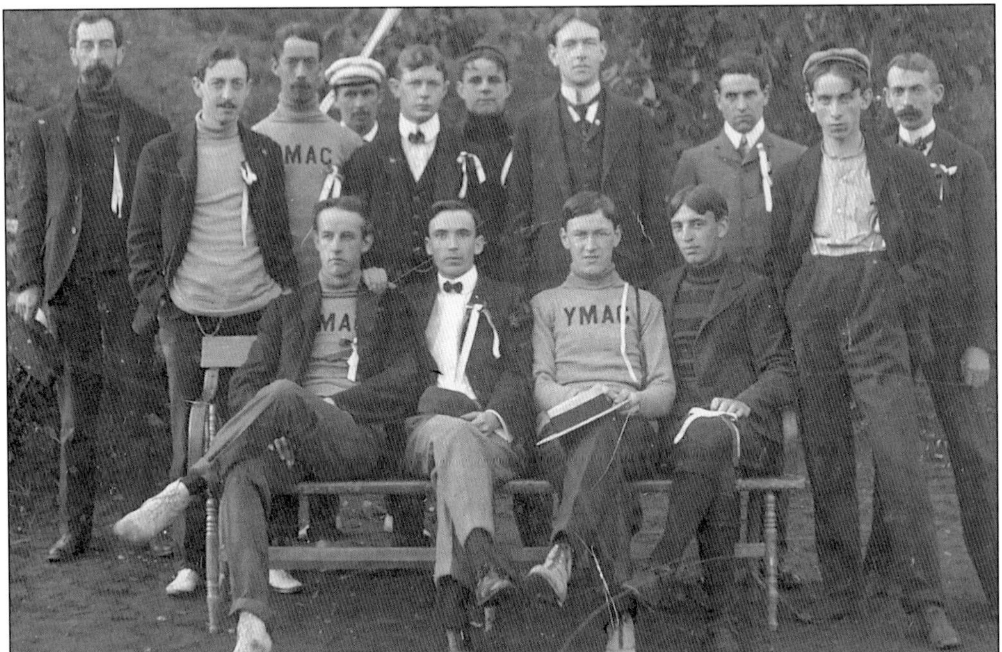

The Congregational Church sponsored the Young Men's Advance Club (YMAC), and this c. 1905 image shows the club at the tennis courts on Spring Street. From left to right are as follows: (front row) unidentified, Philip MacDonald, Bill Lister, and unidentified; (back row) Rev. B. Alfred Dumm, unidentified, William Chapman, Nathan Chapman, unidentified, Ernest Bell, Ethan Delano, ? French, James Munroe, and Arthur Jones.

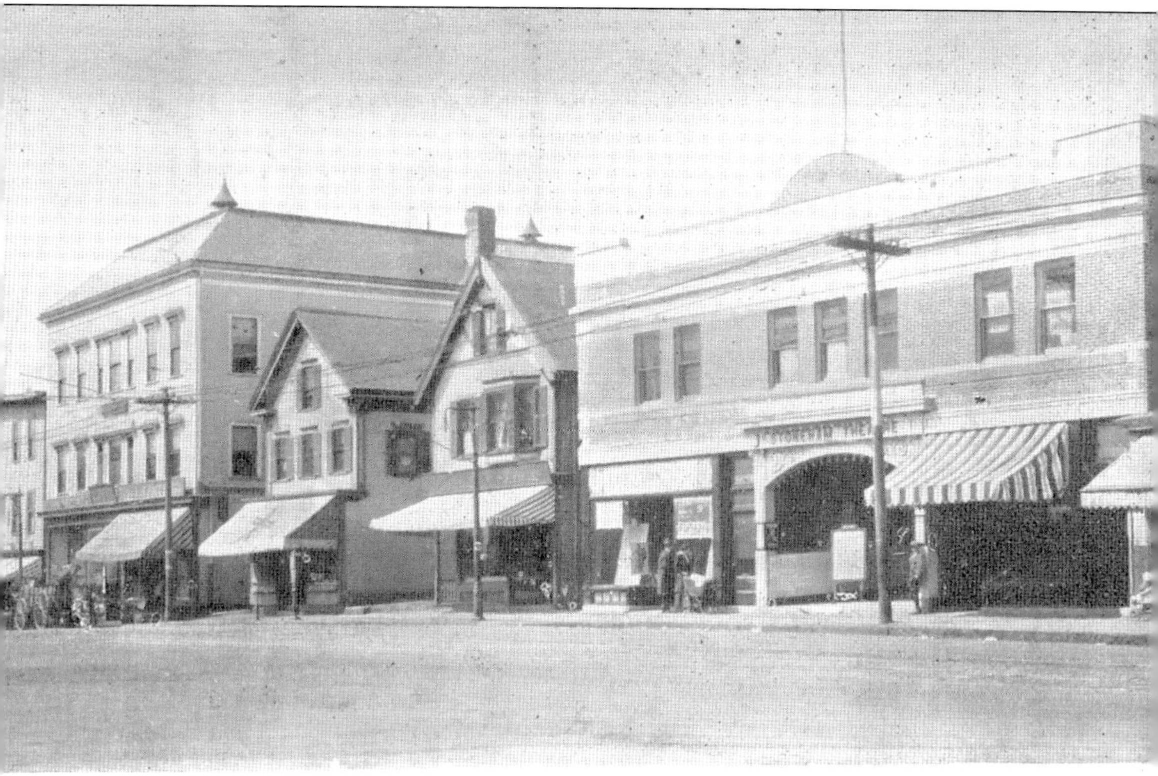

New Stoneham Theatre, Stoneham, Mass.

The Stoneham, built by Joseph Defarrari, opened on November 2, 1917, and was the first building in Stoneham designed specifically for movies. Though equipped for movies, the building also housed vaudeville, lectures, concerts, and plays. Through the years various owners tried to keep pace with advancing technology, but drive-in movies and television took a toll on attendance. In later years, the Stoneham was operated by non-residents interested in presenting adult entertainment. Local authorities revoked licenses, seized films, fought court battles, and finally closed the Stoneham. For many year this building, known affectionately as Oscar's Palace, was an important part of our small-town American culture. It has now been closed nearly a quarter of a century. A building full of memories has fallen into disrepair, but hope remains strong that it will soon be restored and reopened.

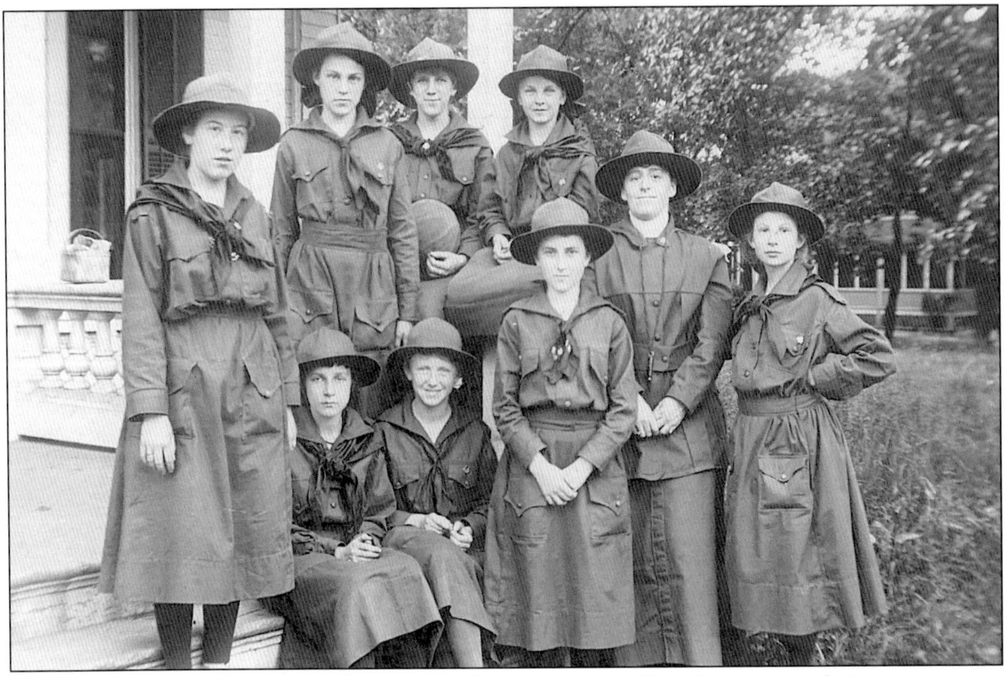

Girl Scouts have had a long and exemplary history here in Stoneham since their organization in 1916. The following year the Girl Scouts came under the sponsorship of the Stoneham Woman's Club and had around 100 members in three troops. Pictured are girls of the Eagle Patrol on June 18, 1917. They are as follows, from left to right: (front row, seated) Martha Terry and Pauline Foss; (front row, standing) Mary Parker, Leader Nellie Patch, and Ruth Massey; (back row) Audrey Parker, Barbara Chase, Marie Burgess, and Marjorie Howe.

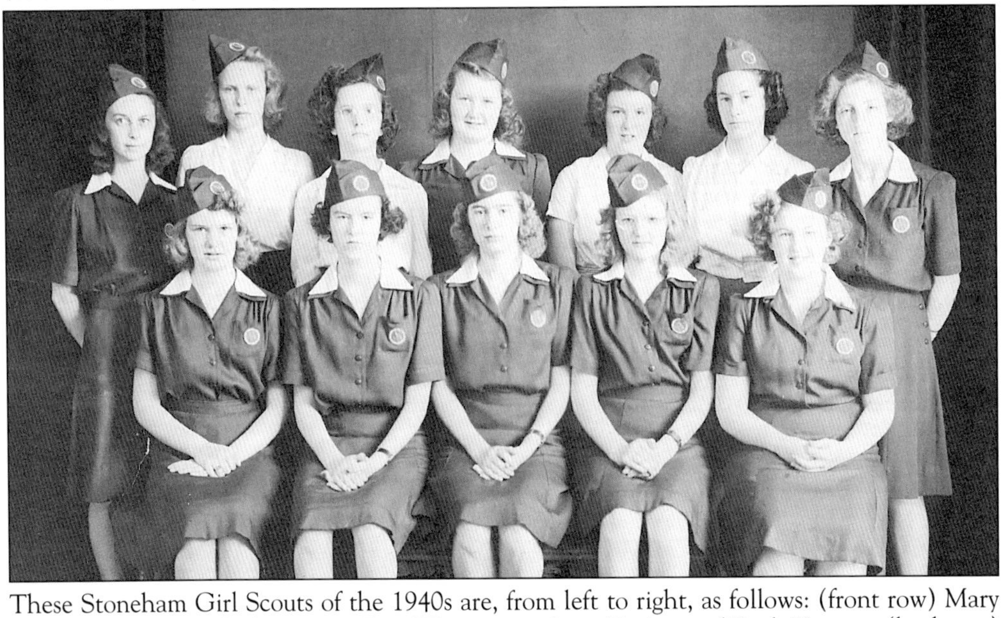

These Stoneham Girl Scouts of the 1940s are, from left to right, as follows: (front row) Mary Lou McGloughlin, Shirley Crane, Dot Whittemore, June Taylor, and Ruth Hanson; (back row) Mona Bruno, Pauline Johnson, Sally Lawson, Eileen Murphy, Dottie Hastings, Marilyn Jelley, and Ruth Buck.

Judith Barnstead of Troop 6, North School, and State Representative Charles Gibbons are shown admiring the 3¢ stamp issued in 1948 to honor Juliette G. Low, founder of the Girl Scouts. Representative Gibbons served as Speaker of the House (1953–54) and was an unsuccessful candidate for both lieutenant governor in 1956 and governor in 1958.

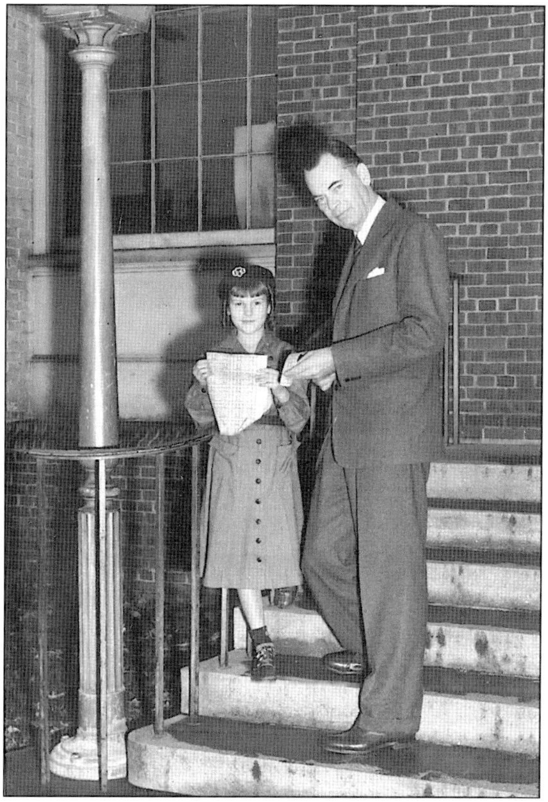

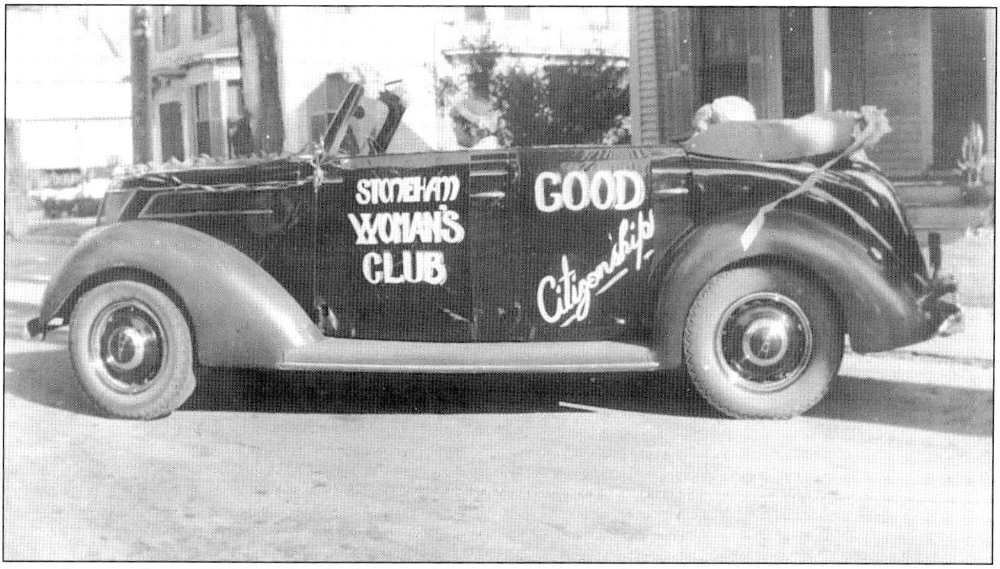

This float in the 1939 Fourth of July Parade sums up the goal of the Stoneham Woman's Club—good citizenship. The club was organized in 1899 as part of a nationwide effort to improve living conditions, starting with your own hometown. These women were active in all national projects including suffrage, temperance, and free postal delivery. Locally, they brought about trash collection, organized the Girl Scouts, and performed many volunteer services in both World War I and World War II.

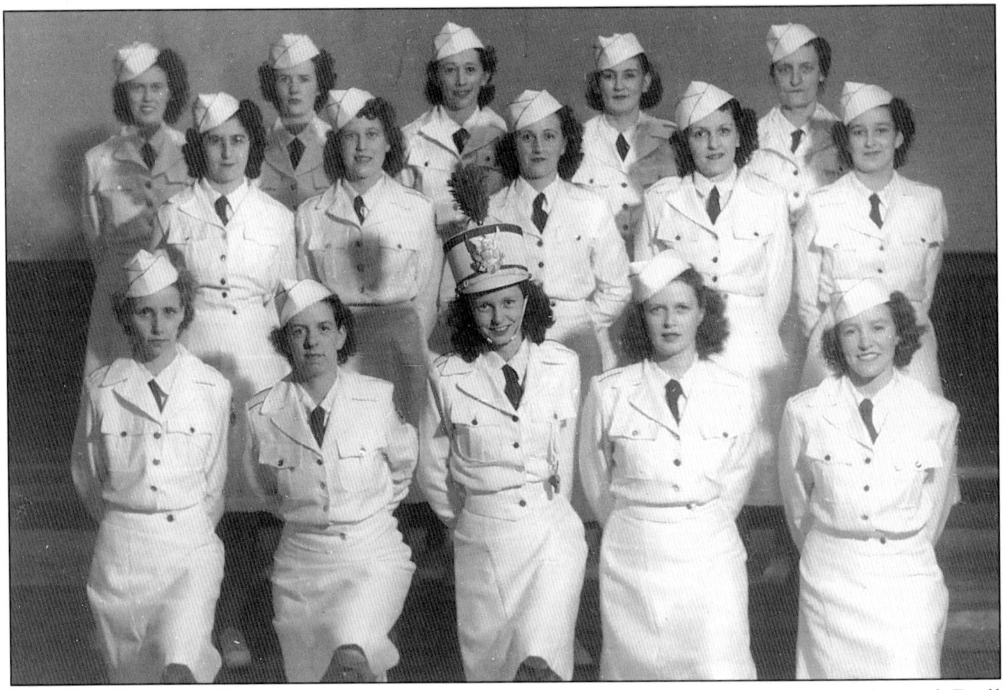

The S/Sgt. George Hall Cadets of Post 620, Auxiliary Veterans of Foreign Wars (VFW) Drill Team are shown here in 1945. They are as follows, from left to right: (front row) Helen Abbott, Jeannette Gile, Alice O'Donnell, Edna O'Donnell, and Kay O'Donnell; (middle row) Louise Savelo, Dorothy Lawson, Elsie Porter, Doris Outram, and Marie O'Donnell; (back row) Marjorie Boudreau, Phylis Kelly, Ann Nagle, Phyllis Tucci, and Edith Cook.

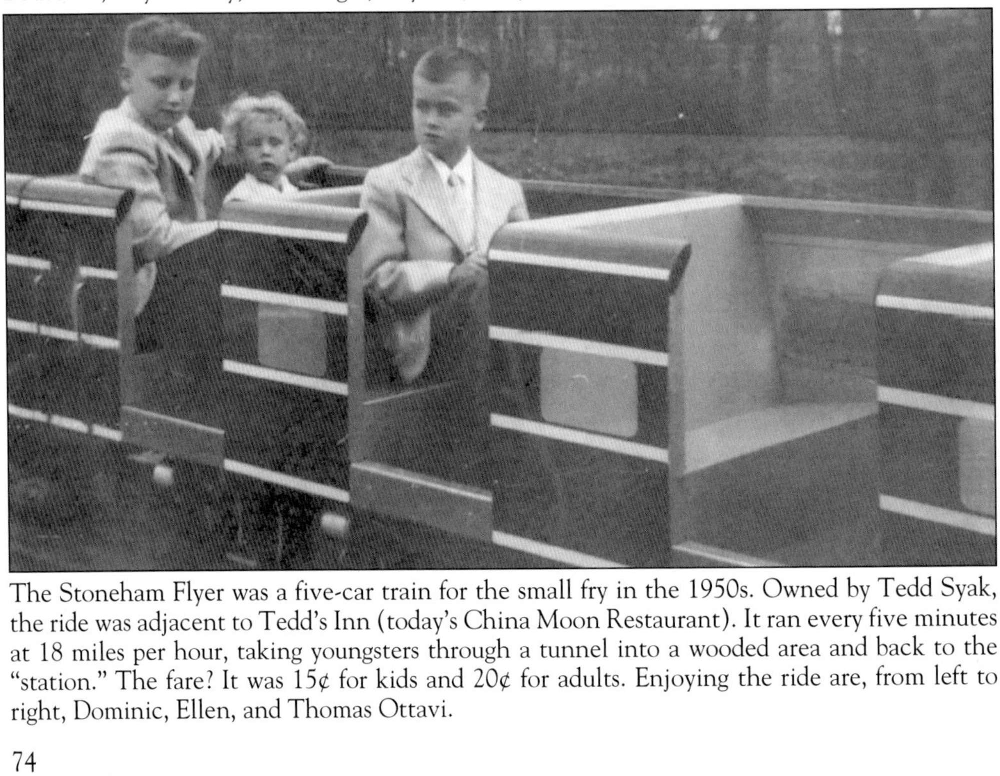

The Stoneham Flyer was a five-car train for the small fry in the 1950s. Owned by Tedd Syak, the ride was adjacent to Tedd's Inn (today's China Moon Restaurant). It ran every five minutes at 18 miles per hour, taking youngsters through a tunnel into a wooded area and back to the "station." The fare? It was 15¢ for kids and 20¢ for adults. Enjoying the ride are, from left to right, Dominic, Ellen, and Thomas Ottavi.

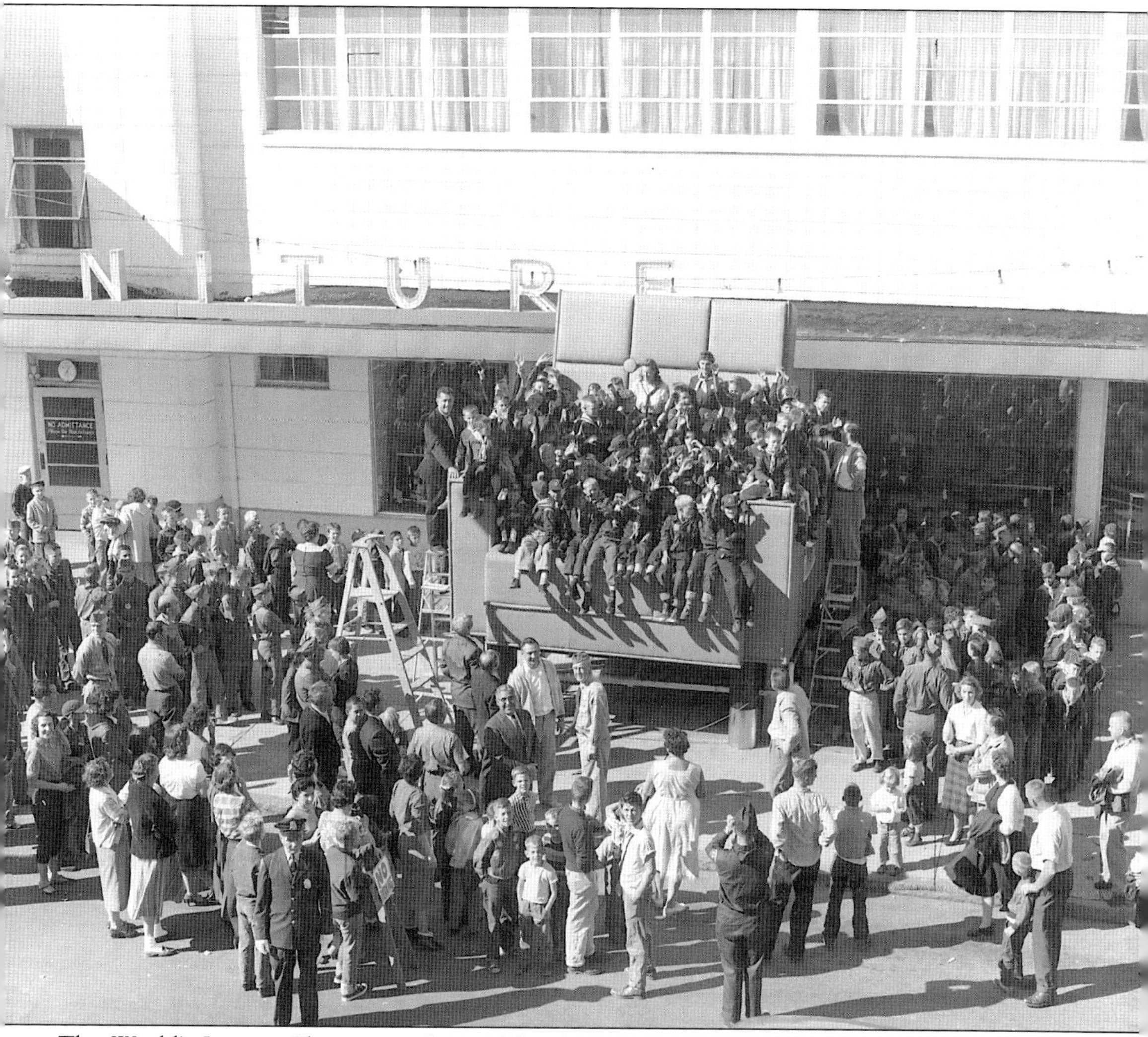

The World's Largest Chair, manufactured by the U.S. Rubber Company, was exhibited for two weeks in front of Barbo's Furniture Store on Main Street in October 1959 and attracted considerable attention. The chair was 10 feet deep, 11 feet wide, and 14 feet high. Eighty yards of fabric and 560 square feet of foam-rubber backing were used in its construction, and 440 man hours were needed to build the giant piece of furniture, which weighed over 2,000 pounds. The Beaver, Panther, and Tiger Troops of the Minuteman Council took part in a "sitdown" competition. The winning Panther Troop was able to seat 102 Boy Scouts in the chair in 5 minutes and 37 seconds. They received a $500 cash award from Mr. Leo Barbo, and donated the prize to the Minuteman Council.

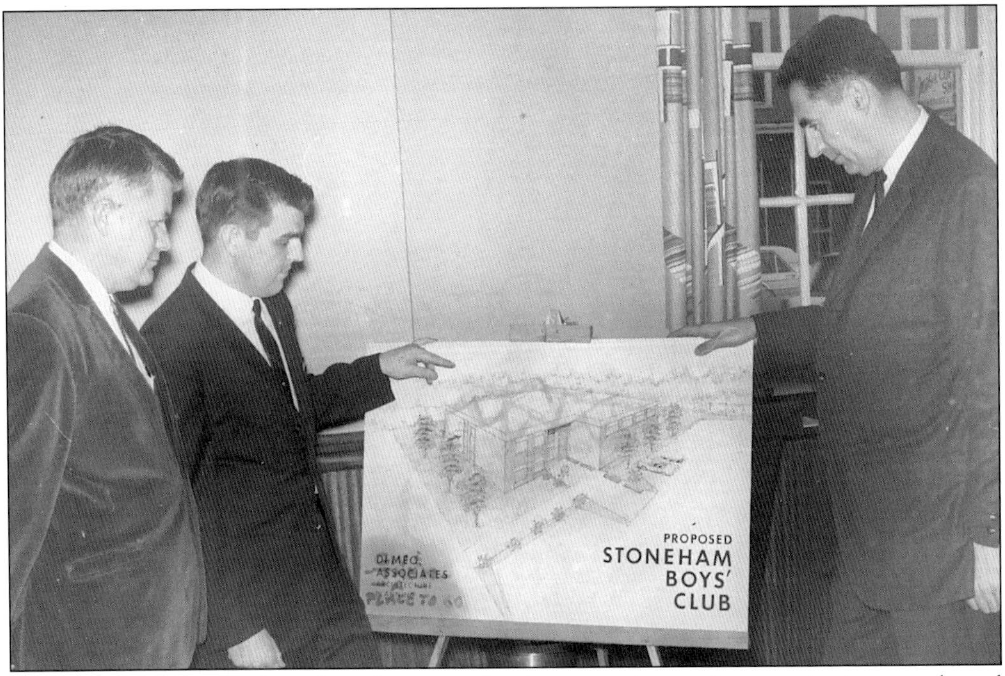

In the early 1960s, the Stoneham Jaycees, a local community service organization, conducted a feasibility study that determined the need for a Boys' Club in Stoneham. Official documents established the Boys' Club of Stoneham, Inc., on January 22, 1965. Next, a suitable location and a proposed design were needed. Examining a plan are, from left to right, Robert O'Neil, Cameron Bain, and Bernie Vacon.

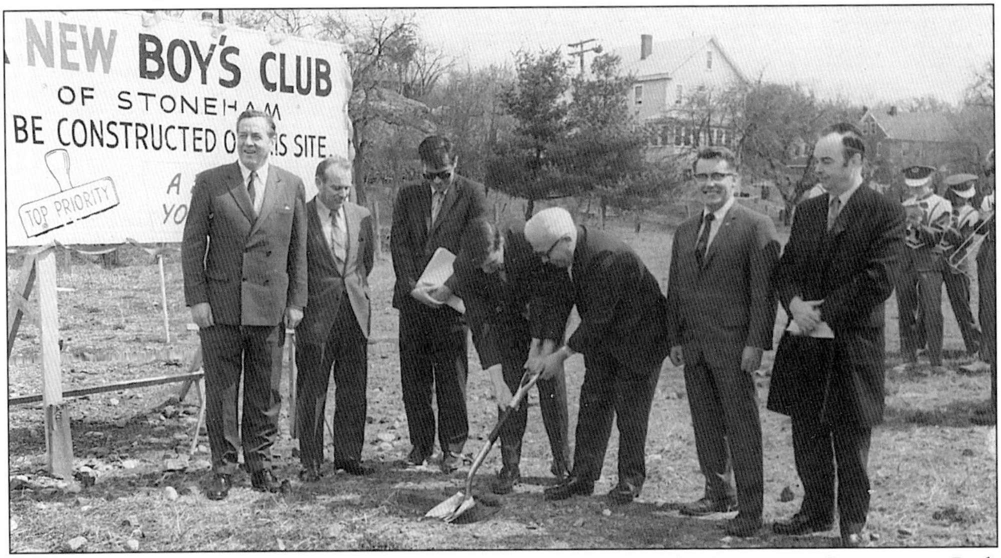

The 1969 town meeting voted to sell town-owned land on Dale Court near Recreation Park to the Boys' Club for one dollar. The deed was officially transferred on June 30, 1969. The building committee accepted the design of Tully Associates and contractor Ted Thomas, and ground was broken on April 25, 1970. Shown are, from left to right, Congressman Torbert H. Macdonald, Norman Houghton, Roland Dion, Cameron Bain, Ernie Clivio, Dan Towse, and State Senator Lamson.

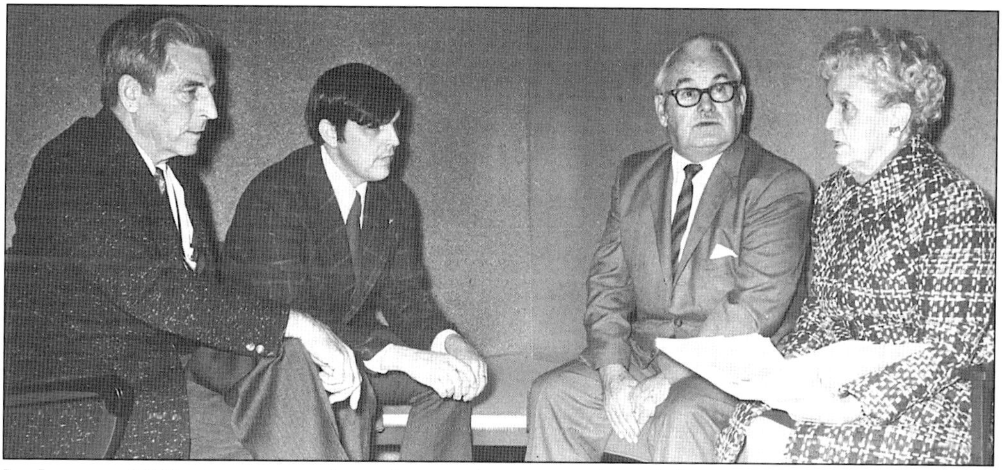

In January 1973, it was voted to donate the remainder of the Home Front Trust Funds to the Stoneham Boys' Club to build a gymnasium. These funds were raised during World War II to help returning Stoneham veterans readjust to civilian life, but not all the funds had been expended. From left to right are Bill Coy, Cameron Bain, Norm Downs, and Kathryn B. English.

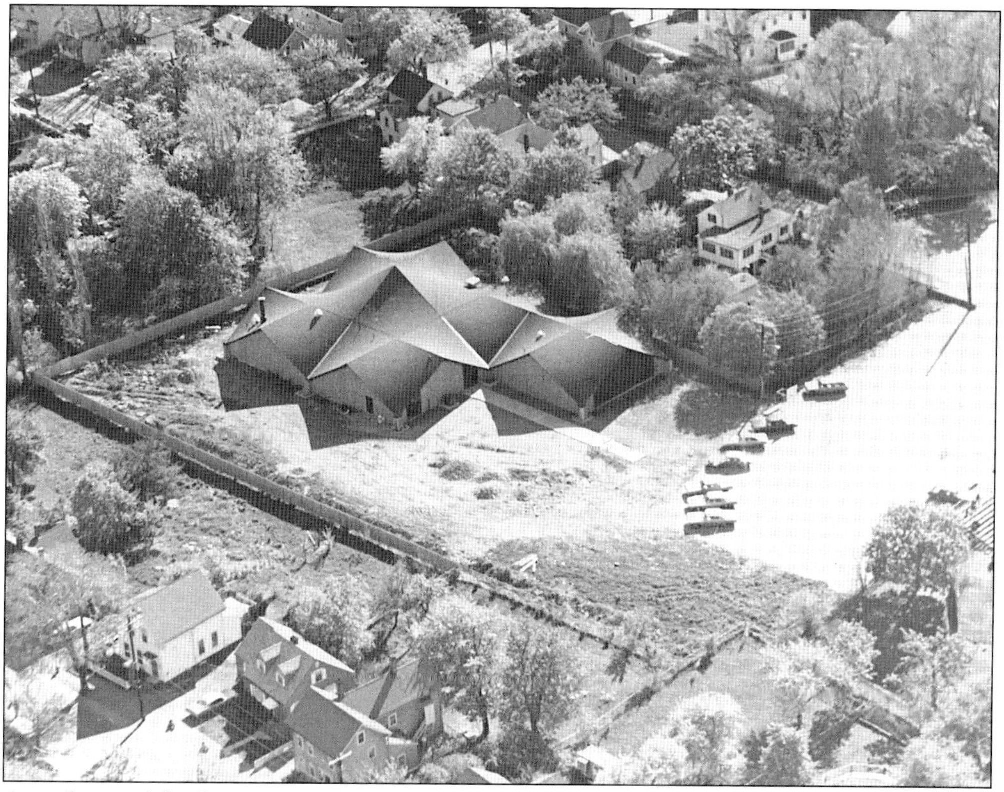

A professional fund-raising organization was selected, and the fund drive began in 1969. With support from memorial gifts, business and organizational donations, and the charity of local residents, a $100,000 matching grant was received from the Charles Hayden Foundation. This aerial view shows the building nearing completion. The official ribbon cutting ceremony was held on February 4, 1973.

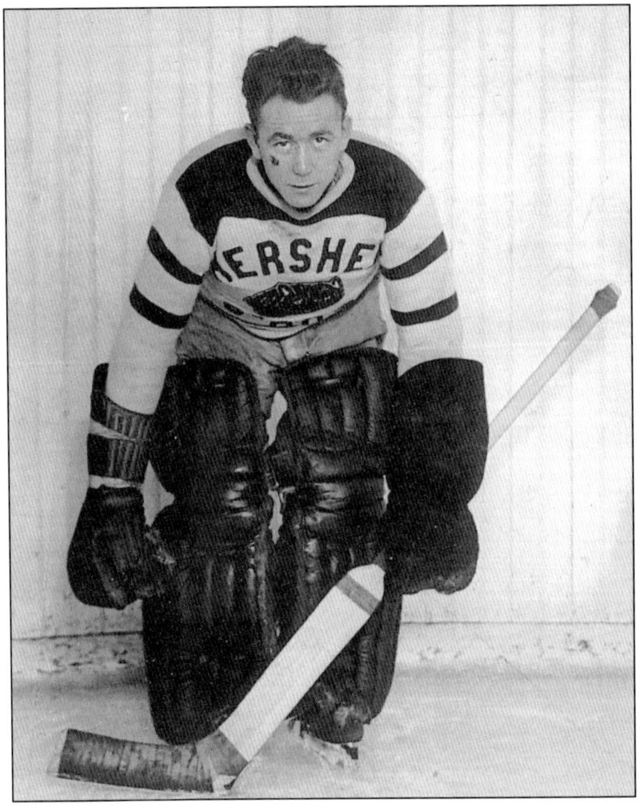

Stoneham's fame as an "Olympic Town" began in 1932 when Edwin H. "Ted" Frazier was chosen as a goalie in the third Winter Olympics, held at Lake Placid, New York. In later years, Ted played for the Atlantic City Seagulls, the Hershey B'ars, and the Boston Olympics.

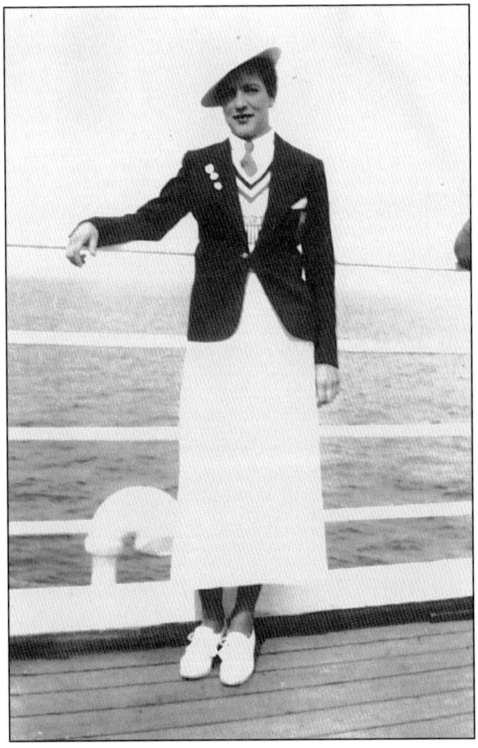

In 1936, the 11th Summer Olympic Games were held in Berlin, Germany. Josephine Warren Madden, now a Park Street resident, was a member of the track and field team. Travel to Europe was by boat, and the team members trained while on board. "Jo" poses here in the official dress uniform for ladies.

"Don" Whiston was a goalie at the sixth Winter Olympics, held in Oslo, Norway, in 1952. Don played for Brown University, where he later coached. He is shown wearing an early face mask, made in 1948 by Dr. Ed Crane, an orthodontic surgeon. The mask was designed to protect some teeth that had recently been knocked out and reinserted. Remember, no ice hockey players wore masks as part of their regular equipment at this time.

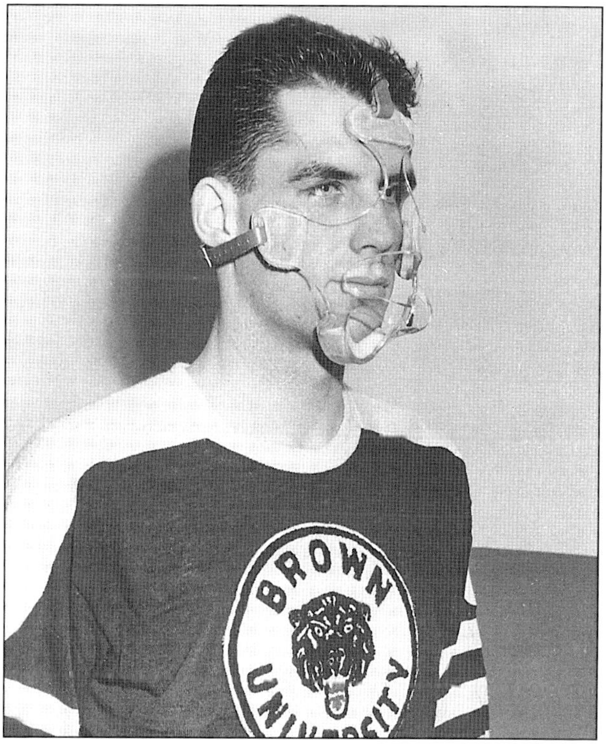

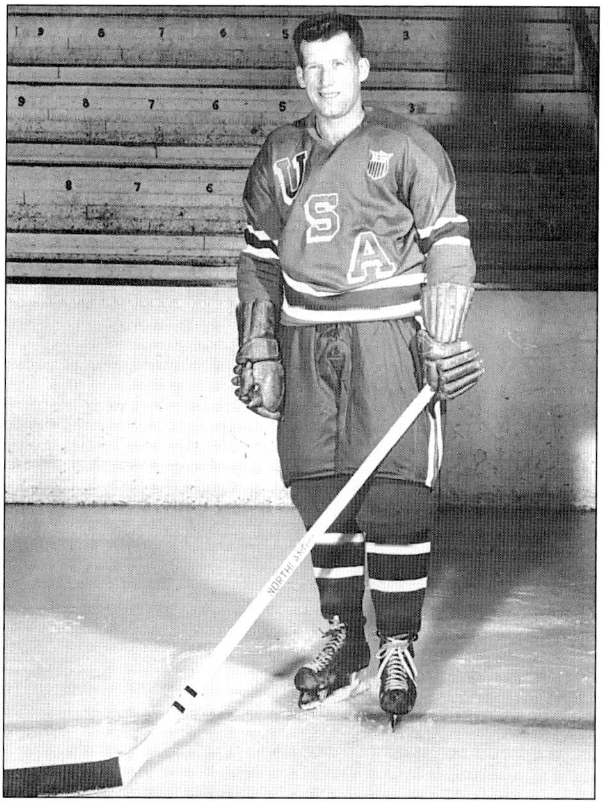

The seventh Winter Olympics Games were held in Cortina d'Ampezzo, Italy, in 1956, and Francis P. "Frank" O'Grady was chosen as a defenseman on the hockey squad. Frank was a graduate of Boston College and later a popular teacher and administrator in the Stoneham Public School System.

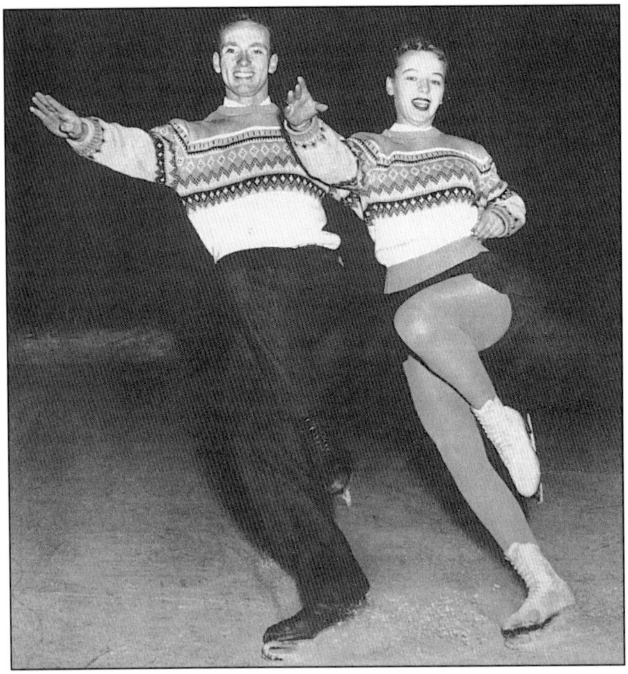

Nancy Rouillard Ludington of Stoneham and her partner, Ronald Ludington, participated in the eighth Winter Olympics, held in Squaw Valley, California, in 1960. The figure-skating couple were National Senior Champions from 1957 through 1960 and won the bronze medal at the 1960 Olympics. Nancy was inducted into the United States Figure Skating Association (USFSA) Hall of Fame in 1993.

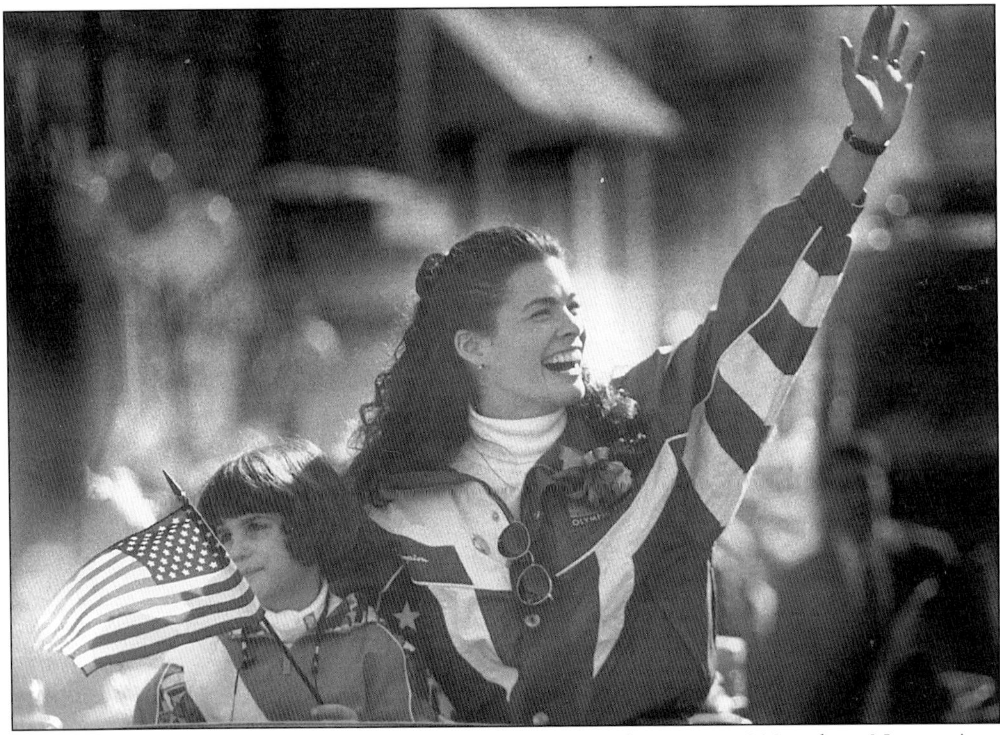

Stoneham's most recent contributions to the Olympics began in 1992, when Nancy Ann Kerrigan won the bronze medal at Albertville, France, during the 16th Winter Olympics. She went on in 1994 to win the silver medal at the 17th Winter Olympics held in Lillehammer, Norway. Nancy is shown riding triumphantly through Stoneham Square in 1992 accompanied by her cousin, Allison Schultz. Nancy was inducted into the USFSA Hall of Fame in 1993.

Five

AGAINST THE FOE

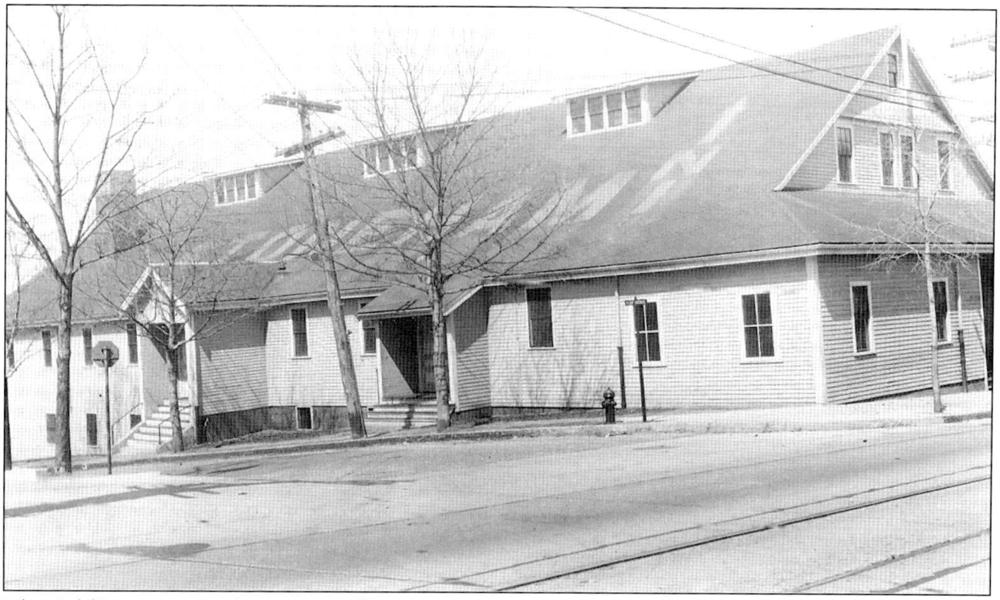

The "old" armory, at the corner of Main Street and Flint Avenue, was built in 1884 as a roller polo rink. It later became the armory for Company H of the Sixth Massachusetts Infantry. After being purchased by the town in 1894, graduations, town meetings, banquets, movies, and other social events were held here until the present town hall was erected in 1939. The wording and arrow indicating "North" in this 1934 photo were removed during World War II for defense purposes. The building was razed in August 1970.

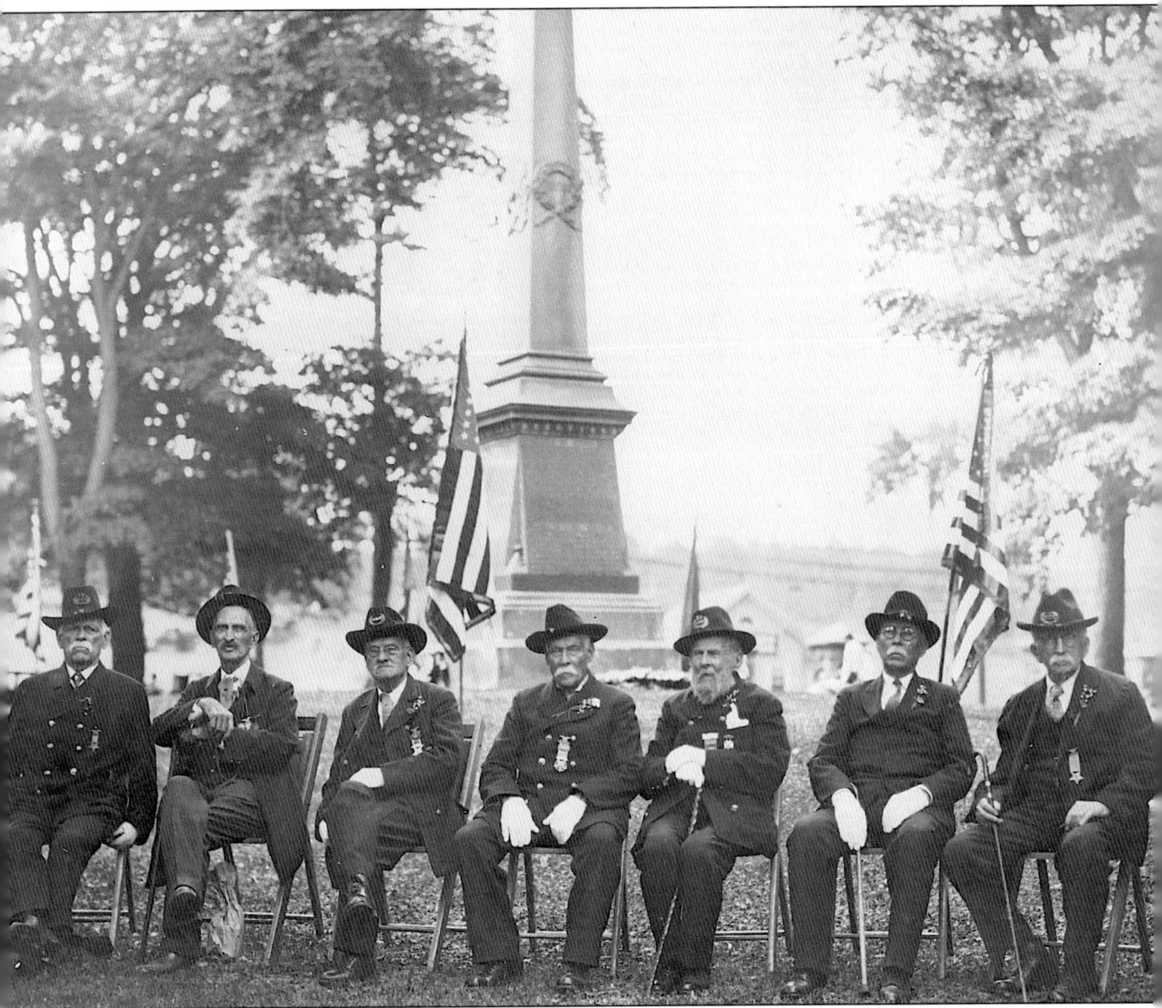

Memorial Day, originally known as Decoration Day, was a special day set aside to remember those who had defended the Union during the Civil War. It was first celebrated in Stoneham on May 30, 1869. The Soldiers' Monument in Lindenwood Cemetery, which was dedicated on August 12, 1869, is the backdrop for the seven remaining Civil War veterans who attended the ceremonies on Memorial Day in 1931. These veterans are, from left to right, George E. Kenson (age 86), Ephraim A. Perry (90), George W. Newhall (86), Rodman F. Davis (87), Samuel C. Trull (94), Henry D. Wallace (91), and Joseph A. Moulton (84). Unfortunately, Ephraim A. Perry became ill and died at his home later that day.

Dr. W. Symington Brown served as a surgeon in both the 33rd and 55th Regiments during the Civil War. The 55th was the second black regiment from Massachusetts. Dr. Brown was instrumental in the organization of Post 75 of the Grand Army of the Republic and was its first commander. Brown and his wife, who was also a doctor, were both educated in their native Scotland.

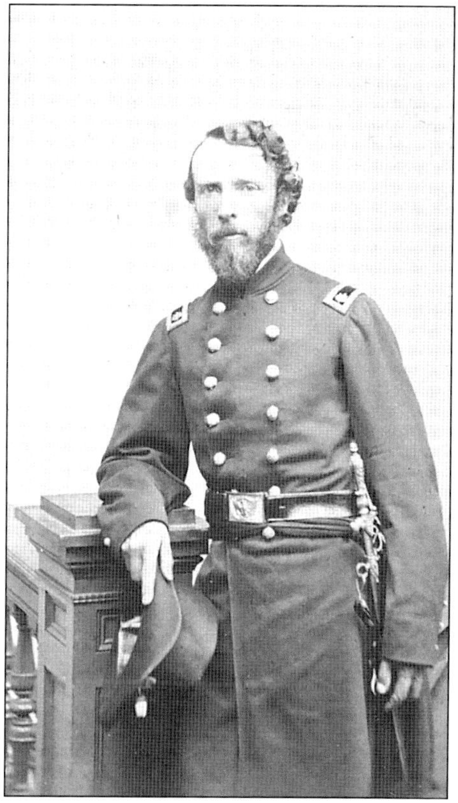

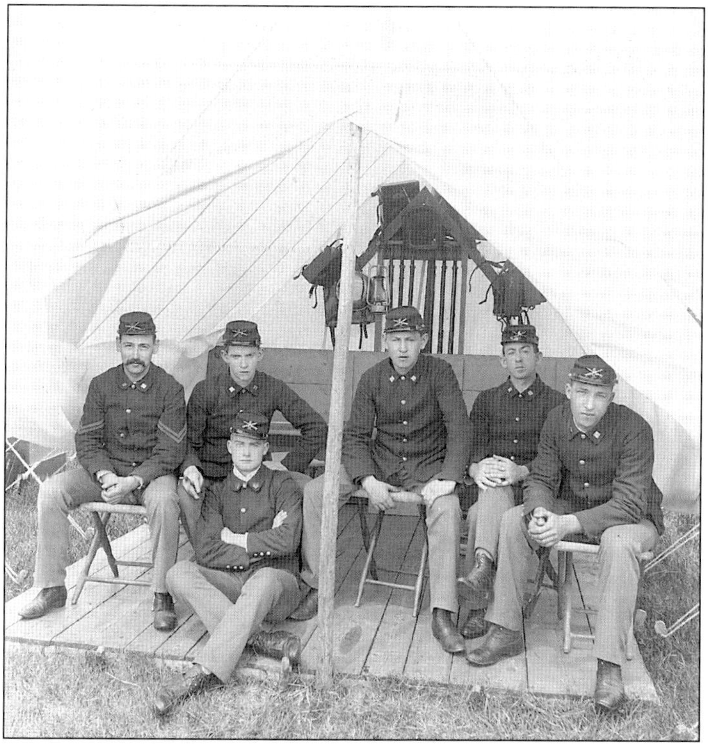

Following the outbreak of the Spanish-American War, the men of Company H, Sixth Massachusetts Infantry, reported to Framingham on May 6, 1898 and in one week were mustered into service. The men who posed for this photograph in Framingham include Jason Quinn, Joe Keenan, Jack Reynolds, Peter Quinn, John Glynn, and ? Temple.

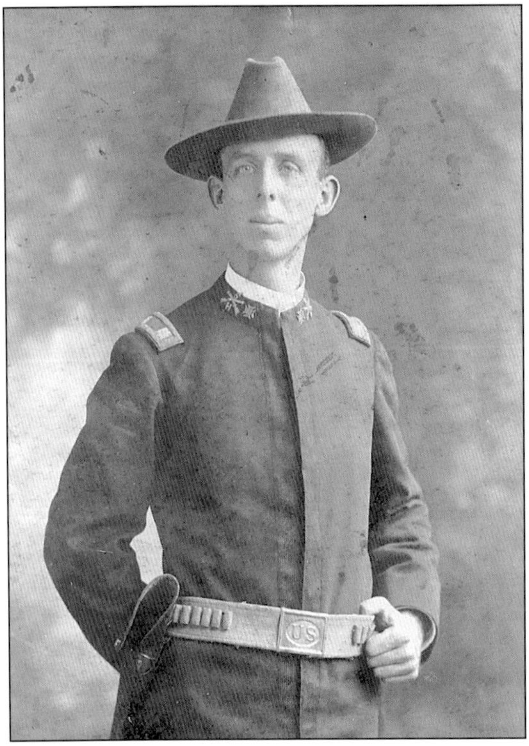

Warren E. Sweetser became the captain of Company H, Sixth Regiment, Massachusetts Volunteer Militia, in January 1897. Thus, he was the captain of the Stoneham Light Infantry, which left town on May 6, 1898, for service in the Spanish-American War. Sweetser was the fifth captain of this company and eventually rose to the rank of colonel.

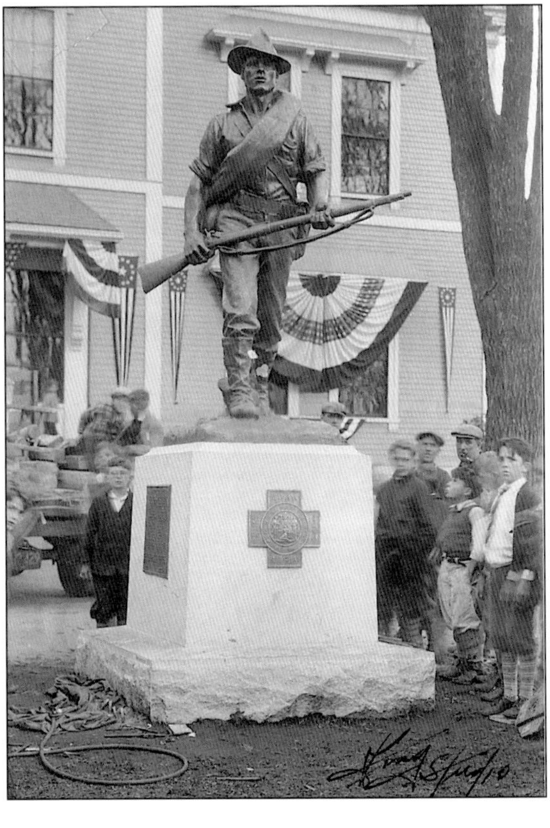

A crowd of interested onlookers gathered in 1928 on the grounds of the Dean School at the corner of Central and Common Streets. A monument, known as the Hiker's Monument, was being put in place to honor the men of Company H, Sixth Regiment, Massachusetts Volunteer Militia, who served in the Spanish-American War. Wearing broad-brimmed hats and carrying canteens and cups, these men served about three months during the hot summer of 1898 hiking over the Puerto Rican countryside. As a result, they nicknamed themselves "Hikers."

These two little flag-waving patriots are Dorothy Richardson (Miss Liberty) and her cousin, Russell Colley (Uncle Sam). There was much to cheer about as the 20th century dawned in Stoneham. The country was again at peace, and the town was filled with patriotic fever.

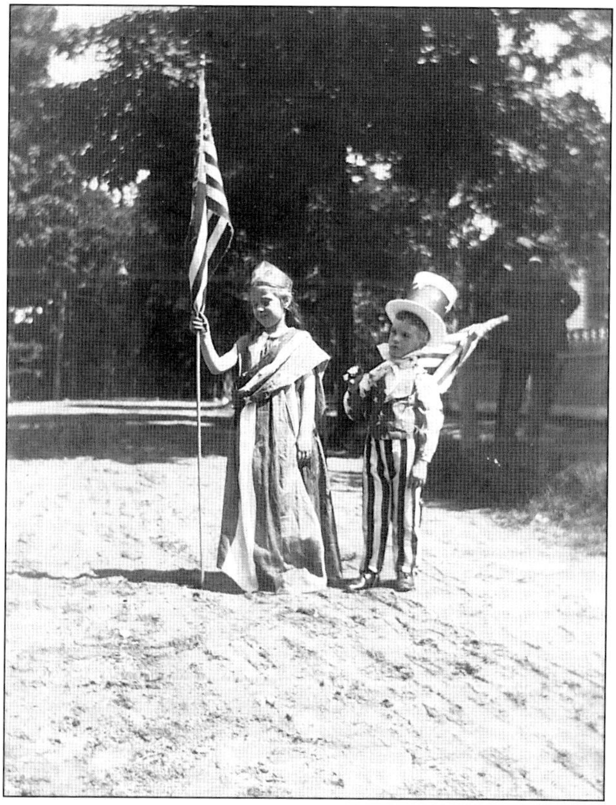

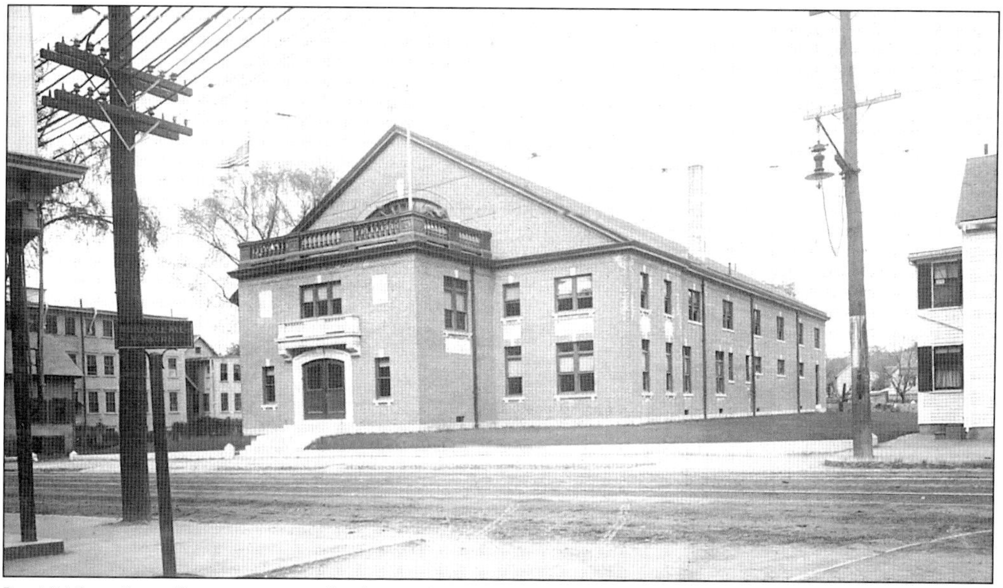

In 1913 a "new" armory was built on Main Street opposite Montvale Avenue. When the building ceased to operate as an armory, the town of Stoneham bought it for one dollar in the mid-1970s. The building was resold in 1978, altered, and opened as a hardware store in the fall of 1980.

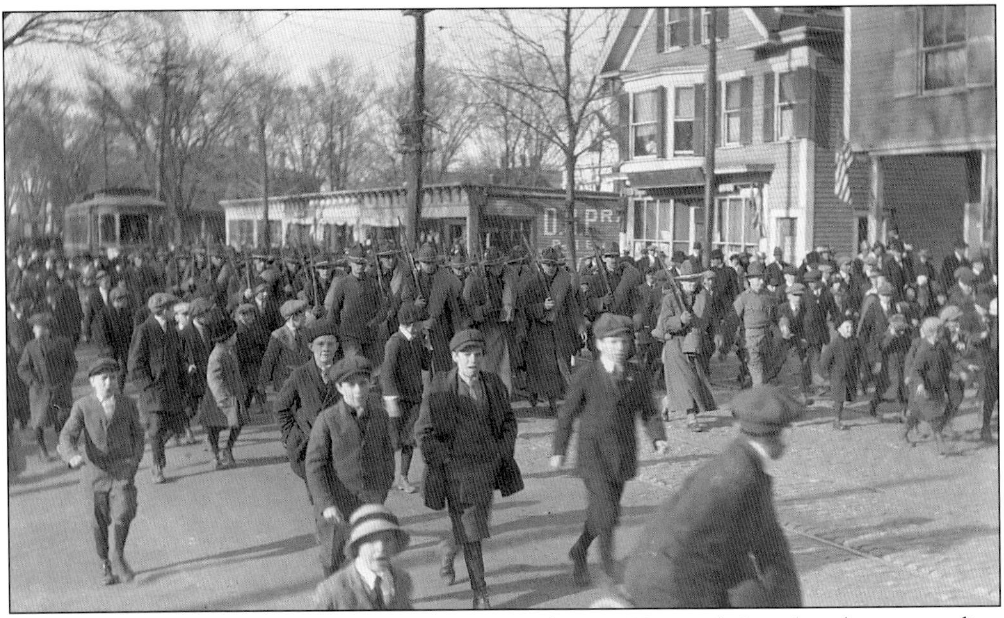

Company H of the Sixth Regiment of the Massachusetts National Guard is shown parading down Main Street from the armory on Sunday, April 8, 1917. These 67 men and three officers, with Captain-elect T. Arthur Ireland in command, are en route to the Franklin Street Station and on to active duty.

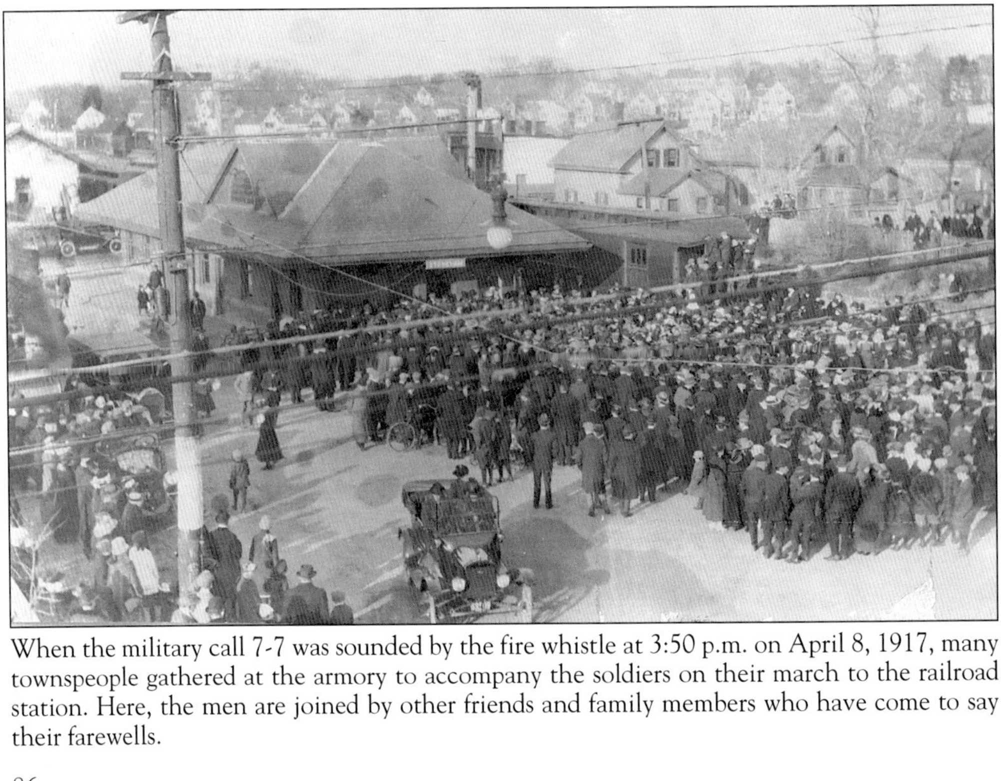

When the military call 7-7 was sounded by the fire whistle at 3:50 p.m. on April 8, 1917, many townspeople gathered at the armory to accompany the soldiers on their march to the railroad station. Here, the men are joined by other friends and family members who have come to say their farewells.

As in other parts of our country, the windows of many homes in Stoneham displayed service flags during both World War I and II. Each star represented a man or woman from that household who had answered the call to duty. In spite of fears for their safety, residents such as this young woman were proud of those who had answered the call.

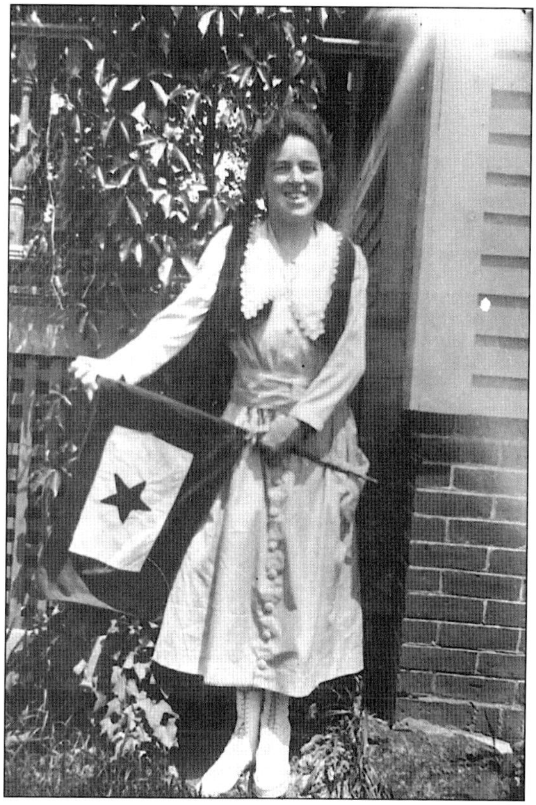

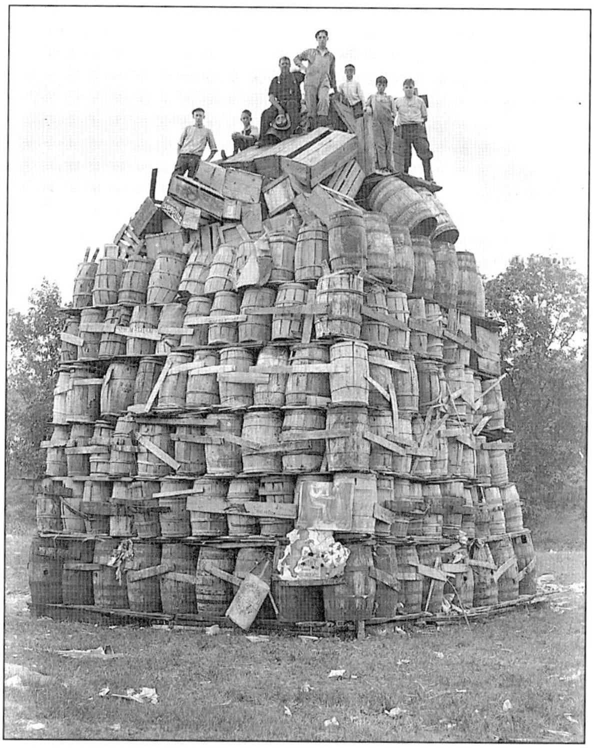

Fourth of July was never complete without a bonfire, and most were held at the Pomeworth Street Playground. In the days prior to the Fourth, the tower was assembled with care, often reaching 50 feet. At midnight it was lit to the delight of the thousands who had gathered.

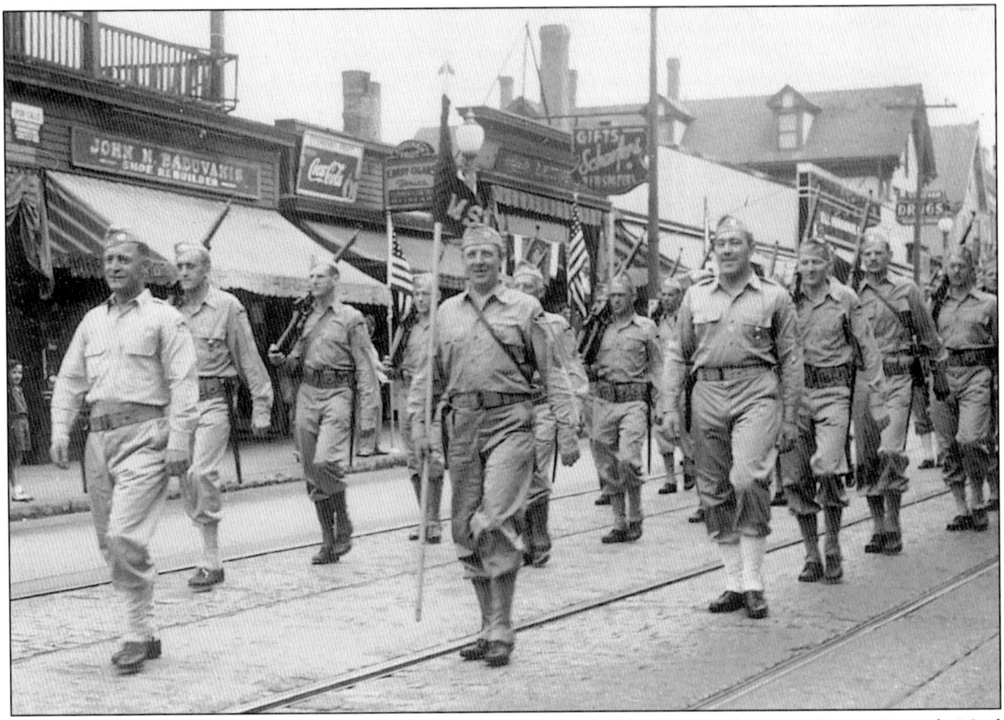

The Fourth of July parade in 1942 featured Company H of the Massachusetts State Guard, 23rd Infantry. This company was organized in 1941 and was the first unit in the state to be inducted as part of the regular army. Lt. Walter H. Strobel is commanding the unit as it marches south out of Stoneham Square.

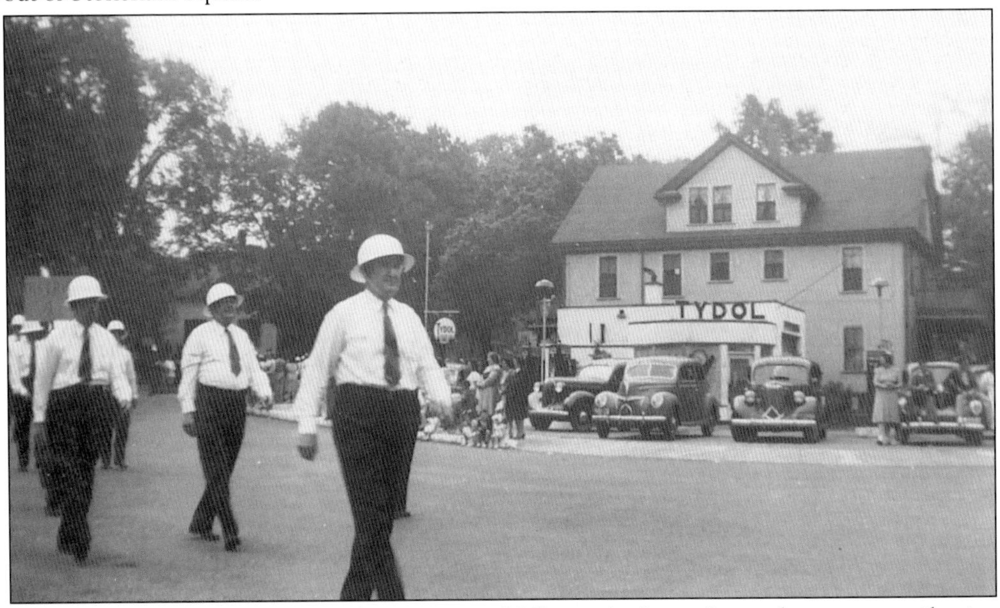

The parade in 1942 also contained many units of folks on the home front who were contributing to the war effort in countless ways. Here, the Air Raid Wardens proudly round the corner from Central Street onto William heading for Main Street. The town was divided into 19 districts, and Fred A. Lawson served as the chief air raid warden.

With young men, such as brother Bob, away on military duty, it fell to young ladies, such as Norma and Helen Lister, to help Dad with the planting and harvesting of crops. Without sufficient food production on the home front, the war efforts would have been severely hampered.

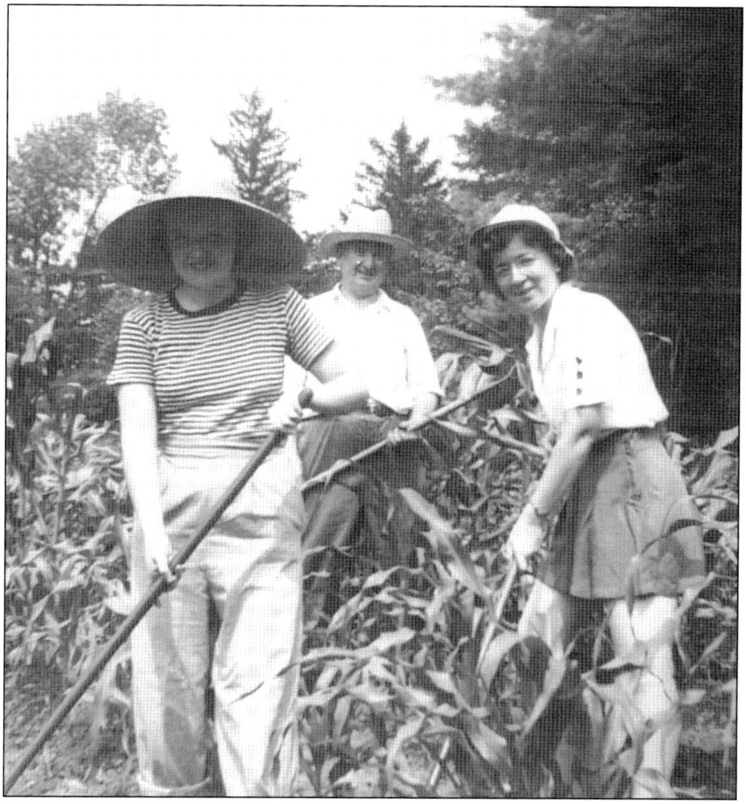

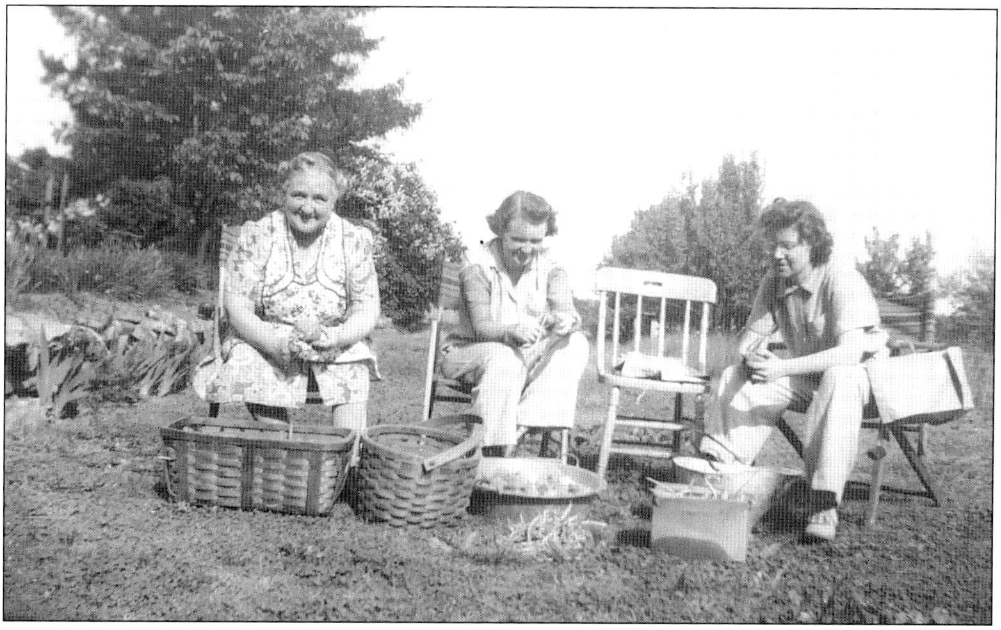

There was a sense of contribution and usefulness in performing even such simple tasks as preparing potatoes for planting. Mom, Norma, and Helen Lister are readying seed potatoes for planting in their Victory Garden. The hard part would come later, when the rows had to be hoed and weeded, and the plants sprayed and checked for bugs.

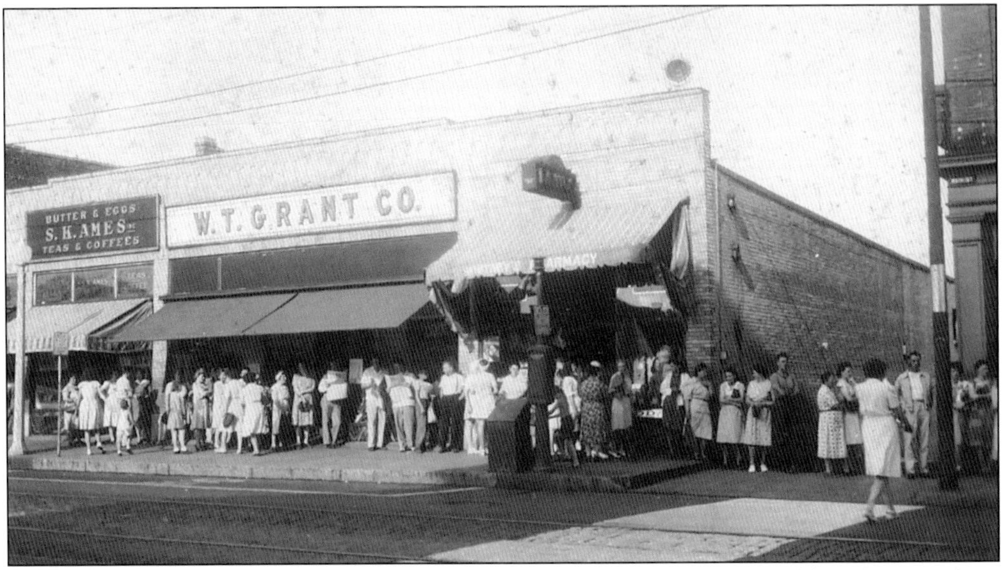

On the home front, shortages of everyday groceries, such as butter, caused long lines to form whenever a store received such a shipment. Here, potential customers are lined along Main Street near the corner of Minot Street in front of W.T. Grant, hoping to reach the grocery store before the butter supply runs out.

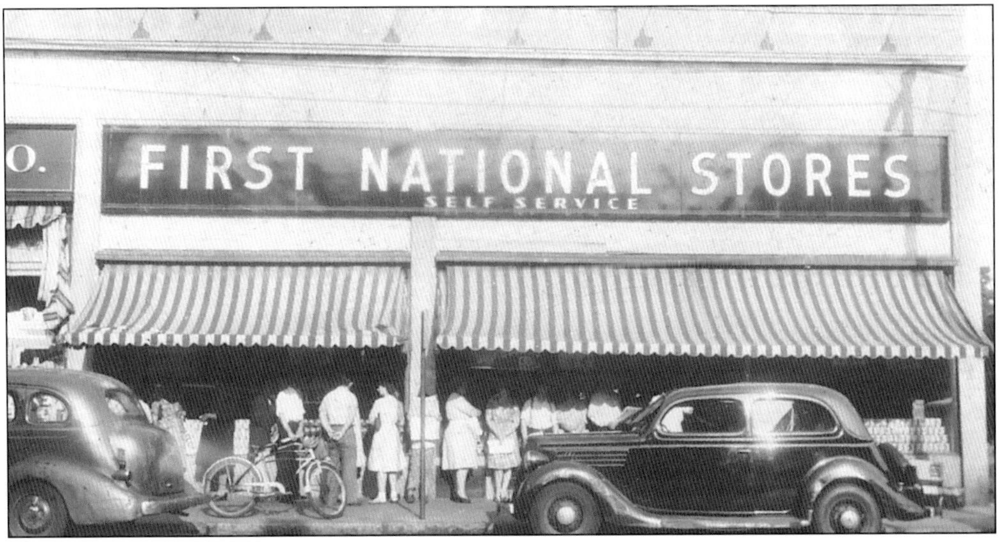

The First National Store was the destination of those lined along Main Street to purchase butter. This grocery store was then located on Main Street at the corner of Hersam Street. Long lines such as these encouraged some consumers to use "oleo," which came with a separate packet that had to be added to create the yellow color.

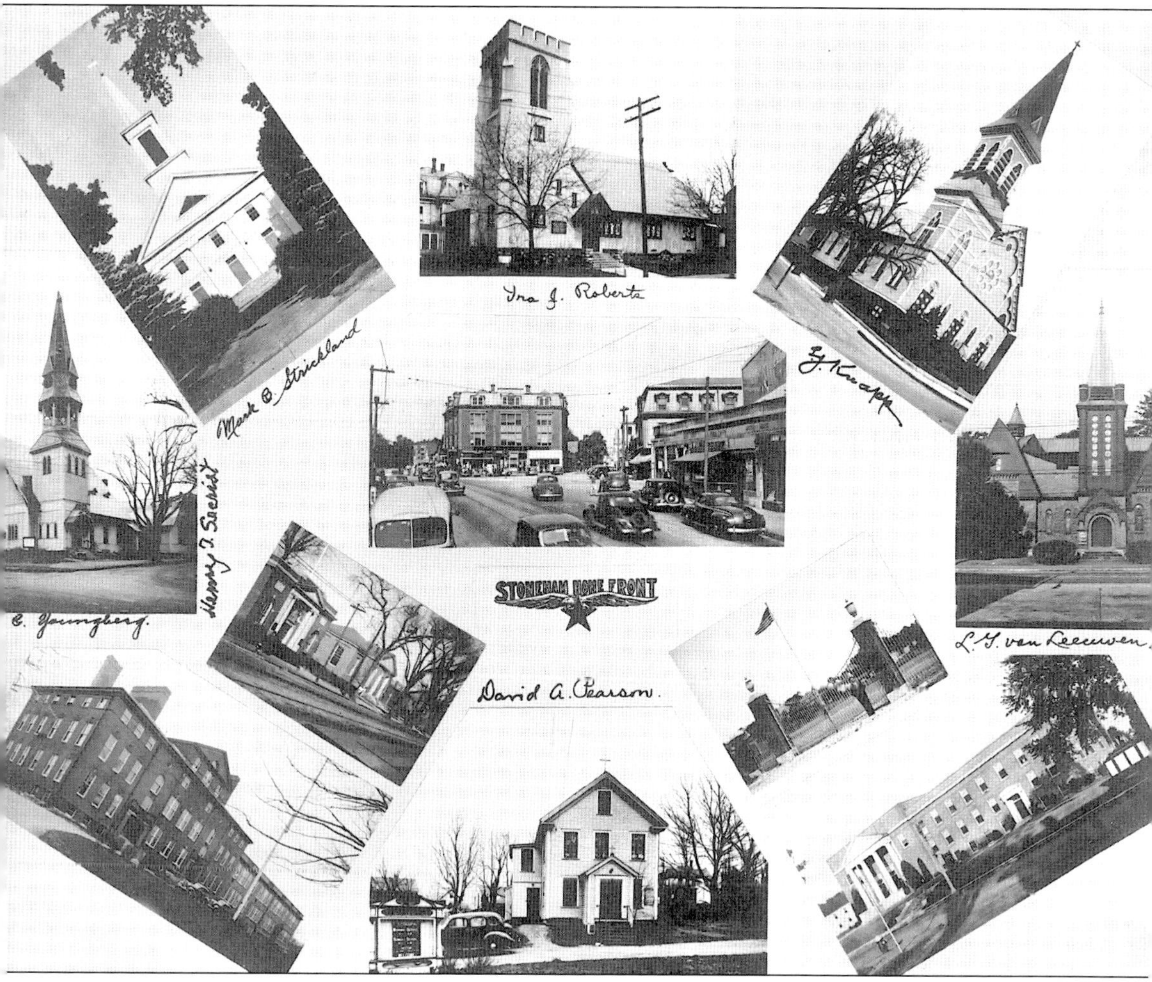

During the summer of 1942, a group of residents organized the Home Front Trust. Among its purposes were to help those in the service and their families during the war years and to offer supportive services as the veterans returned to civilian life. Funds to support the program were raised by bean suppers, concerts, scrap drives, and dances. Efforts were made to be in contact with all Stonehamites serving in the armed forces. This card with photos of the post office, high school, Recreation Park, town hall, the Square, and churches with the clergymen's signatures was to remind them of their town and its concerns for them. Fortunately, the federal government anticipated the needs of returning veterans and the GI Bill addressed many of the needs that the Home Front Trust had foreseen.

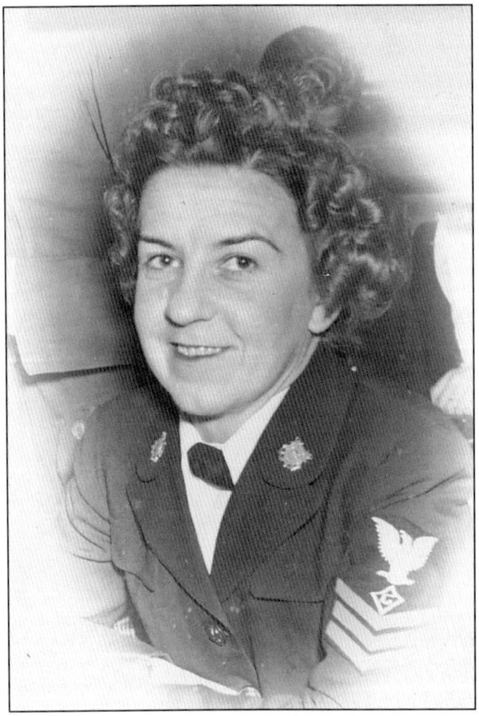

In the spring of 1943, Rosemary Hamill (Levangie) took a military leave from her fourth-grade teaching position at Emerson School to become a SPAR. Having summered at Plum Island for many years, Hamill joined the Coast Guard as her way of helping in the war effort. Her experience as a teacher led her to be stationed at the training division in Washington, D.C. Rosemary held the rank of Specialist C and she served until October 1945.

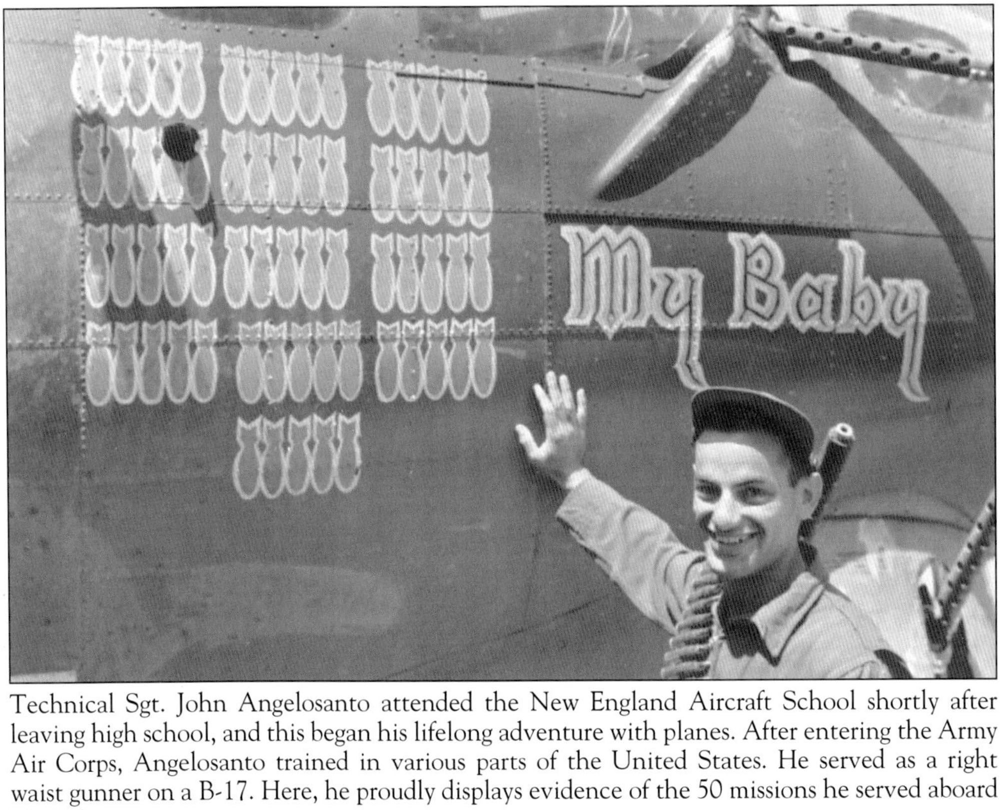

Technical Sgt. John Angelosanto attended the New England Aircraft School shortly after leaving high school, and this began his lifelong adventure with planes. After entering the Army Air Corps, Angelosanto trained in various parts of the United States. He served as a right waist gunner on a B-17. Here, he proudly displays evidence of the 50 missions he served aboard *My Baby*.

First Lt. Herbert E. Mahn was a platoon leader in the 751st Tank Battalion. Tanks, with their ability to climb and descend slopes as steep as 30 degrees and to turn around within their own length, were invaluable in mountainous areas such as Italy. Lt. Mahn served with the Fifth Army from Anzio to the Alps, where he was wounded and hospitalized.

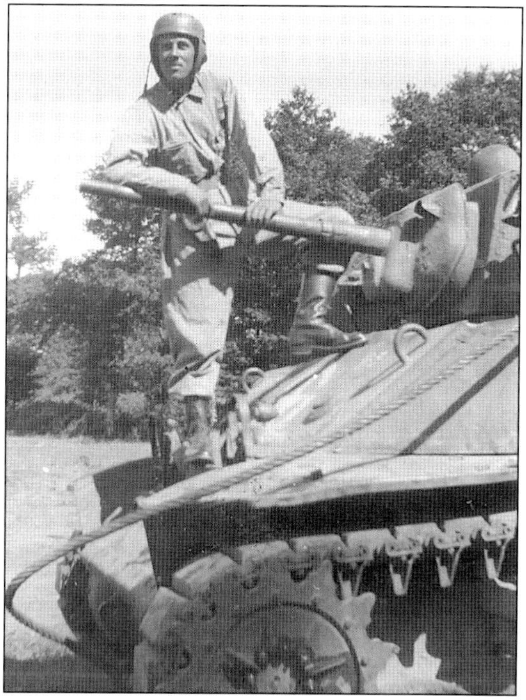

Yeoman Ed Palmer is shown at left aboard the USS *Massachusetts*, where he ran the ship's library, assisted the chaplain, and was the ship's disc jockey. Ed was later a member of the Memorial Committee, which in 1965 succeeded in making this ship the official memorial for the sons and daughters of the Commonwealth who served in World War II. All who visit the ship in Fall River should be reminded of the Massachusetts men and women who responded to the call to arms.

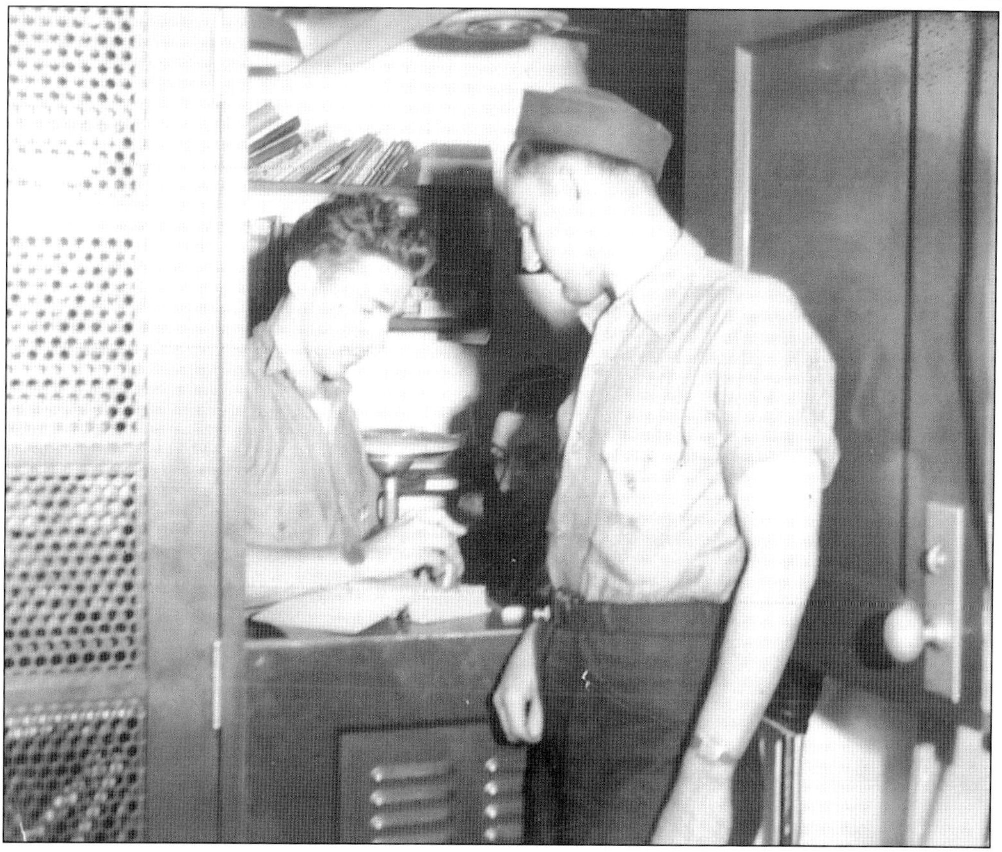

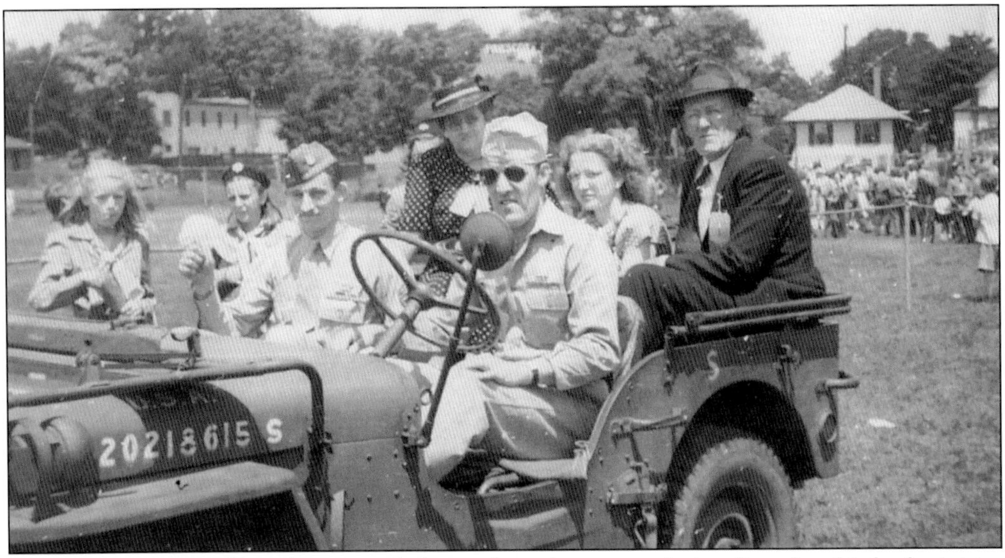

S/Sgt. George J. Hall is shown with his wife and parents during Fourth of July festivities dedicated to him in 1945. Hall had received the Congressional Medal of Honor on April 6, 1945, for his fearlessness and determined fighting spirit in wiping out enemy machine gun nests near Anzio, Italy, on May 23, 1944. Hall was able to kill seven of the enemy and cause nine others to surrender, but it was at great cost to himself.

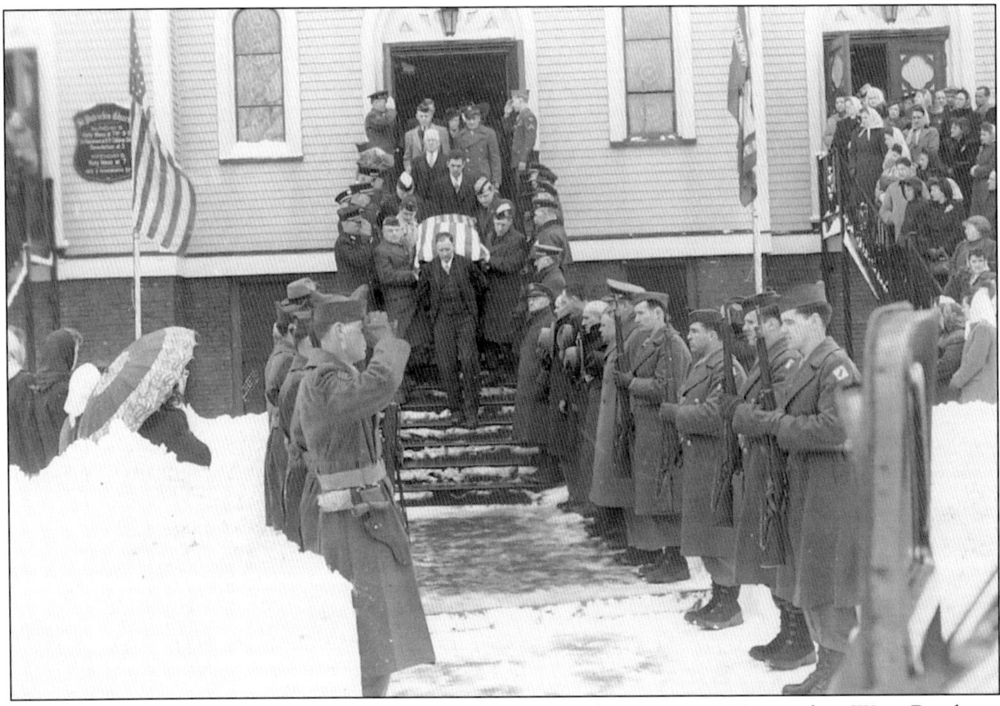

Sadly, S/Sgt. Hall's injuries proved fatal, and he died at the Veterans Hospital in West Roxbury on February 16, 1946. His funeral with full military honors was held at St. Patrick's Church, and he was buried in St. Patrick's Cemetery. The MDC (Metropolitan District Commission) Swimming Pool on North Border Road was dedicated to him on July 4, 1951. The "triangle" at the junction of East and Spring Streets honors him, as does the local VFW post.

Six

About Trade and Travel

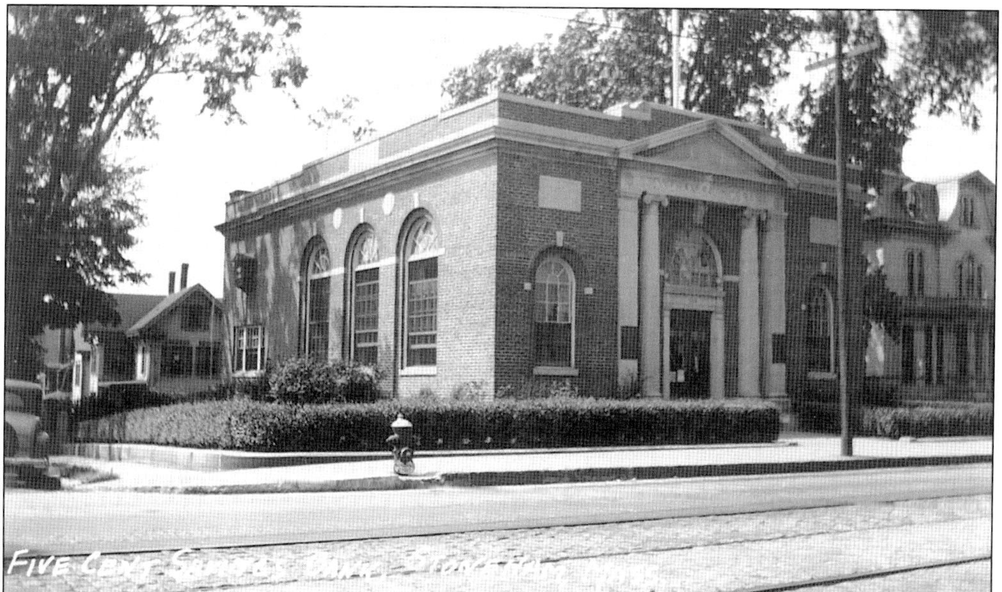

The Stoneham 5¢ Savings Bank was incorporated in March 1855, making it the oldest bank (and business) in town. This building was erected in 1927 at the corner of Main and Hersam Streets. Additions in 1998 included a drive-up window along the Hersam Street side and a parking deck.

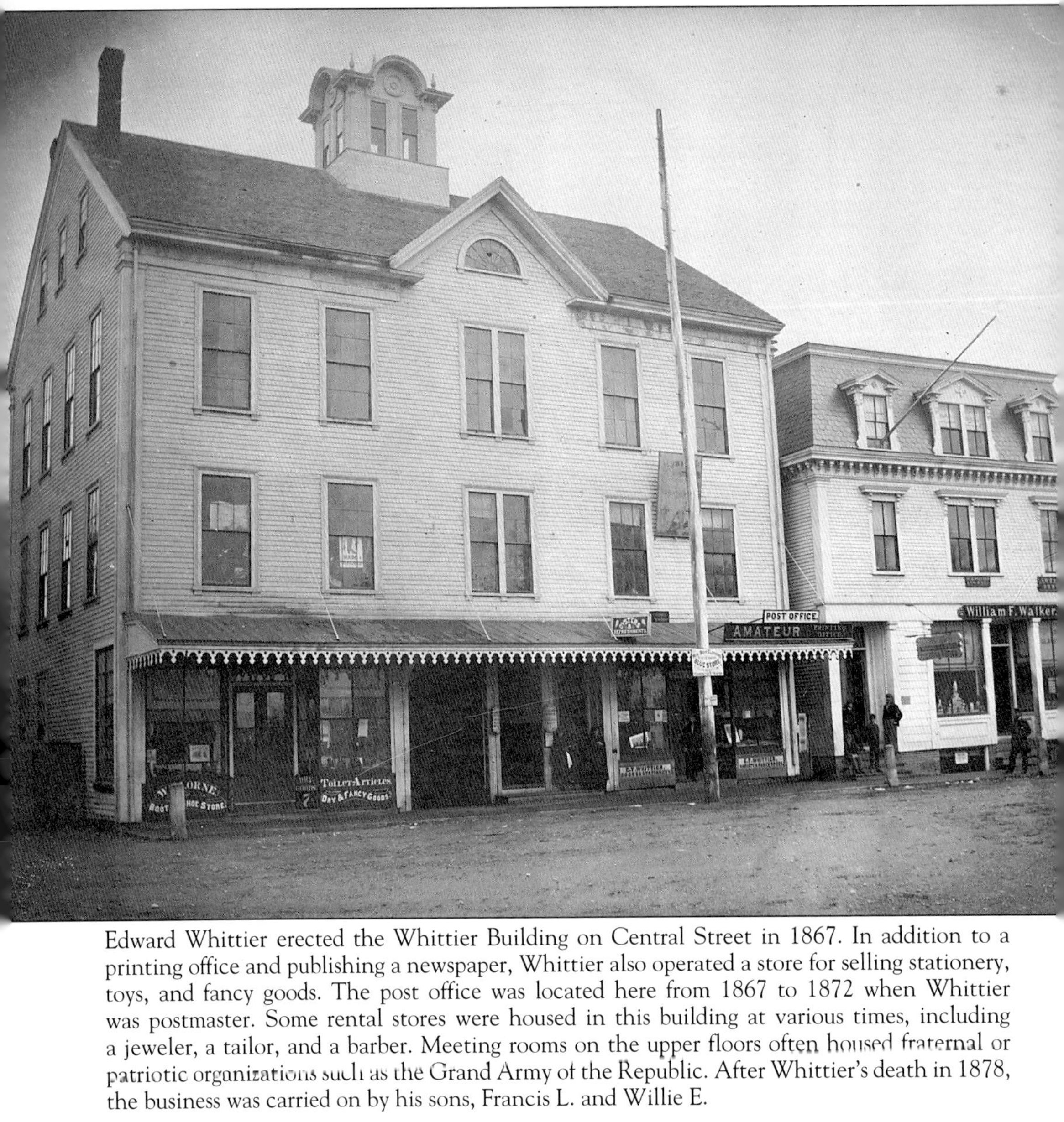

Edward Whittier erected the Whittier Building on Central Street in 1867. In addition to a printing office and publishing a newspaper, Whittier also operated a store for selling stationery, toys, and fancy goods. The post office was located here from 1867 to 1872 when Whittier was postmaster. Some rental stores were housed in this building at various times, including a jeweler, a tailor, and a barber. Meeting rooms on the upper floors often housed fraternal or patriotic organizations such as the Grand Army of the Republic. After Whittier's death in 1878, the business was carried on by his sons, Francis L. and Willie E.

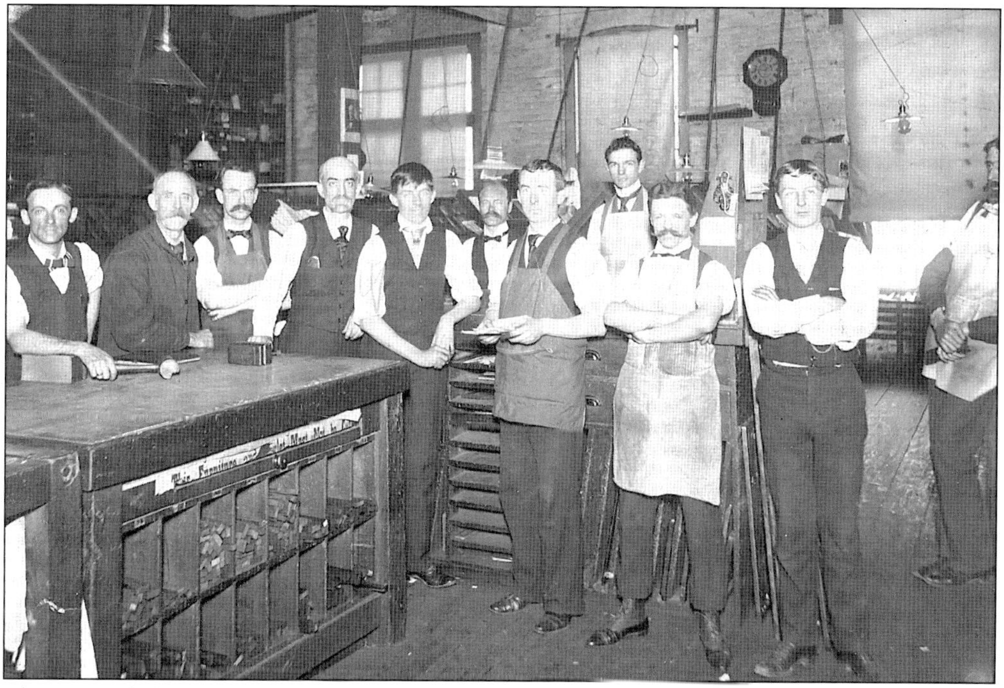

These men helped keep the presses rolling for the *Stoneham Independent* many years ago. This weekly newspaper was an outgrowth of the *Stoneham Amateur*, which was started in 1870 by Edward T. Whittier. The named was changed to the *Stoneham Independent* in 1874. For many years the printing was done in the ell of Whittier's Building.

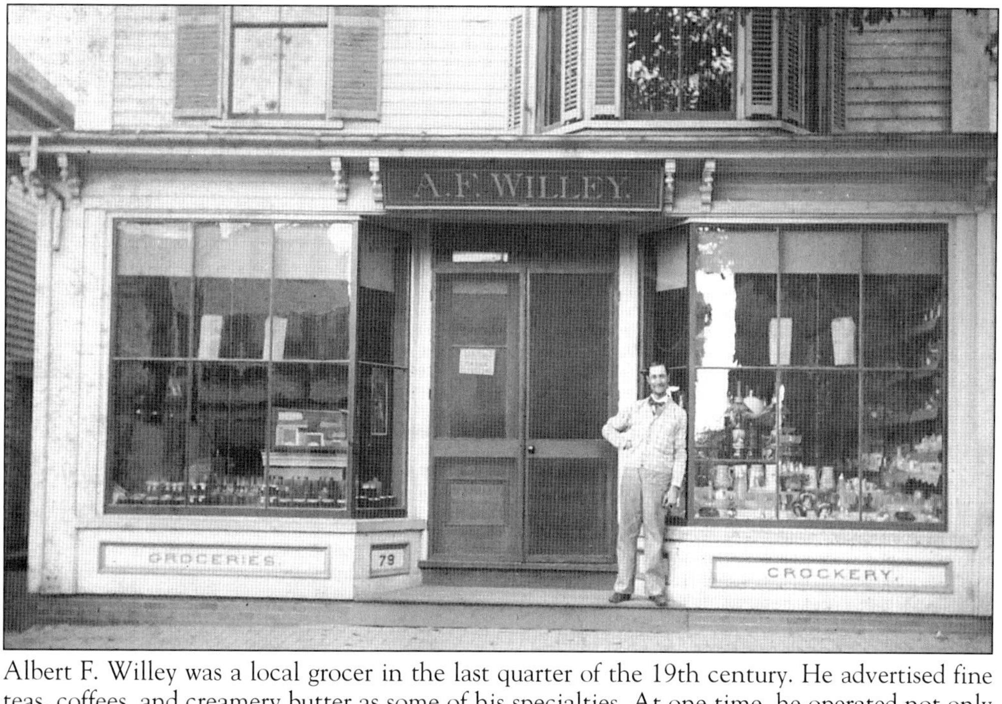

Albert F. Willey was a local grocer in the last quarter of the 19th century. He advertised fine teas, coffees, and creamery butter as some of his specialties. At one time, he operated not only this store on Main Street, but one on Gould Street as well.

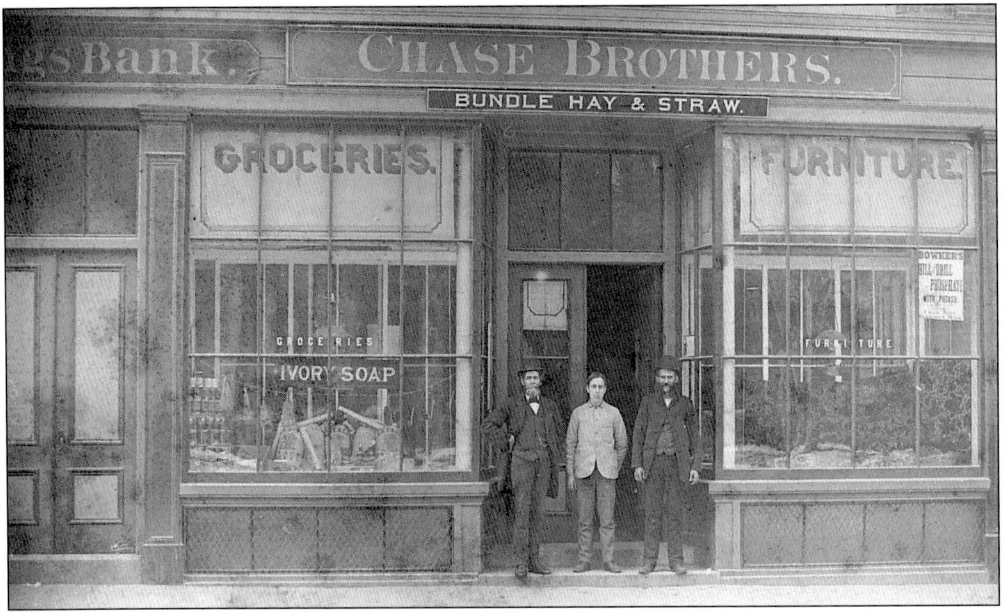

The Chase Brothers, J. Clinton and A. Alfred, went into business together in 1864, and ten years later they built the Chase Block in the Square. The pair occupied one of the large stores until *c.* 1890, selling a variety of items such as groceries, grain and flour, crockery, glass, furniture, mirrors, and mattresses. Through the years this location has also been home to businesses such as banks, dentists, and even the post office.

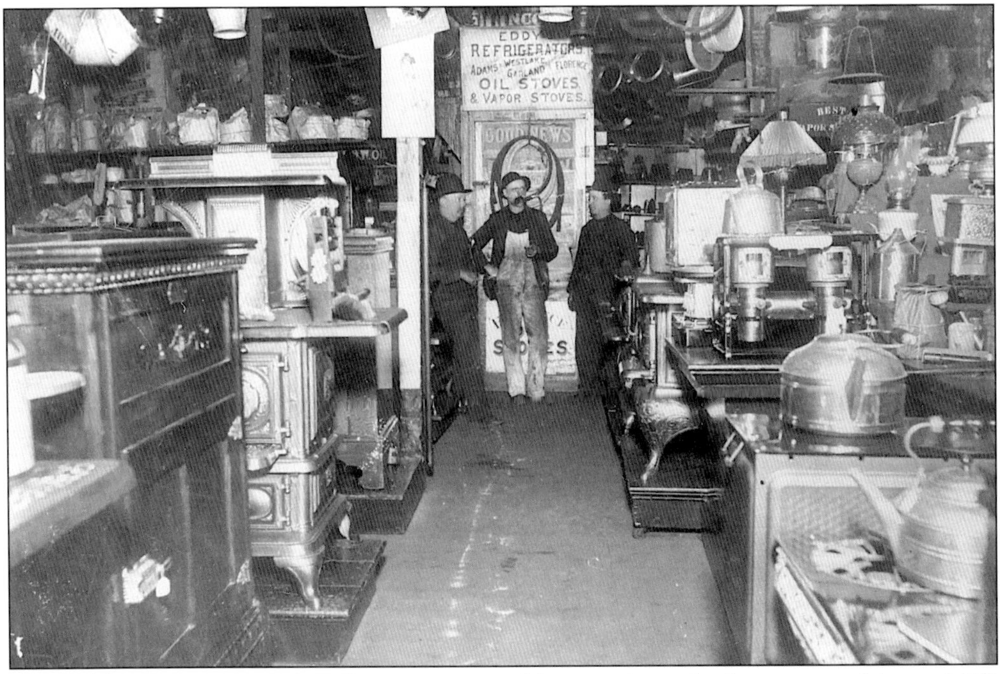

Theobald's store was on Main Street, opposite Hersam. A jingle that appeared in an 1883 advertisement said, "If you would find where stoves are sold, visit the store of Theobald. Though quick in speech, yet he is fair, and buys his stock with greatest care." You can see the great variety of stock sold by Theobald, his son Joe, and James A. Valler.

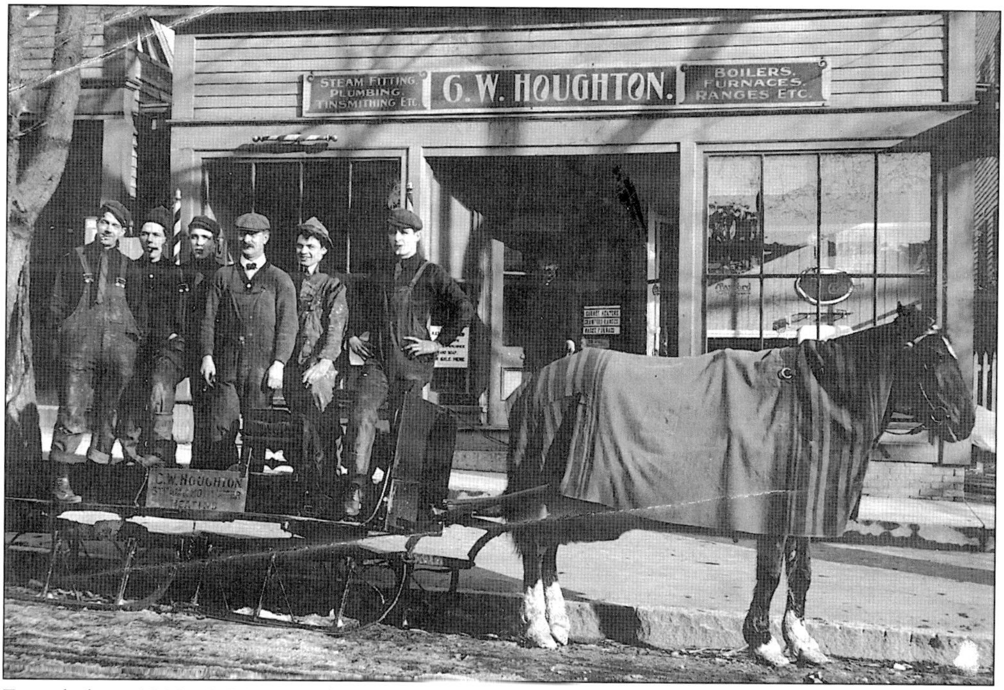

Founded in 1882, C.W. Houghton Plumbing and Heating is still in business today, though at a different location. The workers shown outside the Main Street store in 1902 are, from left to right, Herbert Morey, Fred Richards, Fred Nichols, C.W. Houghton, Harry Brady, and Laurence Byron.

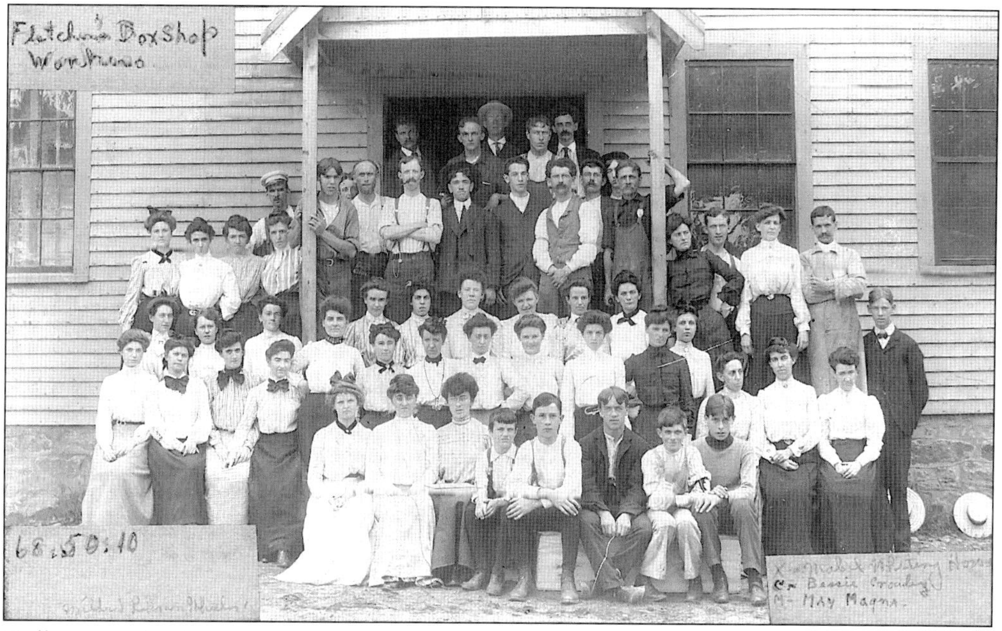

William P. Fletcher founded the Fletcher Box Company in Woburn in 1881. He moved to Stoneham in 1884, and in February 1891 he opened a new factory in Stoneham on Pleasant Street. By 1895, Fletcher employed 40 to 50 people and made about 12,000 paper boxes per day, mostly for local trade.

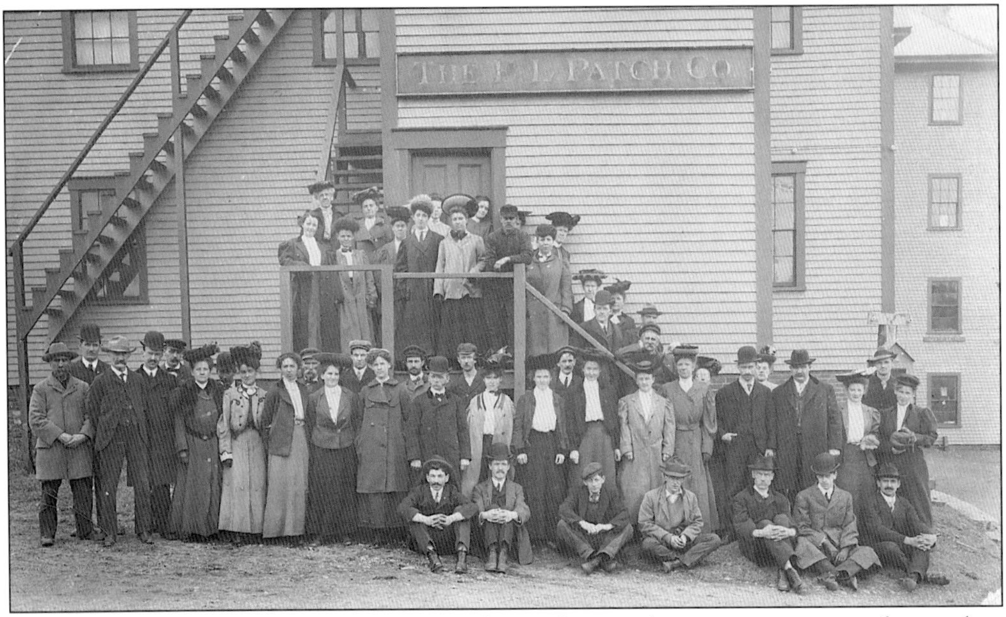

In 1888, the E.L. Patch Co., a pharmaceutical manufacturer, began operations in a former shoe shop on Montvale Avenue. Some of the firm's earliest workers, nicknamed "Patchworkers," are pictured here in 1903. In time, the company became Stoneham's largest employer and offered a variety of jobs to both men and women.

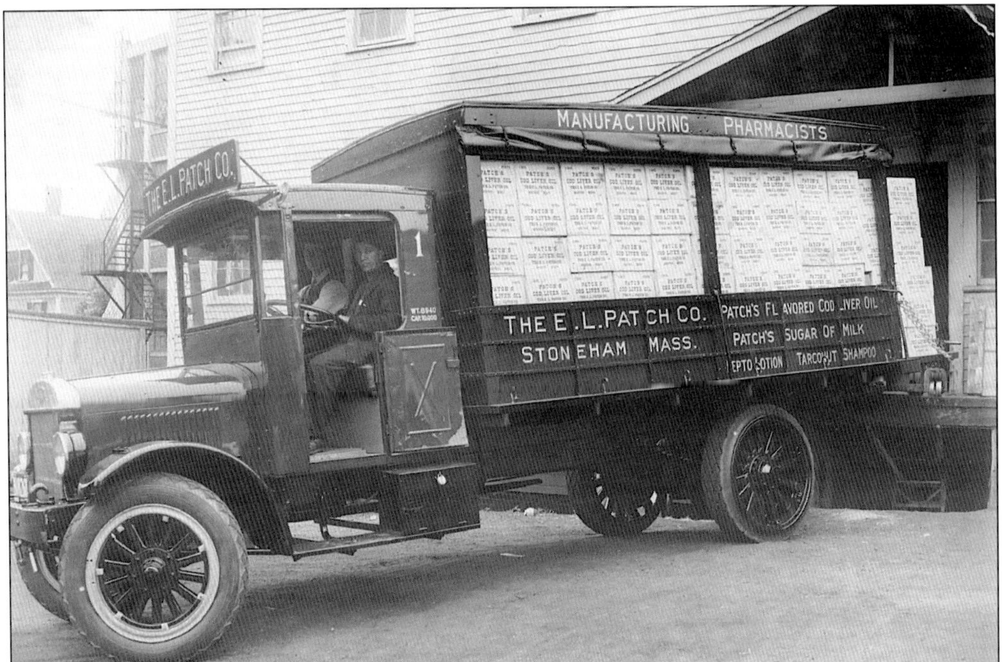

In the 1920s and 1930s, Patch's Flavored Cod Liver Oil became known throughout the country. It was the first flavored cod liver oil on the market. In 1924, Patch's was the first cod liver oil to be accepted by the Council on Pharmacy and Chemistry of the American Medical Association.

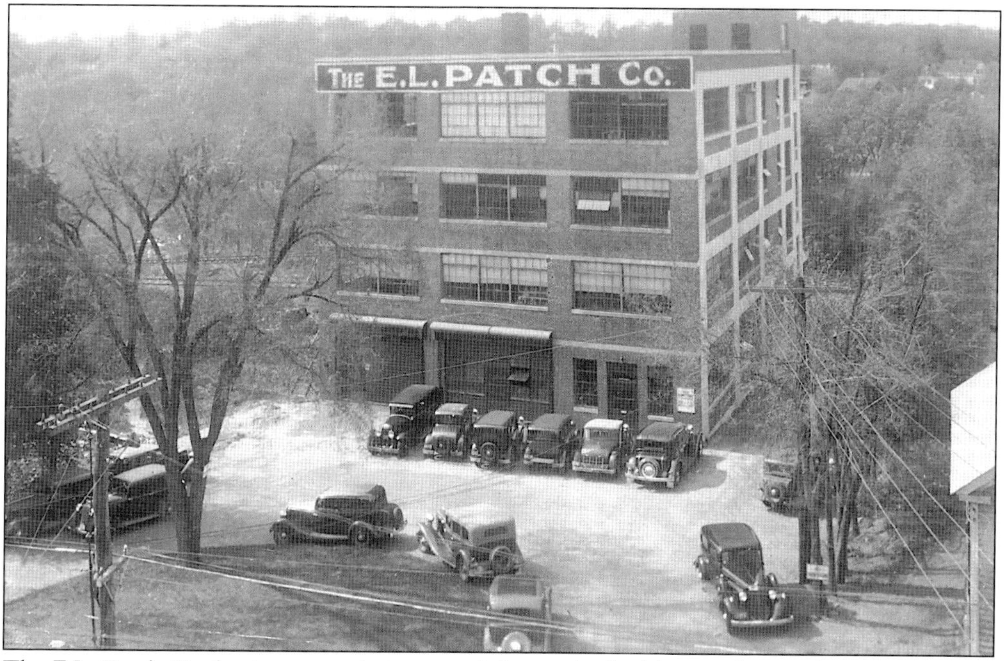

The E.L. Patch Co. business greatly increased due to the highly popular Patch's Flavored Cod Liver Oil. This led to the construction of a new four-story building across the street, where research was conducted on animals to show the effects of cod liver oil. Later owners of the building added a fifth floor to the structure.

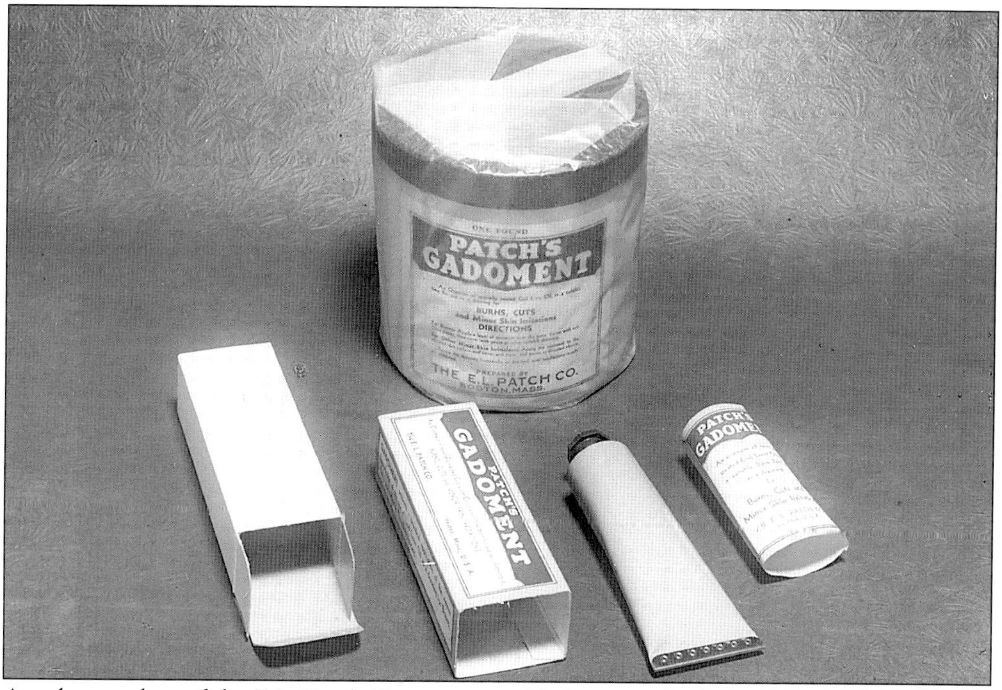

Another product of the E.L. Patch Company was Gadoment, which was composed of 70% cod liver oil. Introduced c. 1934, it was helpful for skin lesions, leg ulcers, and burns. Many victims of the Cocoanut Grove fire in 1942 were treated with Gadoment.

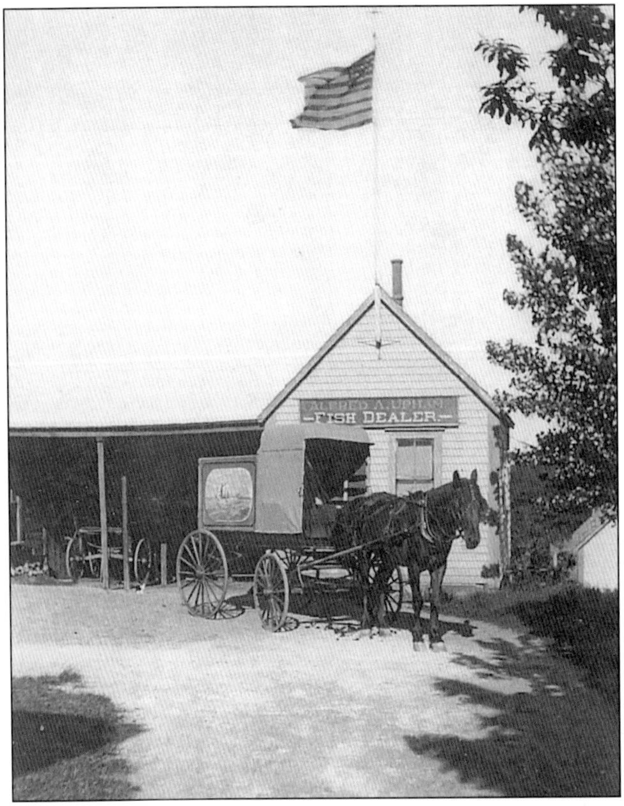

Alfred Upham's Fish Market was located on Bow Street but also offered delivery service. Upham provided fresh fish to Stoneham households from the late 1890s to the mid-1930s. His market survives as a private home on Bow Street.

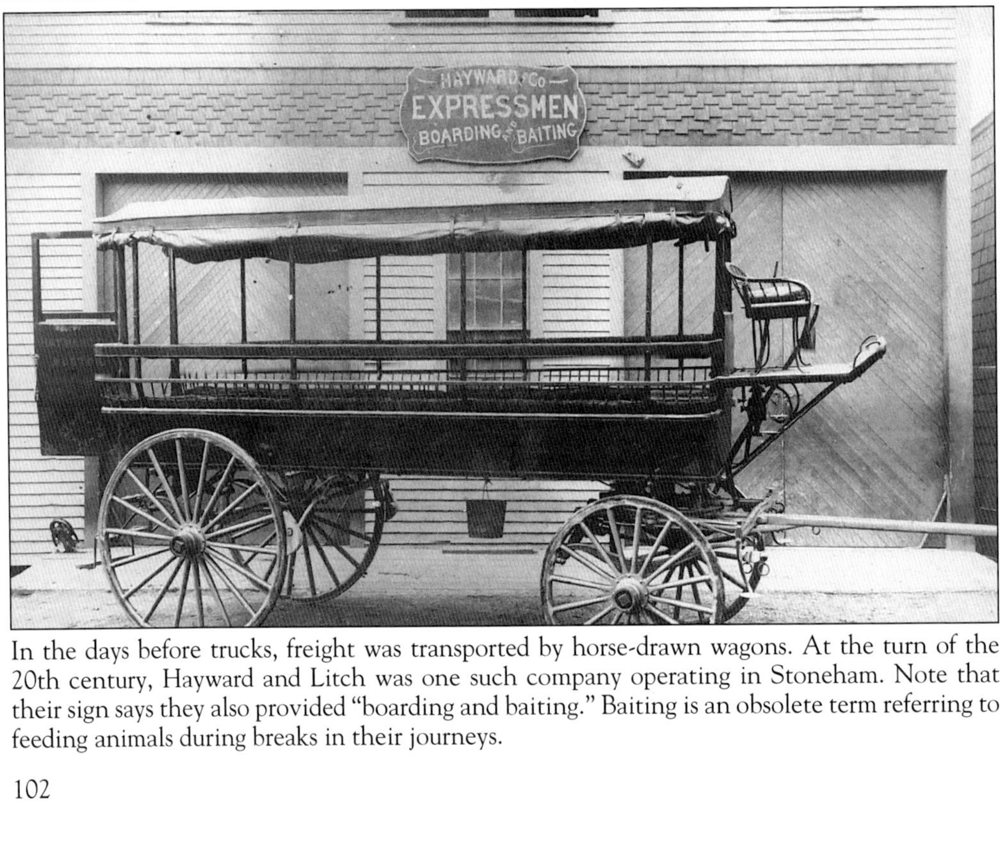

In the days before trucks, freight was transported by horse-drawn wagons. At the turn of the 20th century, Hayward and Litch was one such company operating in Stoneham. Note that their sign says they also provided "boarding and baiting." Baiting is an obsolete term referring to feeding animals during breaks in their journeys.

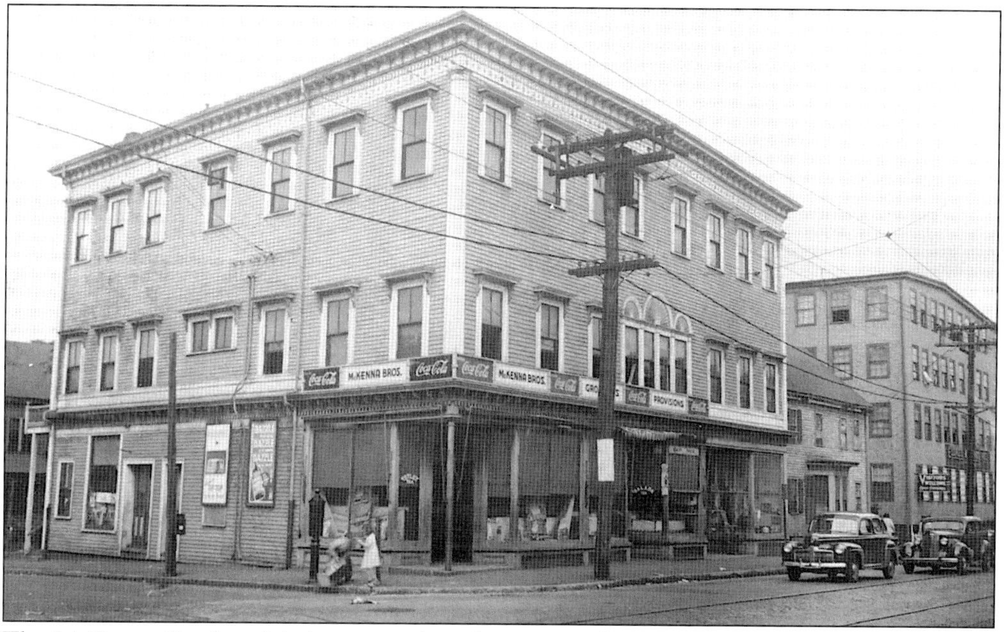

The McKenna Brothers Market opened at the corner of Main Street and Montvale Avenue on January 1, 1898. The upper floors of the building were used for meetings and dances. After nearly 50 years of operation, the market closed in July 1945 and was razed to make way for Barbo's Furniture Store.

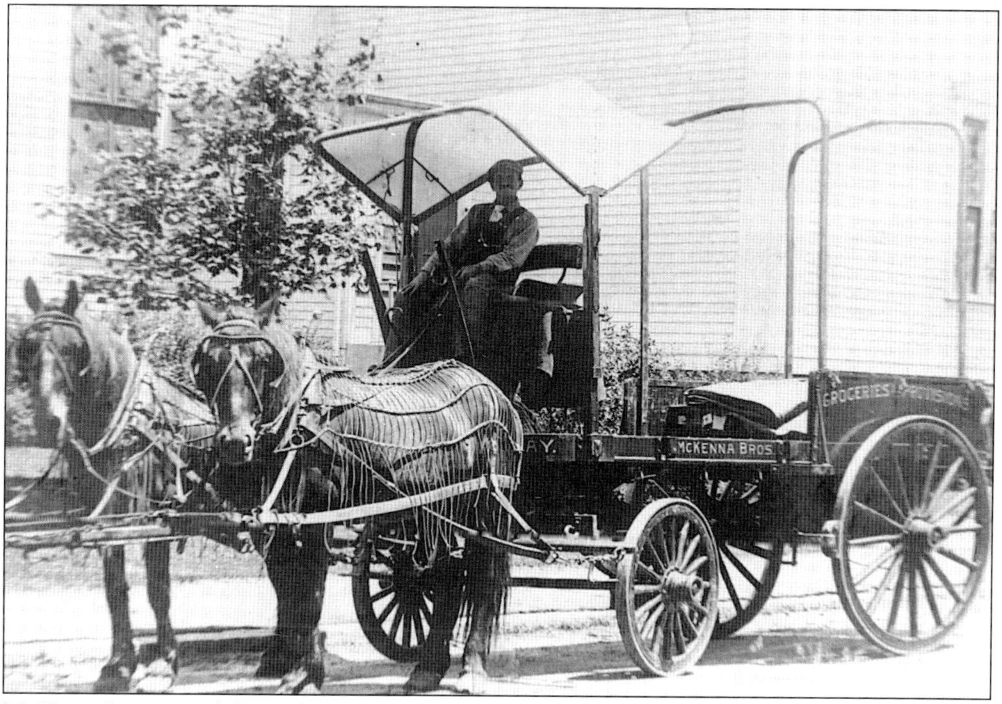

McKenna's wagon delivered groceries throughout the town. The driver, Frank Jennings, is shaded from the summer sun by an umbrella. Note the special harnesses on the horses, designed to keep the flies away.

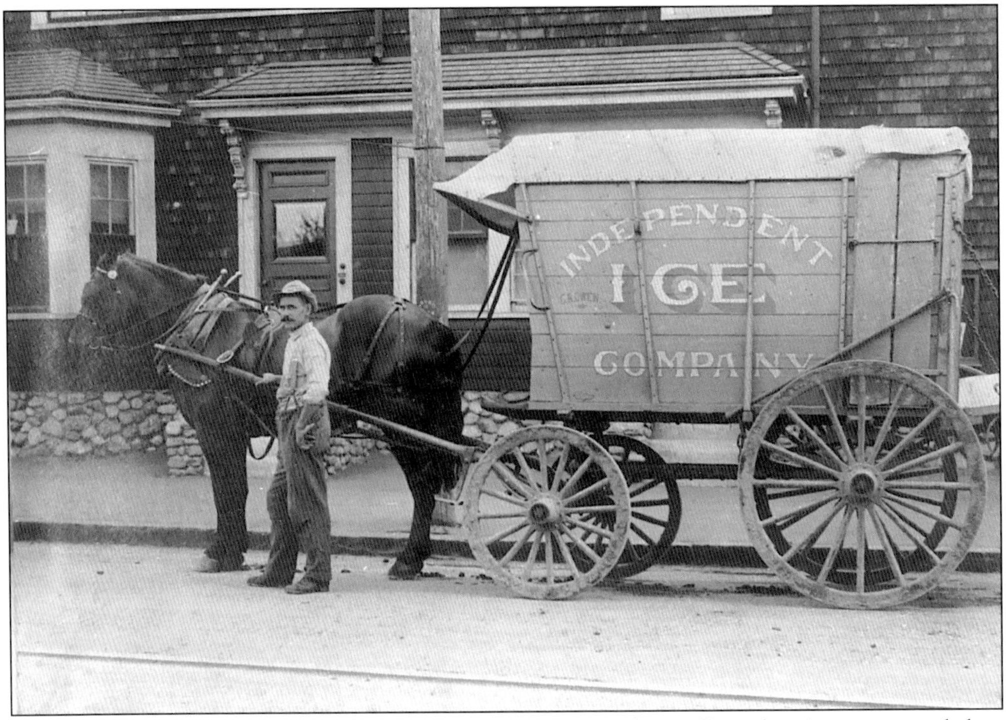

During the warmer months ice wagons were a common sight on Stoneham's streets, and they often delivered ice that had been cut on Stoneham ponds. The Independent Ice Co. was owned by Charles A. Owen. Note the ice card in the window.

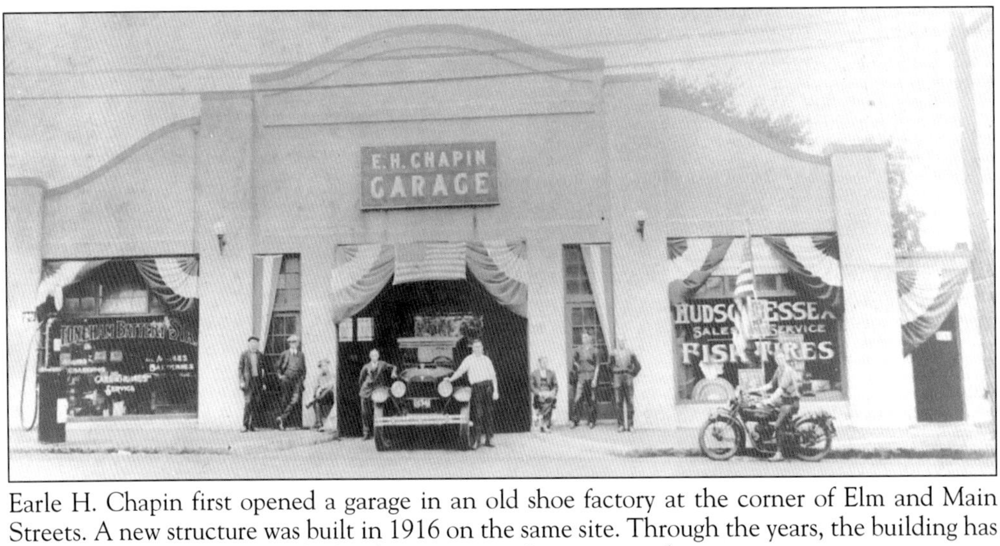

Earle H. Chapin first opened a garage in an old shoe factory at the corner of Elm and Main Streets. A new structure was built in 1916 on the same site. Through the years, the building has also been a bowling alley and a lumber company. It is now a video store.

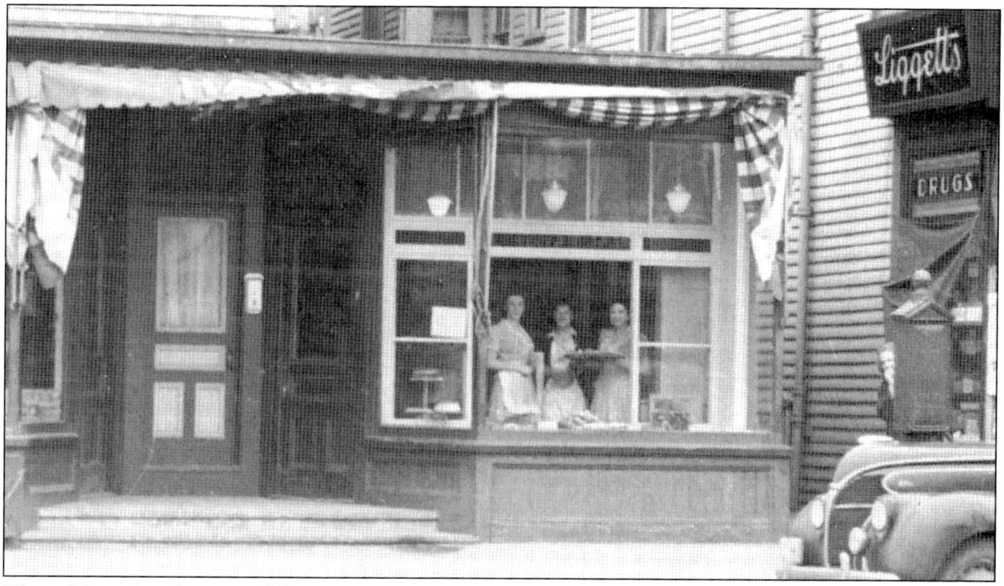

The oldest family-owned business in Central Square is Hanks Bakery, shown in this 1930s view. Warren Hatch and Denslow V. Hanks purchased the shop in 1913. In later years, it was operated solely by Mr. Hanks, and after his death, by his widow, Jennie Beane Hanks. In the 1940s, she sold the business to her nephew, Gwynne "Baron" Beane. Today, the bakery is operated by Baron's son Joe and Joe's wife, Beverly.

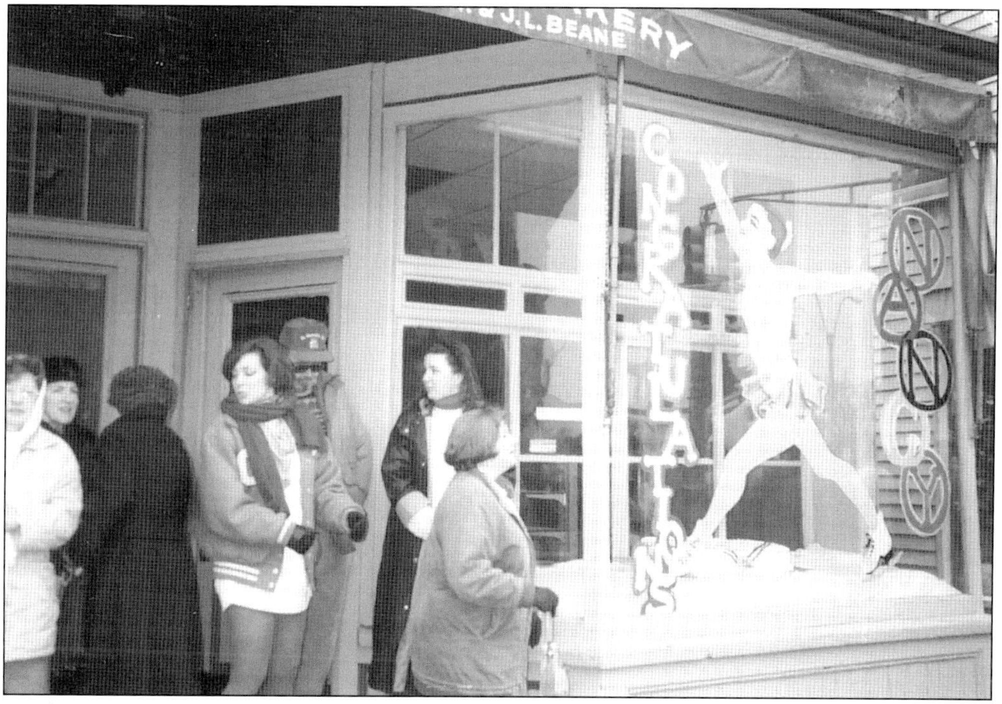

Hanks Bakery continues its tradition of being a "scratch" shop, probably accounting for the homemade taste. A visit to Hanks is a visual treat, with so many sweets to look at and choose from. In addition, daughter Linda's artistic window paintings are a treat to behold. This one congratulates local Olympian Nancy Kerrigan on her efforts in the 1990s.

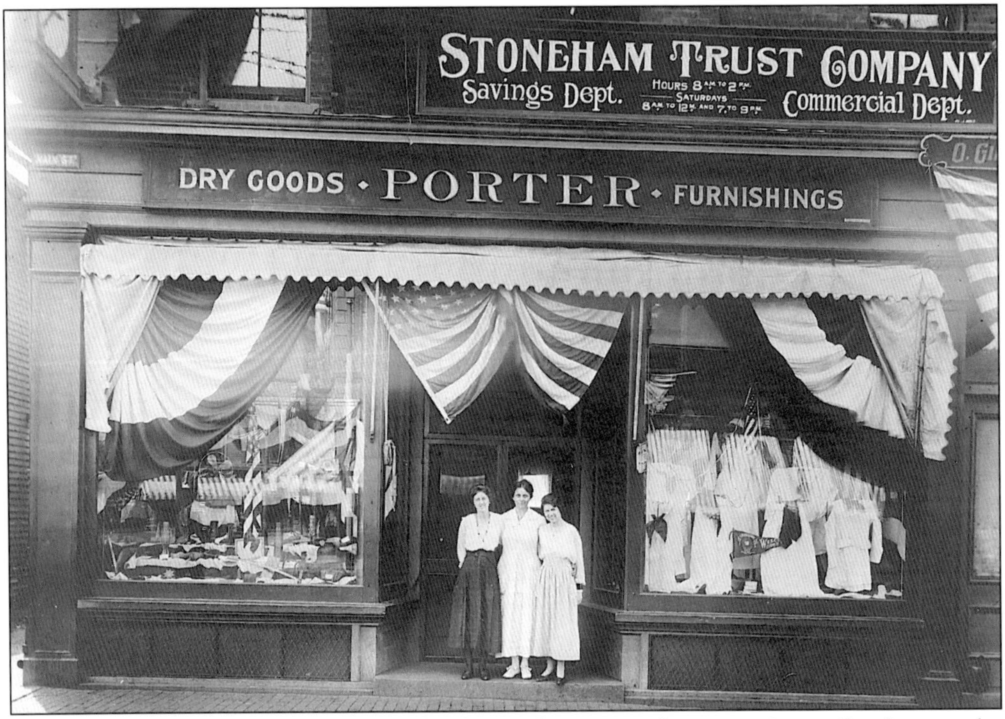

Frank B. and Minnie M. Porter operated a dry goods company known as Porter Co., Inc., in the Chase Block. This was where the ladies of Stoneham could buy items such as cloth, thread, and cloth products. Mrs. Porter and her clerks are saying "Welcome Home" to those returning from World War I. This parade and celebration were held on June 17, 1919.

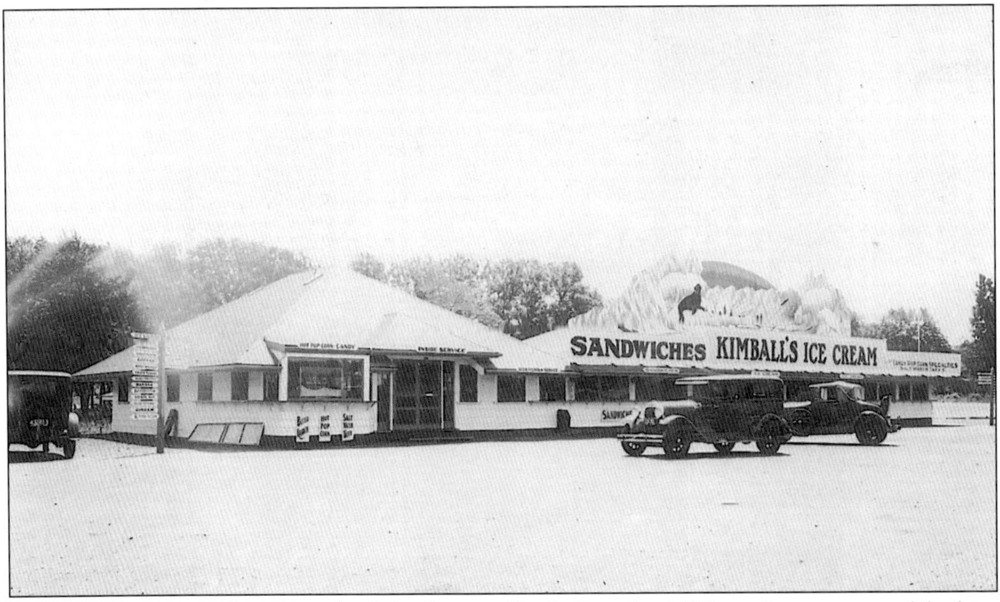

Kimball's Ice Cream Stand was built by George Kimball in the 1920s and was managed for him by Leon and Celia Zibell. Across the street were Kimball's Pond and icehouses. In 1936, Tedd Syak purchased this property, and he and his sister Victoria operated it as Tedd's Inn. In 1953, the building became China Moon.

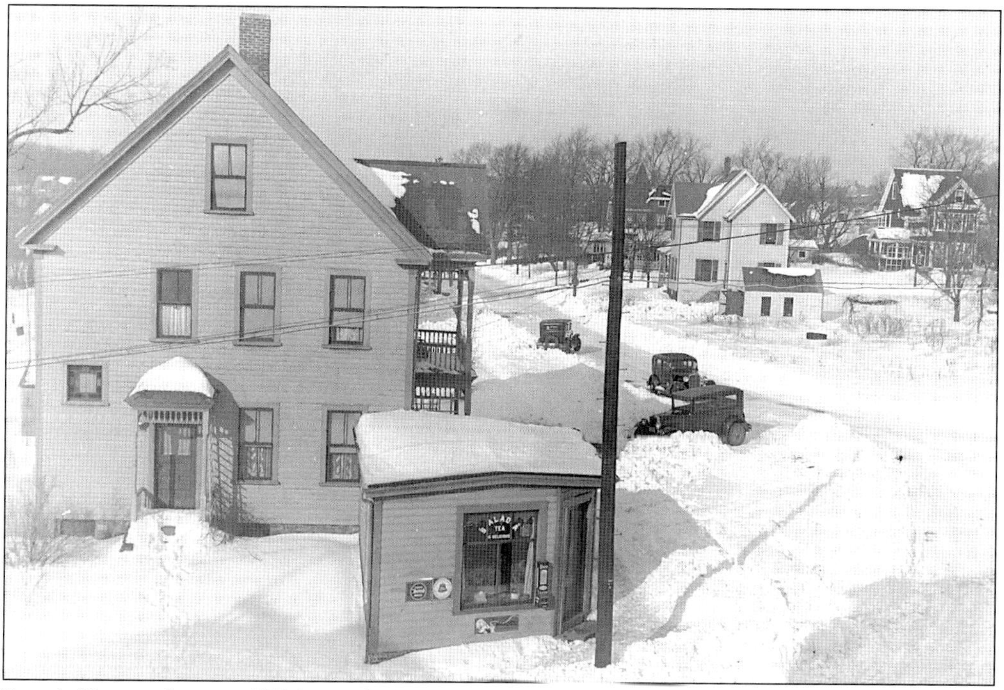

Piper's Variety Store at 37 Montvale Avenue was typical of the many small variety stores found in every part of Stoneham 50 to 75 years ago. Matthew C. Piper and his family operated their store over 25 years, beginning in the late 1920s.

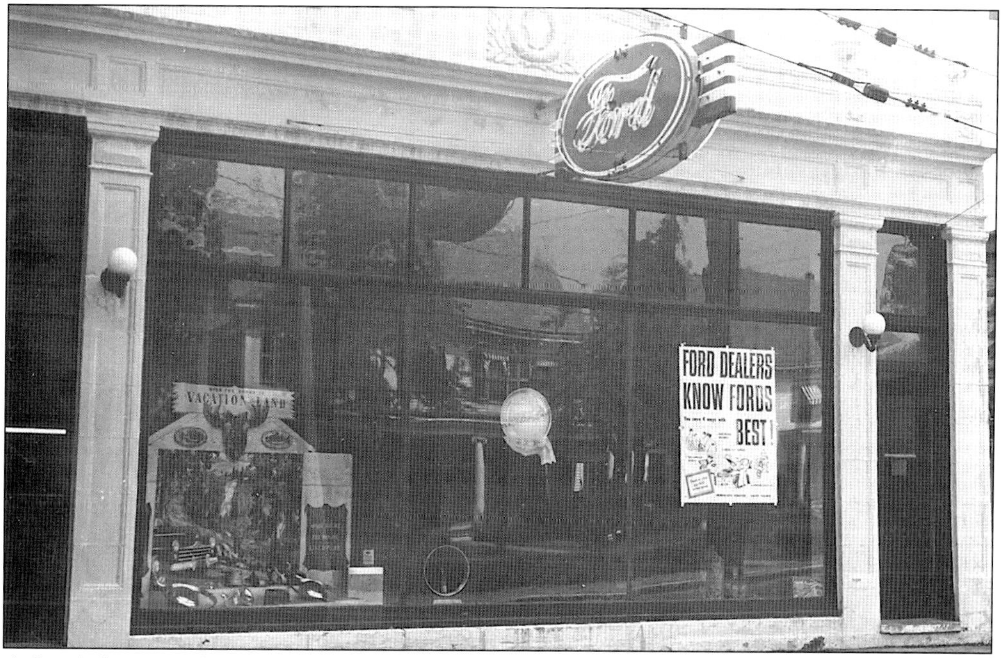

A family business that can operate for four generations has to have a good product! Apparently the Melkonian family did when they opened their first Ford garage on Franklin Street in 1917. The garage is shown here in the late 1940s just prior to their relocation to Main Street, where the business has continued to expand.

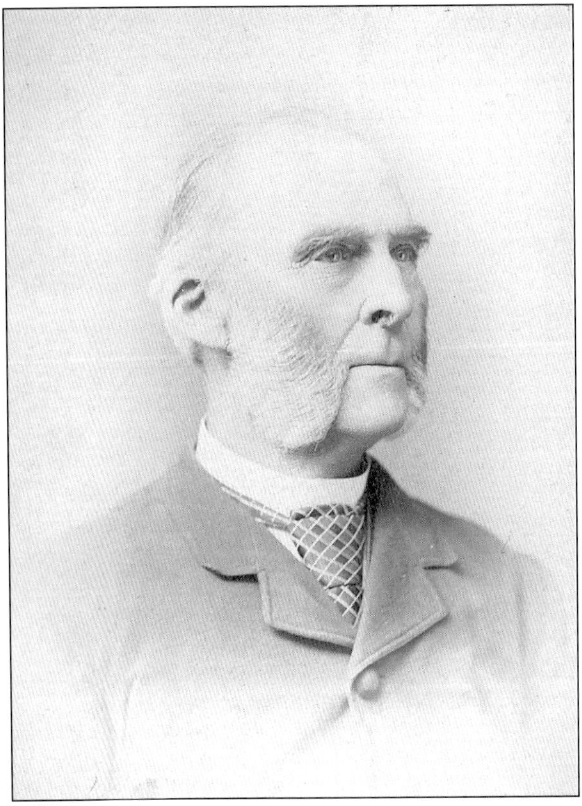

Padilla Beard (1821–1902) was certainly a man who kept pace with the times. In 1839, he became the driver of the tri-weekly stagecoach from North Reading through Stoneham and Medford to Boston. Beard became a railroad conductor on the Stoneham Branch of the Boston and Lowell Railroad in 1861 and retired in 1892.

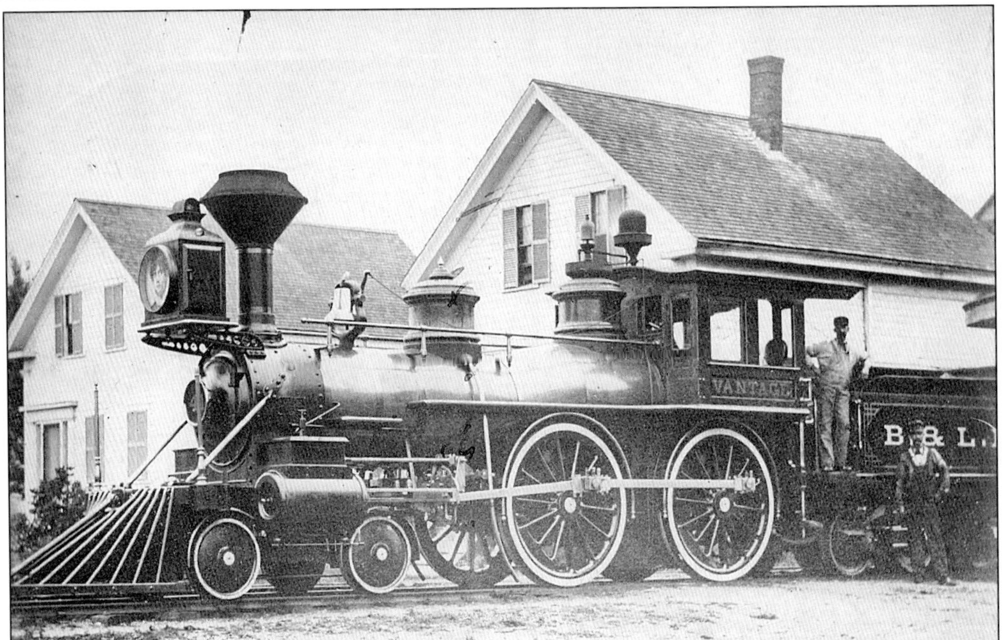

"Vantage" was a railroad engine of the late 19th century on the Boston and Lowell Railway. Note the "pin-up girl" portrait in the headlight! Engineer George W. Blood is beside the engine while Harry Newhall, the fireman, stands on the cab steps.

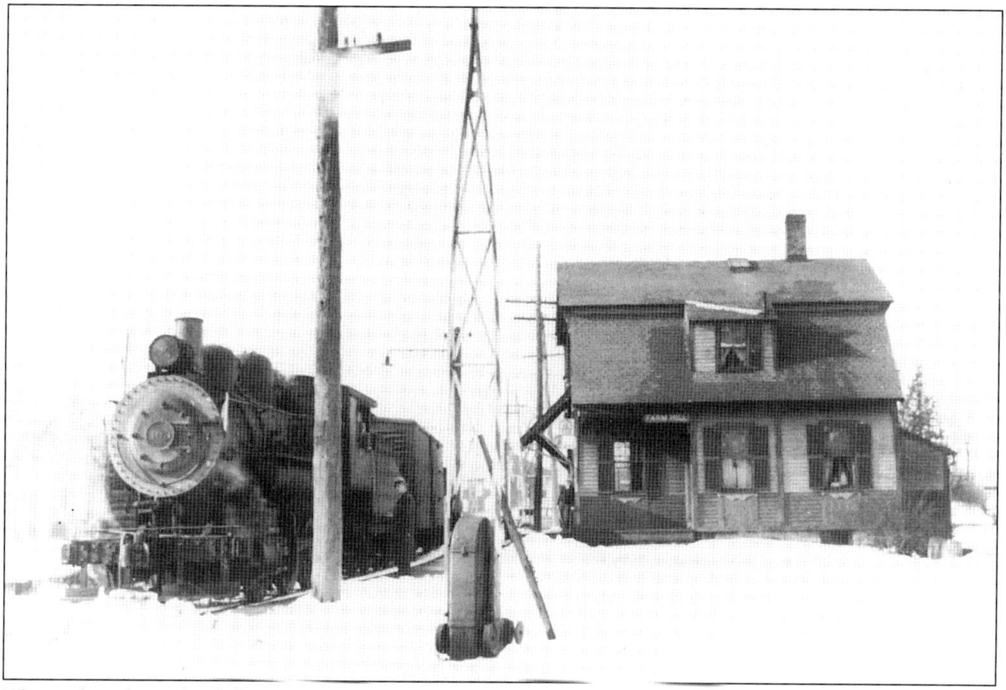

The railroad reached the Farm Hill section of Stoneham in 1861. The earliest station burned in 1880, and the one shown here was built the following year. The station was moved in May 1948 to become a private home on Central Street.

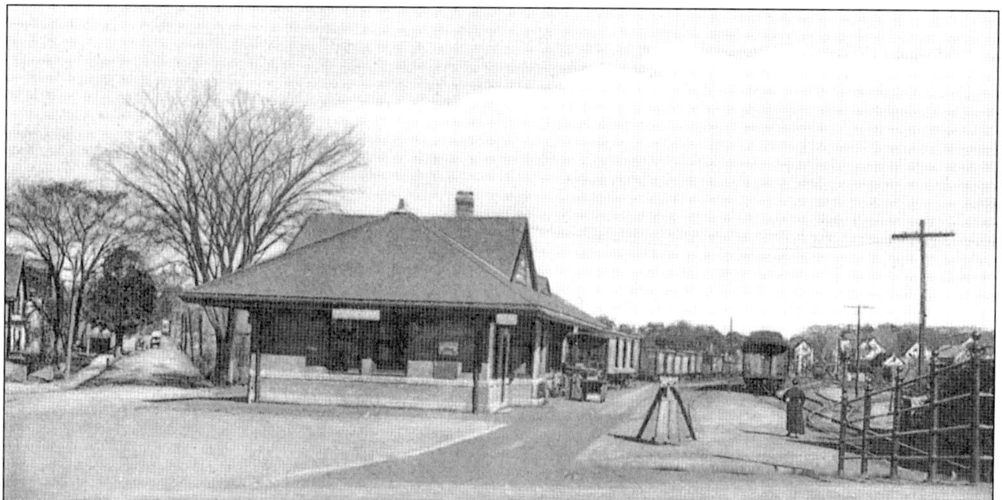

The railroad was extended to Pine and Franklin Streets in 1863. The first station at this location was a wooden structure and was said to be "ugly." It was replaced by a new station, which opened in September 1896. Passenger service on this line was suspended in mid-May 1958. The Stoneham Municipal Employees Federal Credit Union now occupies this old Stoneham station.

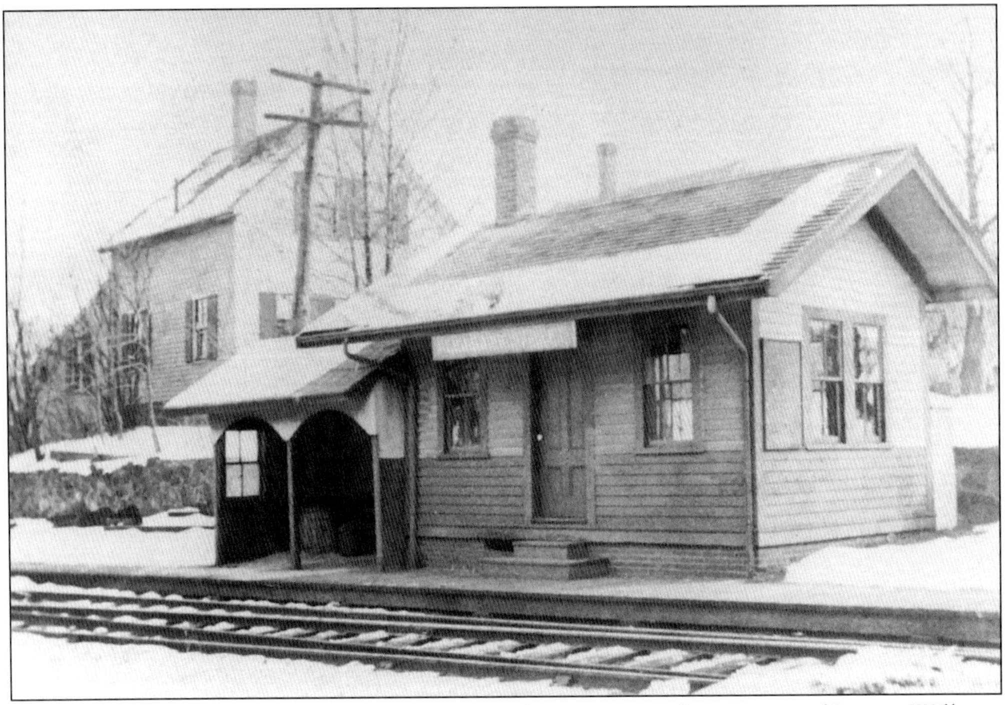

The Pleasant Street Railroad Station was built in the 1870s near the junction of Spring, William, and Pleasant Streets. Although only a few minutes from either Farm Hill Station or Stoneham Station, railroad patrons appreciated this added stop. The decline in rail transportation brought about the station's closure in the 1950s.

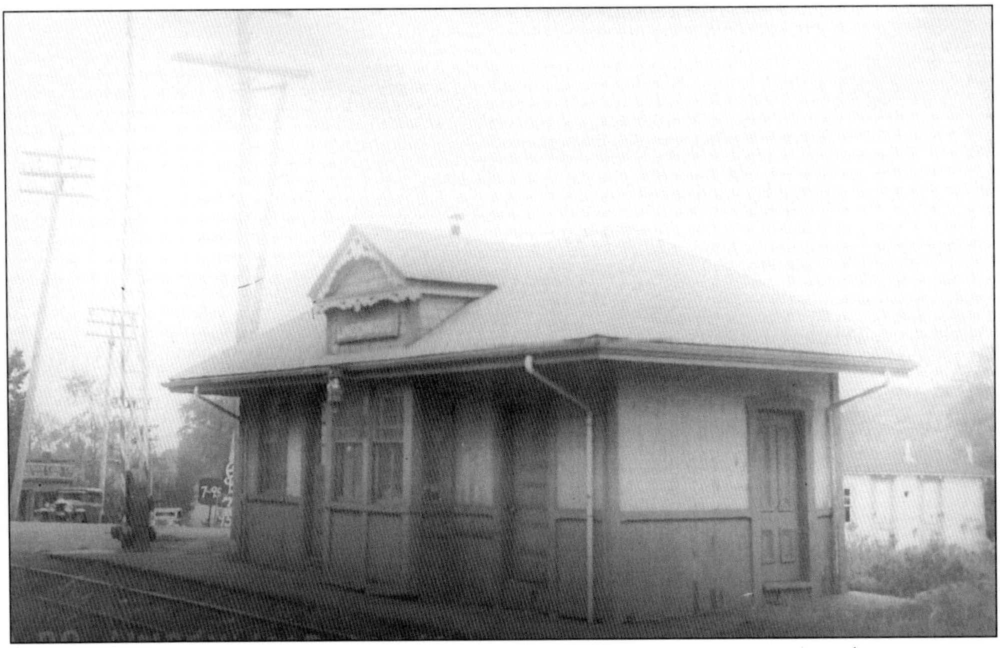

The Lindenwood Railroad Station was built in the early 1880s to accommodate the commuters who lived in the part of Stoneham near Montvale Avenue, Lindenwood Road, and on Nobility Hill. The decline of railroad travel caused this station to close in the mid-1900s.

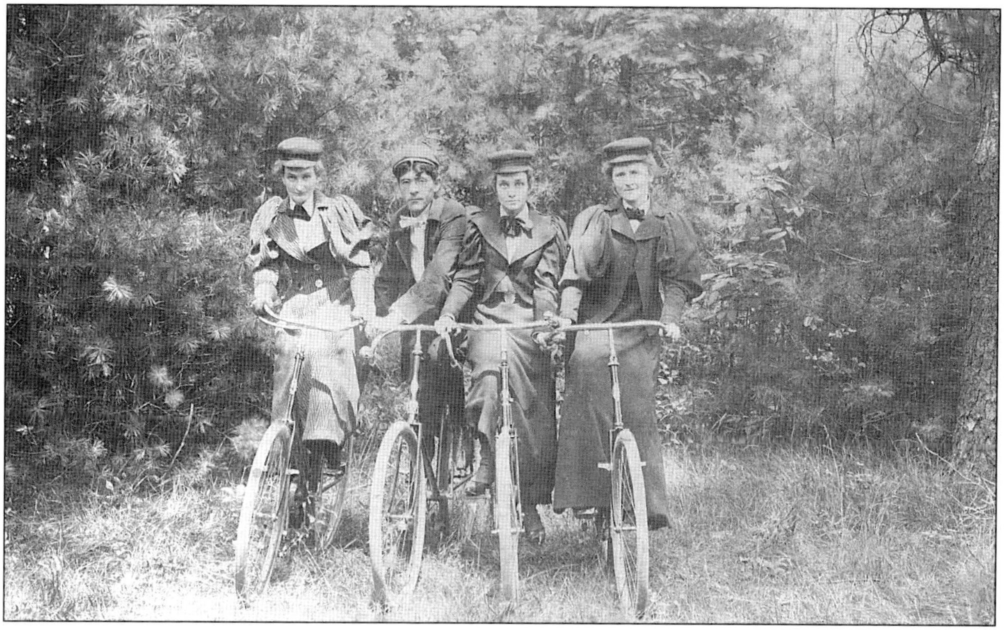

Four members of the Wayside Bicycle Club are shown in costume astride their "machines." They are, from left to right, Mattie Green, Fred Doucette, Lizzie Green Stinson, and Katherine Collins. Bicycles were so popular that in 1896 the town of Stoneham taxed them. These were each probably valued at $50 and cost their owners a tax of $1.02.

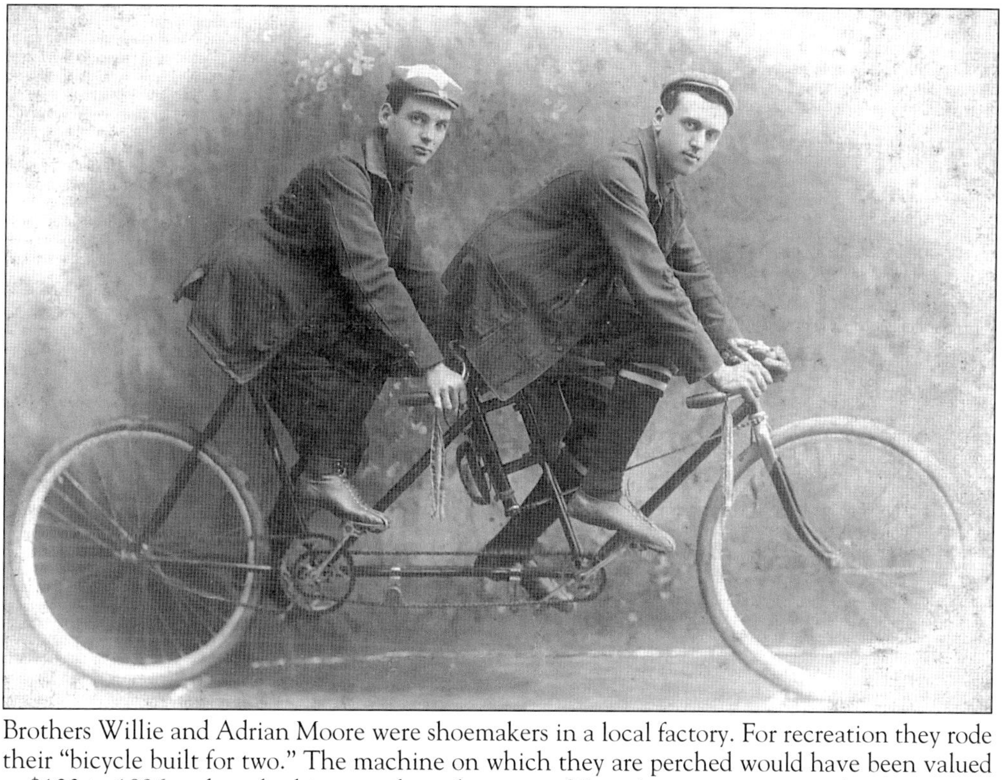

Brothers Willie and Adrian Moore were shoemakers in a local factory. For recreation they rode their "bicycle built for two." The machine on which they are perched would have been valued at $100 in 1896 and resulted in a tax from the town of Stoneham amounting to $2.04

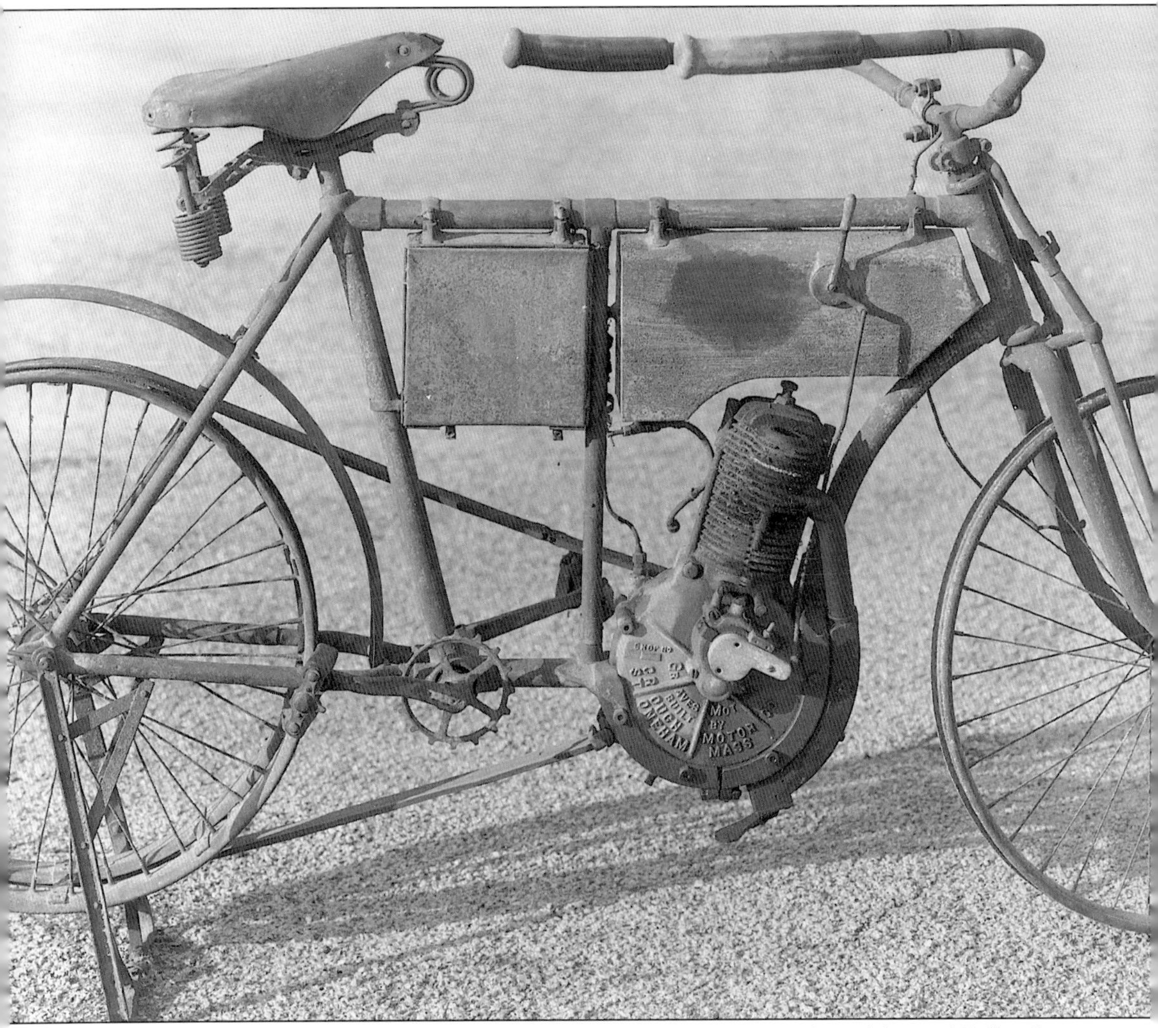

In the spring of 1897, Stillman Crouch built a shop at the corner of Franklin and Fuller Streets for the sale of bicycles and bicycle supplies, and by 1903, he was in the motorcycle business. Note how much this early motorcycle resembles a bicycle. This model had 3.5 horsepower, weighed 130 pounds, and cost $200 when new. In March 1906, two Crouch motorcycles were on exhibit at the Boston Auto Show. One was a 1905 model, and the other was billed as "a new and improved 1906 machine." By 1909, Crouch was exhibiting in New York City as well. Robert Messer and Arthur Johnson demonstrated these machines for Crouch at the shows. Crouch motorcycles became well known, and one was in the collection of actor Steve McQueen. The rapid advancement of the automobile industry probably led to a decreased interest in motorcycles, and Crouch closed his business. In the following years, he worked as an engineer in the A.E. Mann and Company Shoe Factory. He was also the engineer for the fire department's Colonel Gould steamer. In 1912, Crouch became the first permanent member of the Stoneham Fire Department, serving until he resigned in 1923.

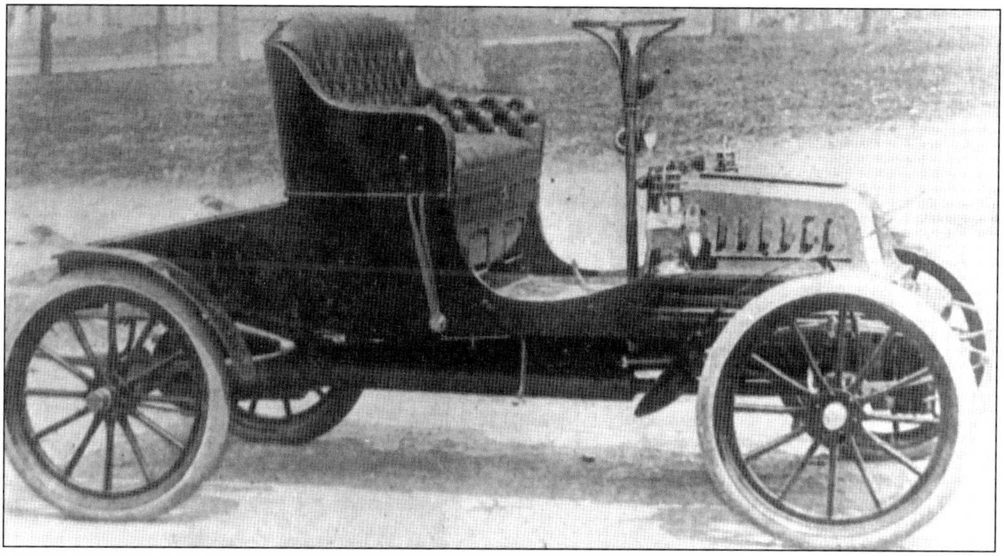

Lucius J. Phelps opened an automobile factory in Stoneham in September 1902. This 1903 touring car had three cylinders and a steering post that tilted. The front part of the body could be raised in about four minutes, making all parts accessible for repair.

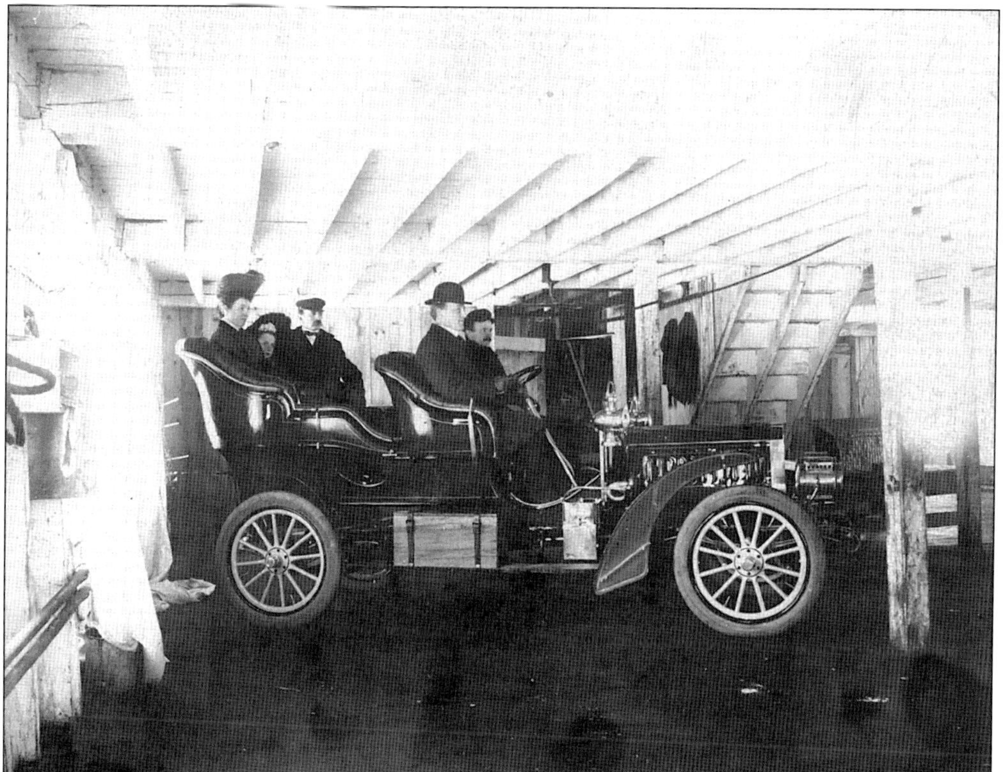

The Phelps touring car of 1905 was priced at $2,500. It came complete with four lamps (two gas and two oil), a horn, and tools. Mr. Phelps guaranteed every car to do 40 miles per hour on any suitable road. The standard color was royal blue with black moldings and yellow stripes.

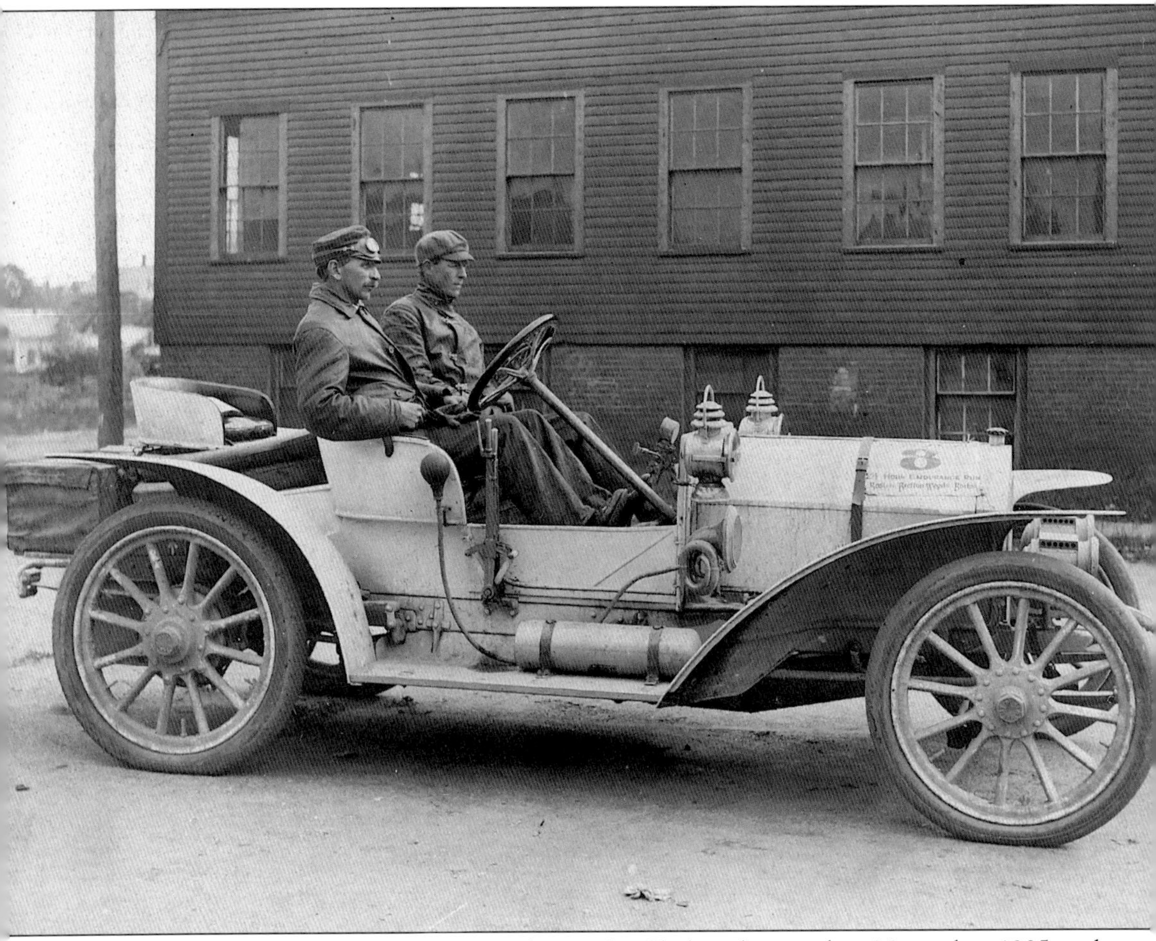

The Shawmut Motor Company moved into the Phelps plant in late November 1905 and produced models in 1906, 1907, and 1908. This car is a 1908 Shawmut Runabout. During this period of development in automobile manufacturing, the emphasis was on endurance. As a result, Shawmut cars such as this one competed in many endurance races, including a 24-hour run from Boston to Bretton Woods, New Hampshire, and back to Boston. From April to October 1908, one car completed the six installments of the Briarcliff Cup Race. The gas tank on the running board powered the headlights. The running lights (where the windshield would be) were powered by kerosene. Note the horn (rubber bulb) and that the steering wheel is on the right. This car sold for $4,750.

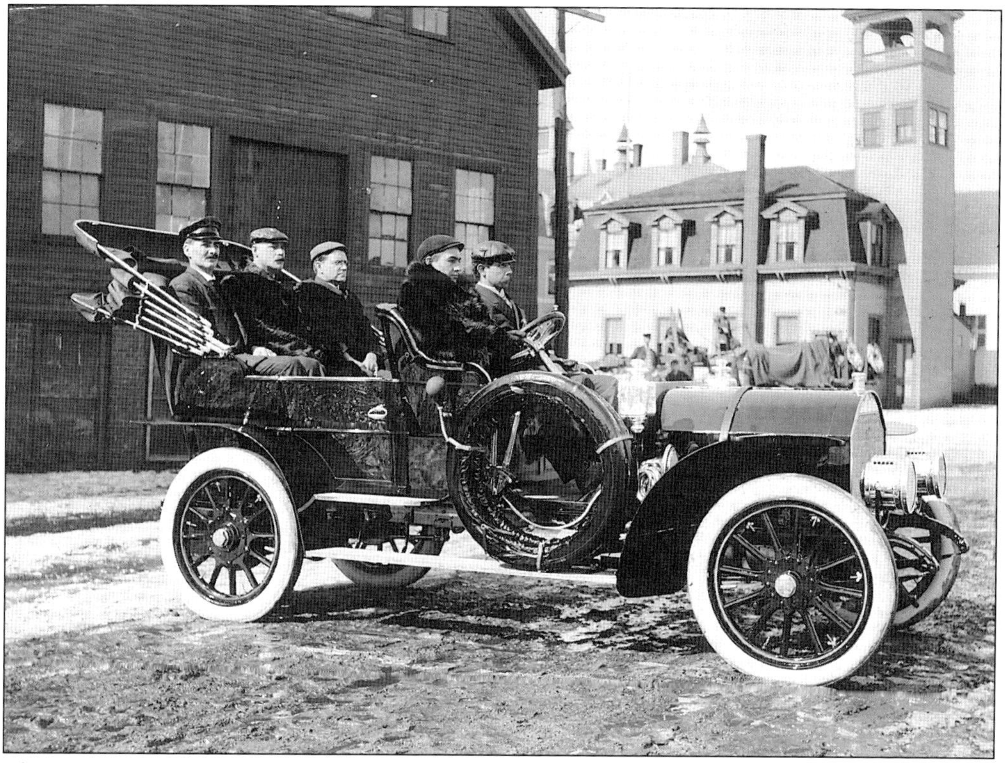

This smart-looking 1908 Shawmut Touring Car is shown outside the factory on Pine Street. The advertising brochure called it "A car for the man who wants only the BEST," and emphasized its reliability, speed, and power, as well as its economy and ease of operation.

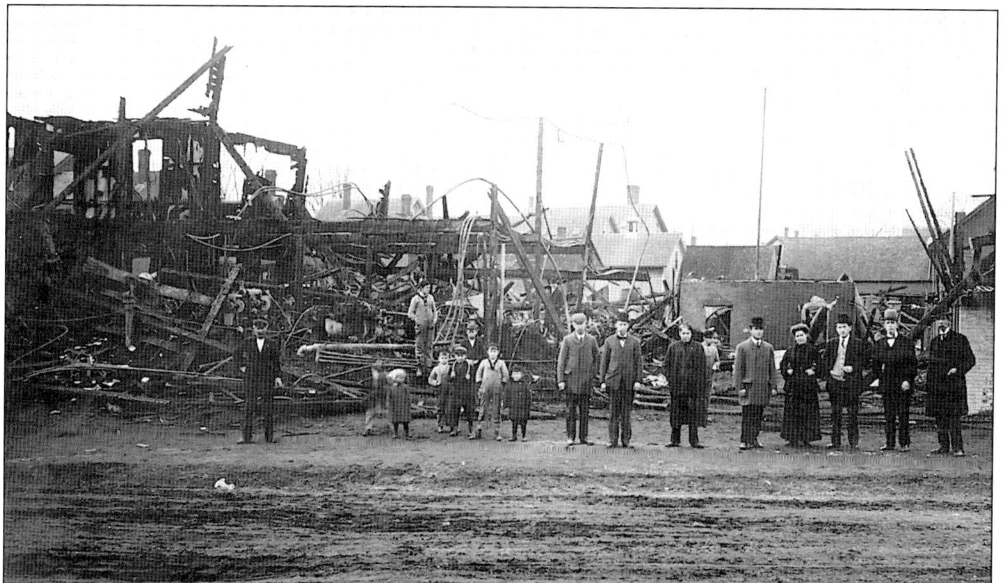

On Friday, November 13, 1908, fire caused by an explosion reduced the old wooden Shawmut factory to ruins. Only the fortunate direction of the wind and the masterly work of the fire department prevented the spread of the fire toward the center of town.

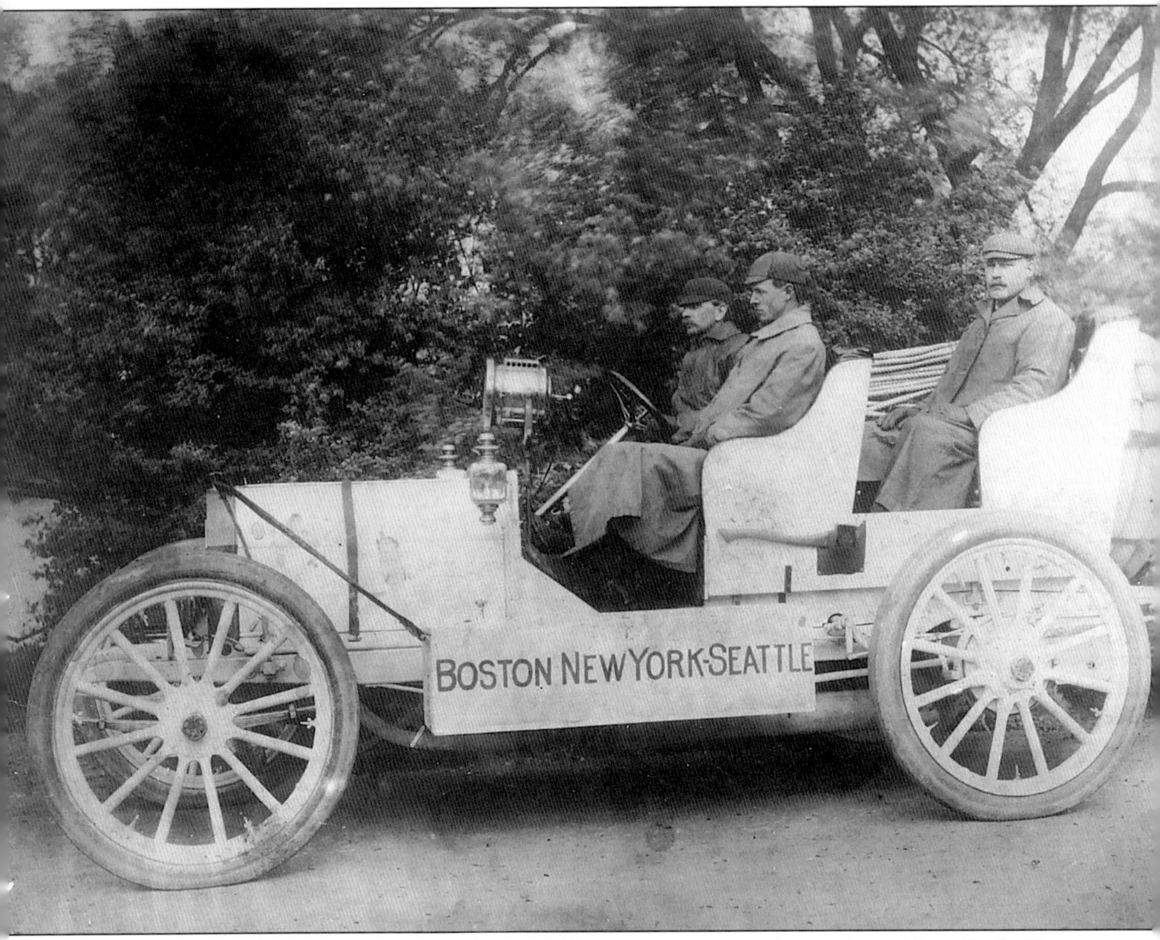

A surviving Shawmut was entered in a 1909 transcontinental race from New York City to Seattle. That car is shown just before the start of the race with T. Arthur Pettengill at the wheel. Beside him is Earle Chapin and seated in the rear is Superintendent F.A. Meier of the Shawmut Motor Company. The race started at 3 p.m. on June 1 when President Taft pressed a gold telegraph key in Washington formally opening the Alaska-Yukon-Pacific Exposition in Seattle and, at the same time, signaling Mayor George B. McClellan to fire the starting pistol. An Acme, an Itala, two Fords, and the Shawmut headed up Broadway for Poughkeepsie. The first week had daily destinations and check-ins due to speeding regulations here in the East. When the cars left St. Louis on Monday, June 7, the race really began.

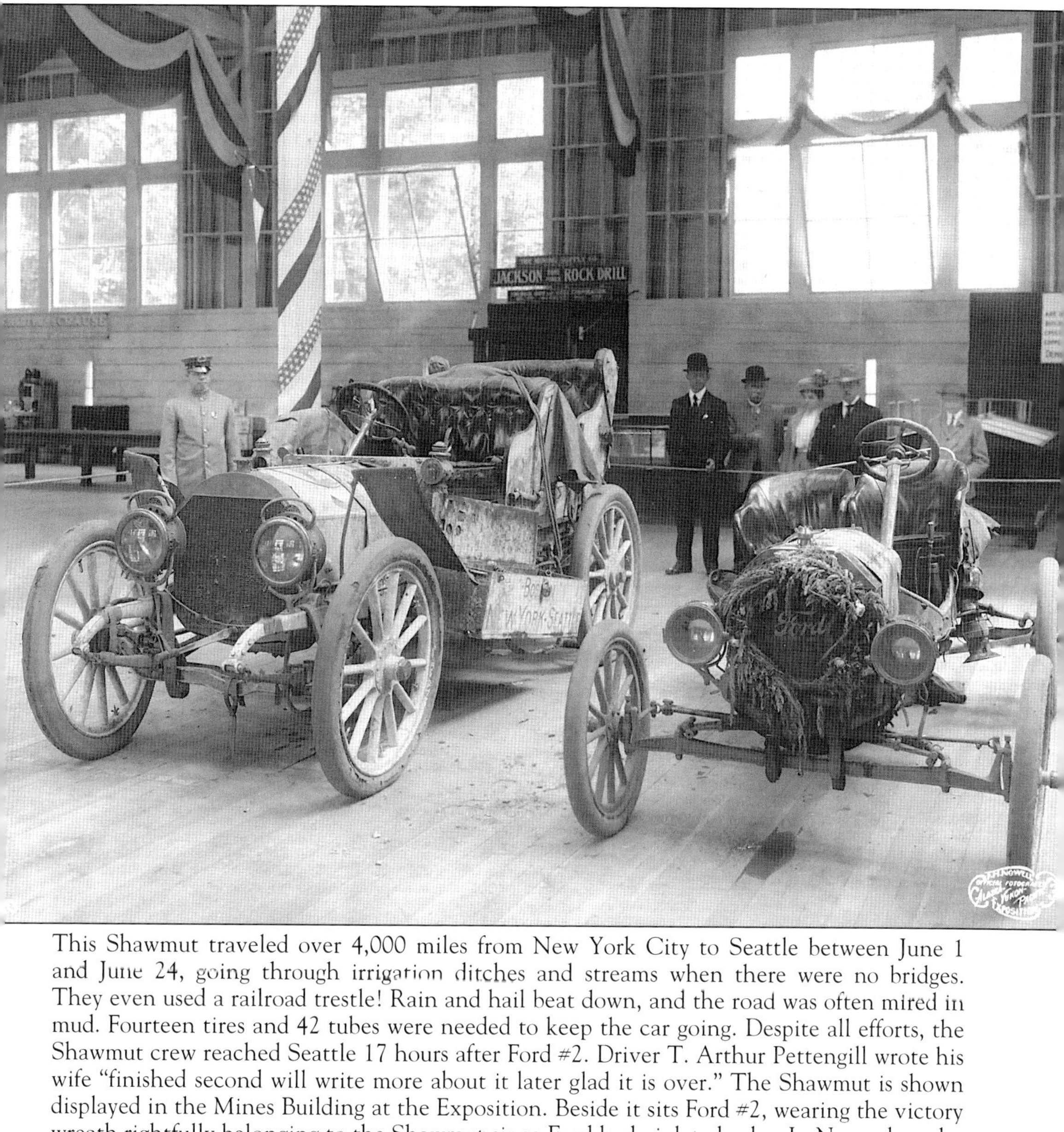

This Shawmut traveled over 4,000 miles from New York City to Seattle between June 1 and June 24, going through irrigation ditches and streams when there were no bridges. They even used a railroad trestle! Rain and hail beat down, and the road was often mired in mud. Fourteen tires and 42 tubes were needed to keep the car going. Despite all efforts, the Shawmut crew reached Seattle 17 hours after Ford #2. Driver T. Arthur Pettengill wrote his wife "finished second will write more about it later glad it is over." The Shawmut is shown displayed in the Mines Building at the Exposition. Beside it sits Ford #2, wearing the victory wreath rightfully belonging to the Shawmut since Ford had violated rules. In November, the Automobile Club of America, the official sponsor of the race, awarded the trophy and first prize money to the Shawmut.

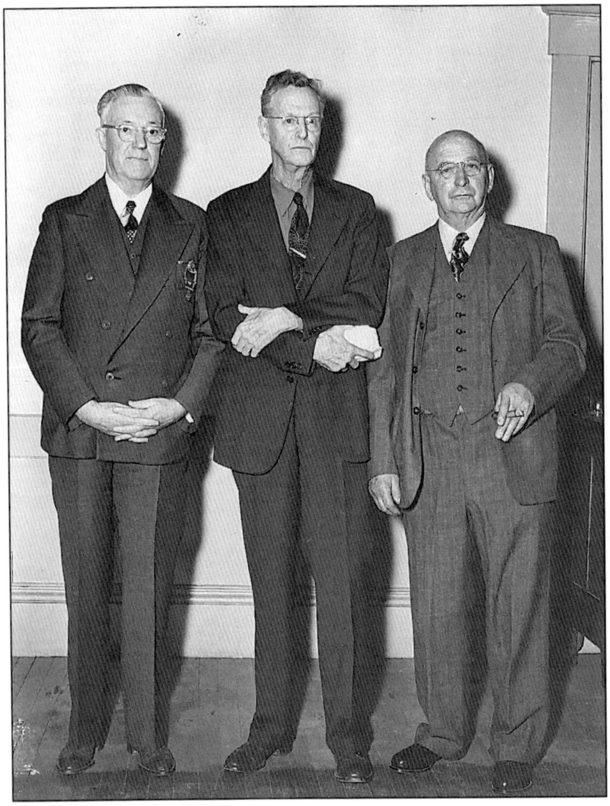

And what of the three pioneers who endured this grueling 1909 race? They related their memories to Stoneham Rotarians in August 1945. The drivers are, from left to right, Robert H. Messer, Earle Chapin, and T. Arthur Pettengill. All three agreed once was enough under those conditions!

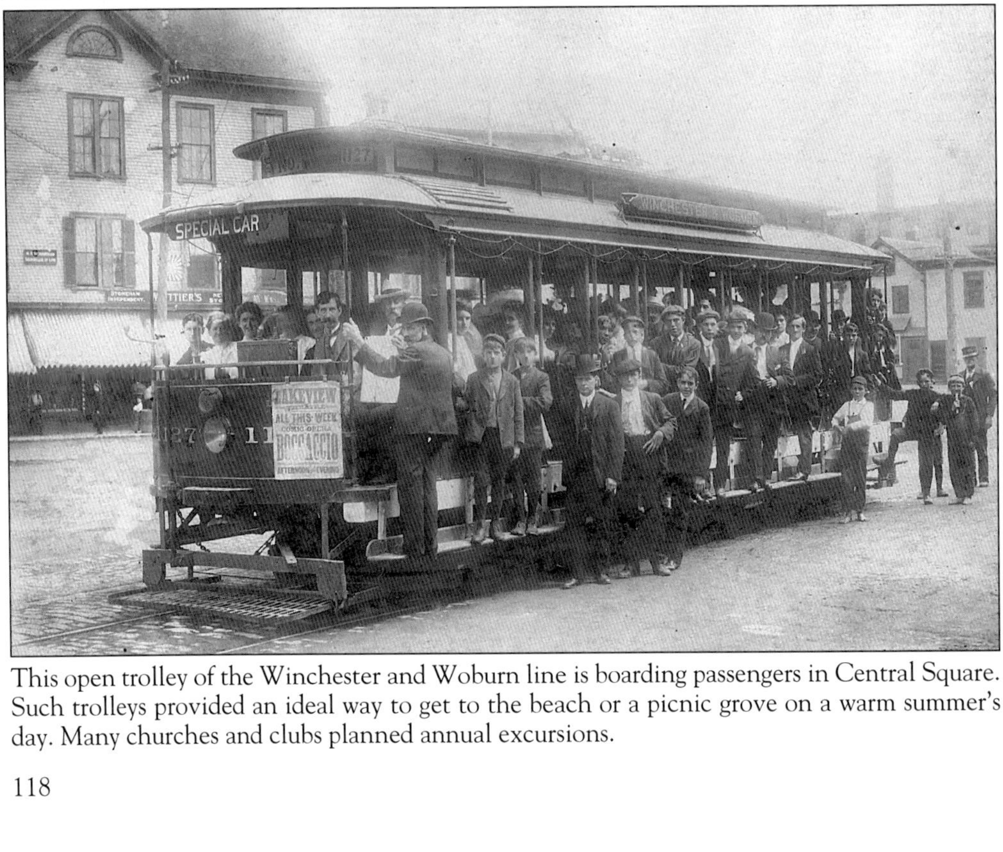

This open trolley of the Winchester and Woburn line is boarding passengers in Central Square. Such trolleys provided an ideal way to get to the beach or a picnic grove on a warm summer's day. Many churches and clubs planned annual excursions.

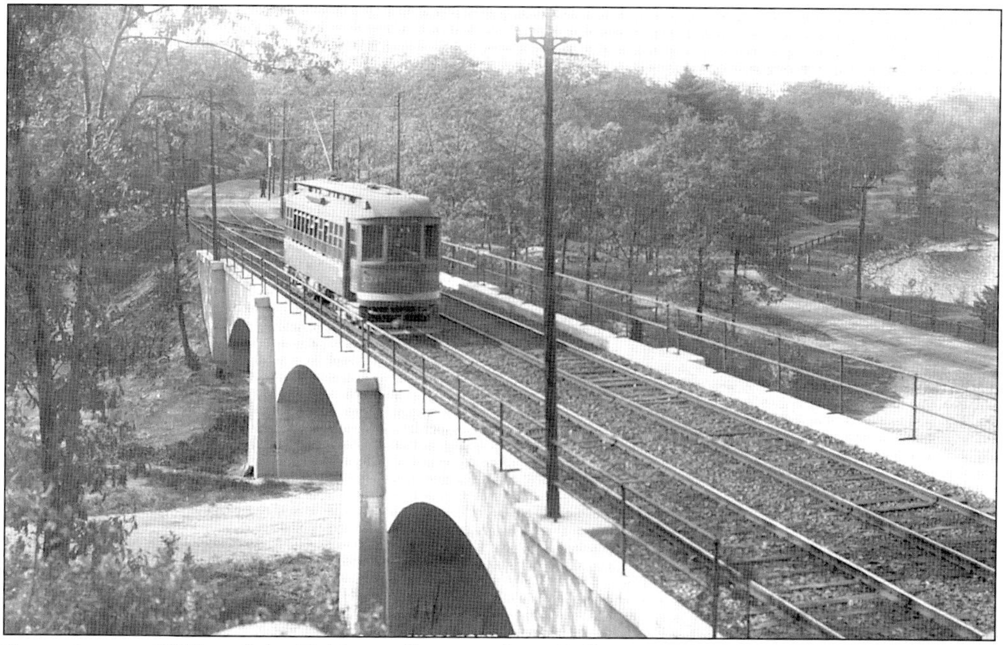

From August 1910 to July 1946 a trolley ran from Sullivan Square in Somerville through a portion of the Middlesex Fells Reservation to Stoneham. Because of its color and the thrills of the ride, this trolley was affectionately called the "Yellow Peril."

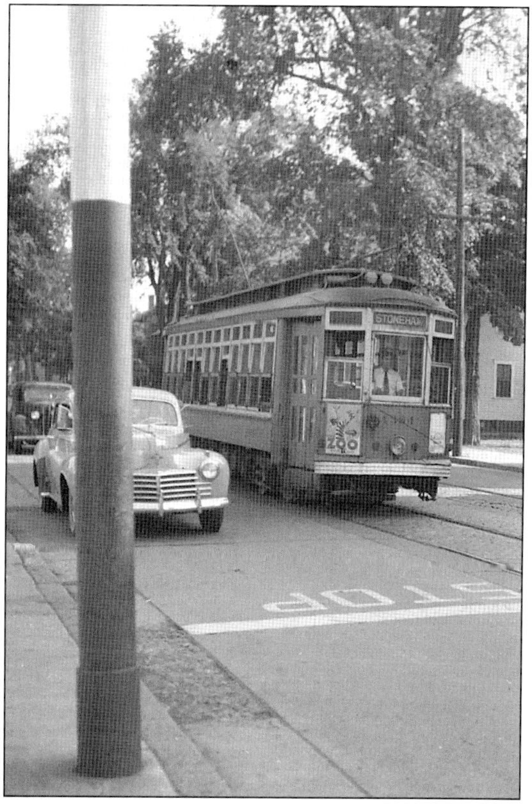

This trolley is heading north on Main Street near Pleasant Street en route to Farm Hill. Although the trolleys have not clanged along Stoneham's streets for over 50 years, it is possible to view one of the same era. In March 1947, a similar car, semi-convertible car number 4387, was taken to be on display at the Seashore Trolley Museum in Kennebunkport, Maine. Through the years it has been visited by many Stonehamites.

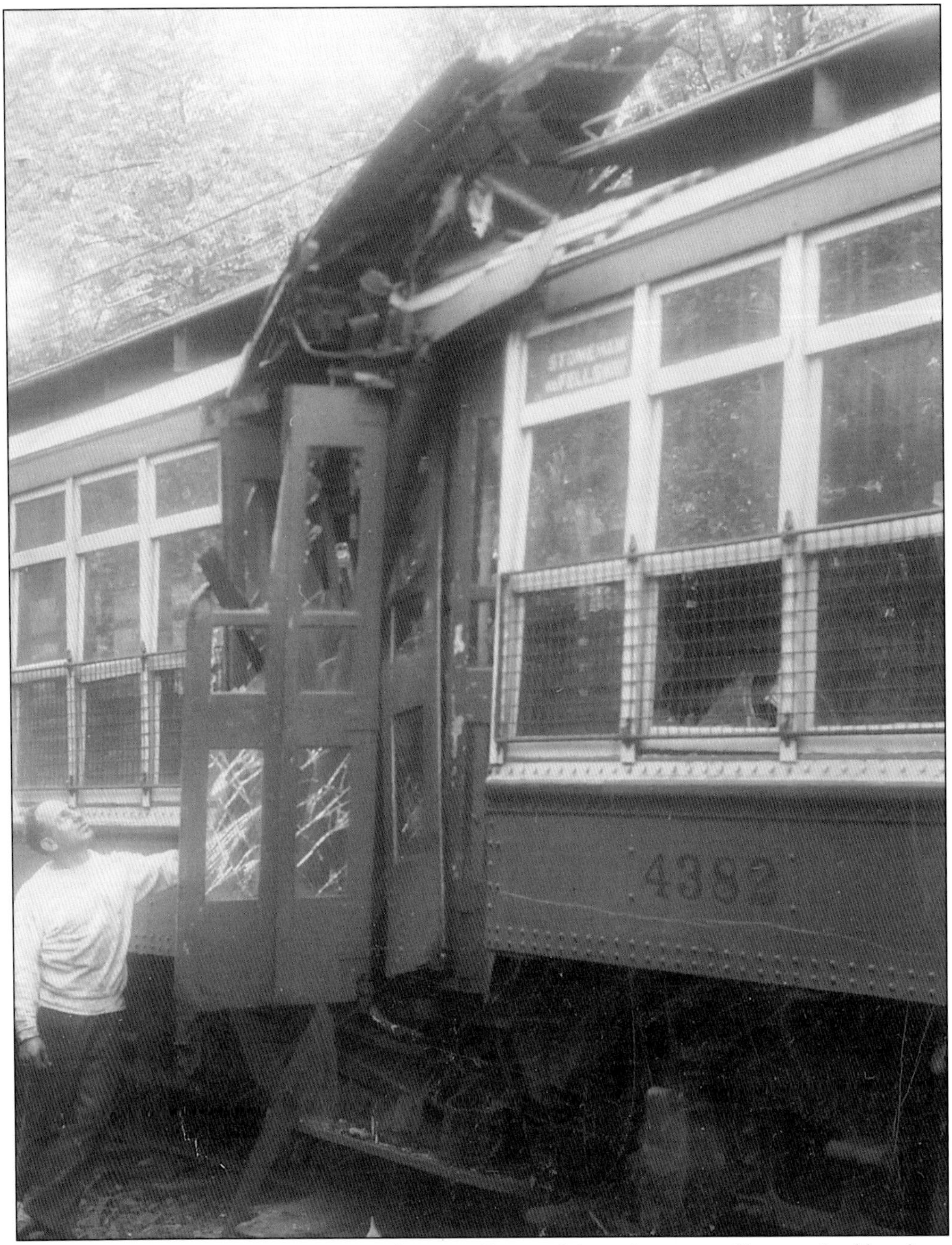

This was the scene on June 12, 1946, when two Eastern Massachusetts trolleys crashed head on. This accident happened near the southern end of Dark Hollow Pond where Bear Hill Road goes under the trestle that carried the trolley tracks. The cars telescoped their front ends, breaking many panes of glass in each car. There were only five passengers on the southbound car, but the northbound car carried 48 passengers. The motorman, James Purtle, was seriously injured and died on July 1. Several passengers were also seriously injured and were taken to the Sanitarium. Many others were shaken up and bruised or cut by flying glass. The line was scheduled to close the following month.

Seven

THROUGH THE YEARS

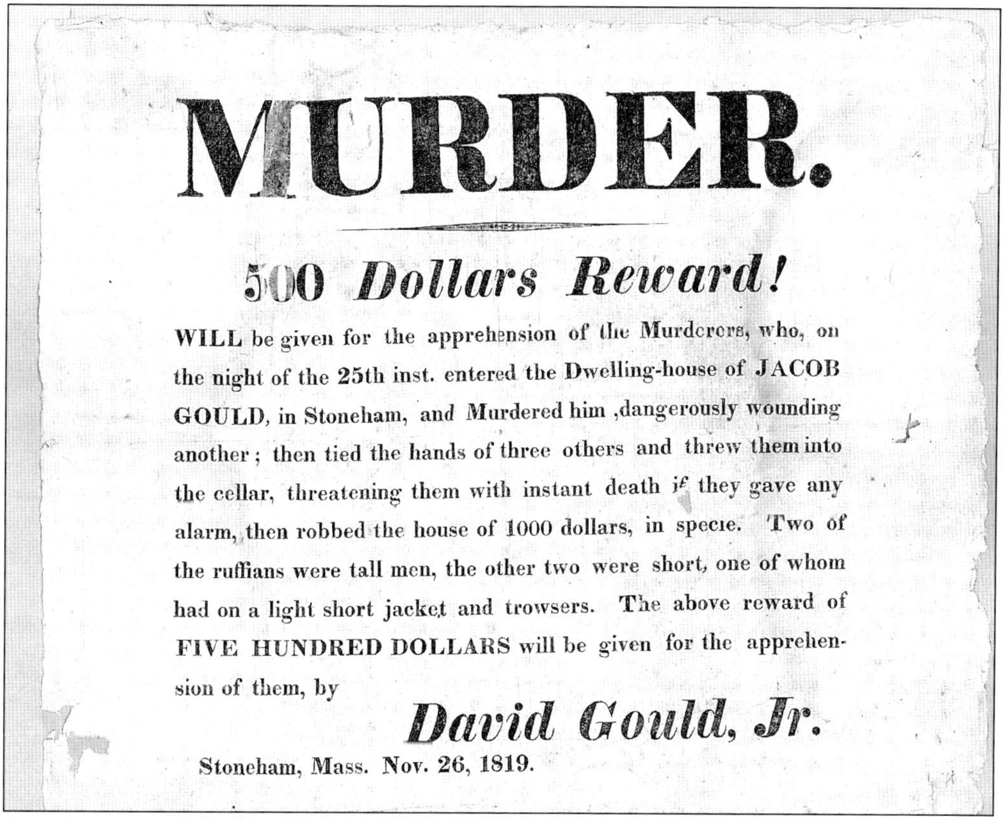

MURDER.

500 *Dollars Reward!*

WILL be given for the apprehension of the Murderers, who, on the night of the 25th inst. entered the Dwelling-house of **JACOB GOULD**, in Stoneham, and Murdered him ,dangerously wounding another ; then tied the hands of three others and threw them into the cellar, threatening them with instant death if they gave any alarm, then robbed the house of 1000 dollars, in specie. Two of the ruffians were tall men, the other two were short, one of whom had on a light short jacket and trowsers. The above reward of **FIVE HUNDRED DOLLARS** will be given for the apprehension of them, by

David Gould, Jr.

Stoneham, Mass. Nov. 26, 1819.

Intruders entered the home of Jacob Gould, his brother David, and their sister Polly on the evening of November 15, 1819. The men tied them up, took their money, and threw them down cellar. When Jacob tried to defend himself, he was stabbed in several places and died before morning. No one was ever convicted for the crime, but a suspect committed suicide in jail. Thus came to an end Stoneham's first recorded murder, a slaying that disturbed townspeople a great deal.

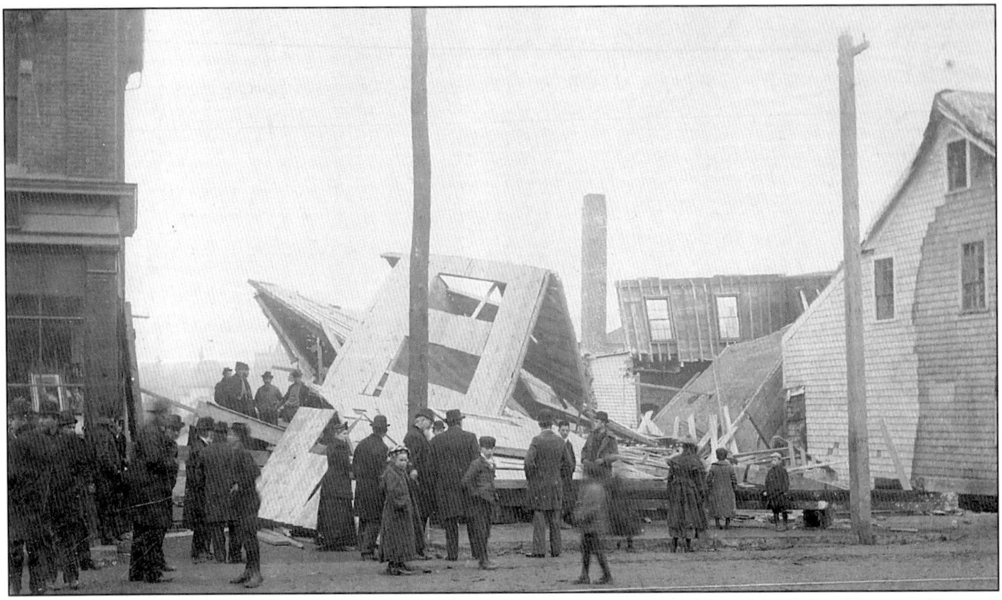

A crash heard for 2 miles signaled the Durkee Disaster on March 7, 1894. A building collapsed while under construction on the T.G. Durkee property at the corner of Main and Minot Streets. Nathaniel Loud, who had gone to investigate the crash, was killed. Several others received bruises from flying debris.

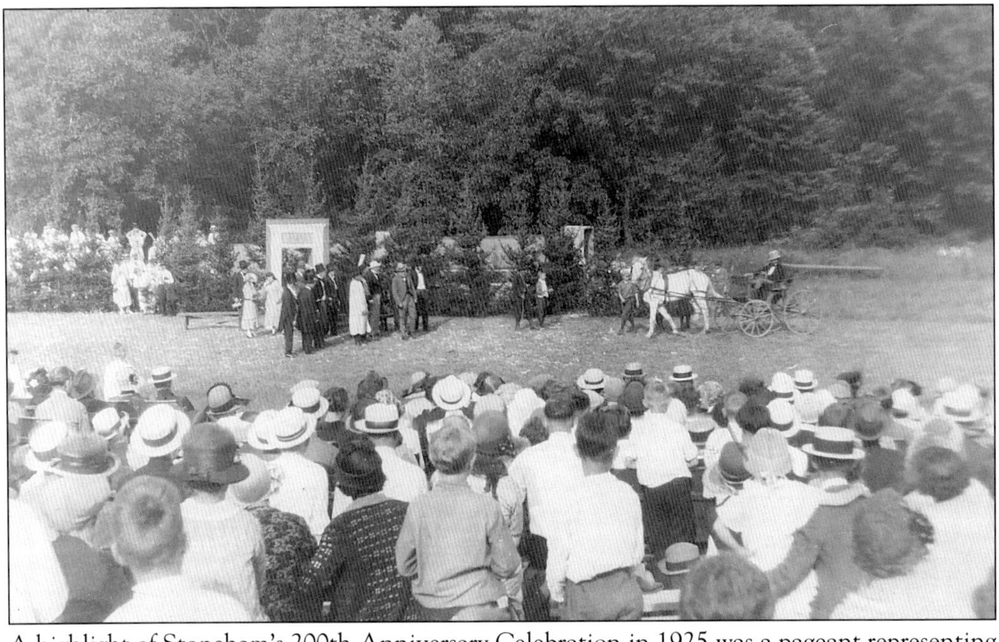

A highlight of Stoneham's 200th Anniversary Celebration in 1925 was a pageant representing various epochs in Stoneham's history. In this scene, Claude Patch makes his entrance as "Pug" Phelps, the town drunkard. Phelps had been sent to Boston to get news about the 1840 presidential election. This was a contest between incumbent Martin Van Buren, seen as an aristocrat, and his challenger, William Henry Harrison, who was presented as a "log cabin and hard cider" candidate.

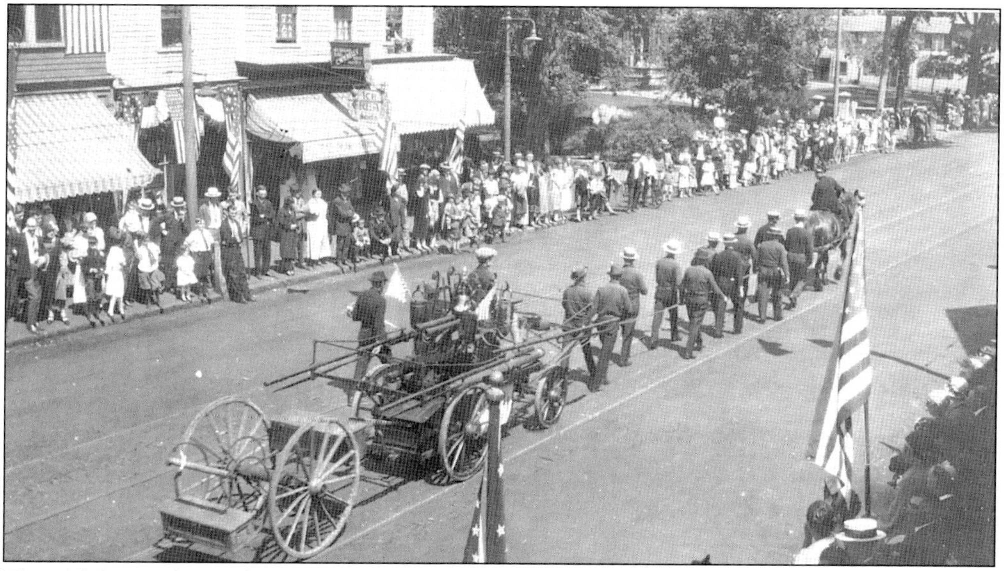

The old General Worth Hand Tub used by Stoneham firemen from 1849 to 1885 returned to participate in Stoneham's 200th Anniversary Parade on June 17, 1925. It was on loan from Goffstown, New Hampshire, and required a $1,000 deposit to guarantee its safe return.

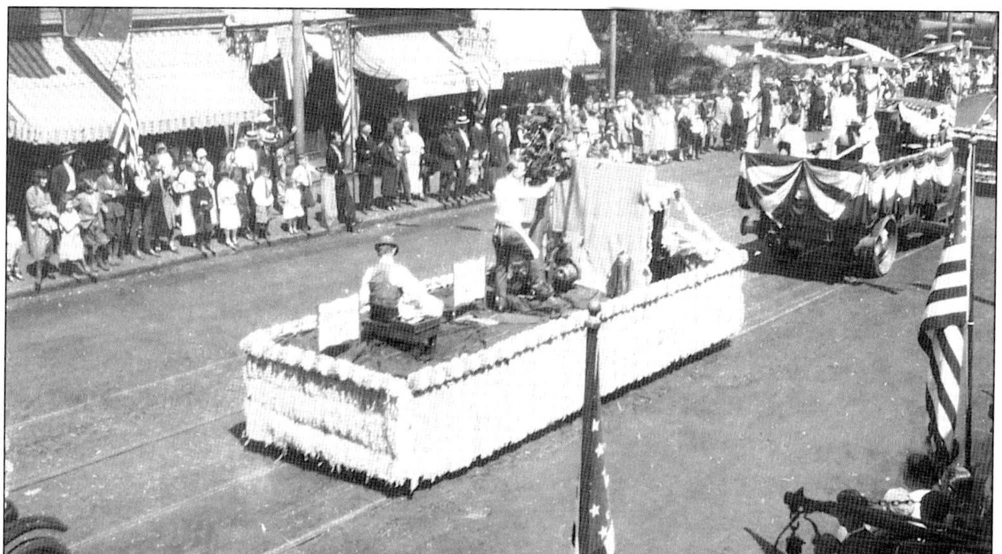

A float in the June 17, 1925 parade depicted differences in shoemaking during Stoneham's 200-year history. At the back of the float, a 1725 cordwainer is seated at his bench, while at the front of the float a 1925 shoe worker tends his machine.

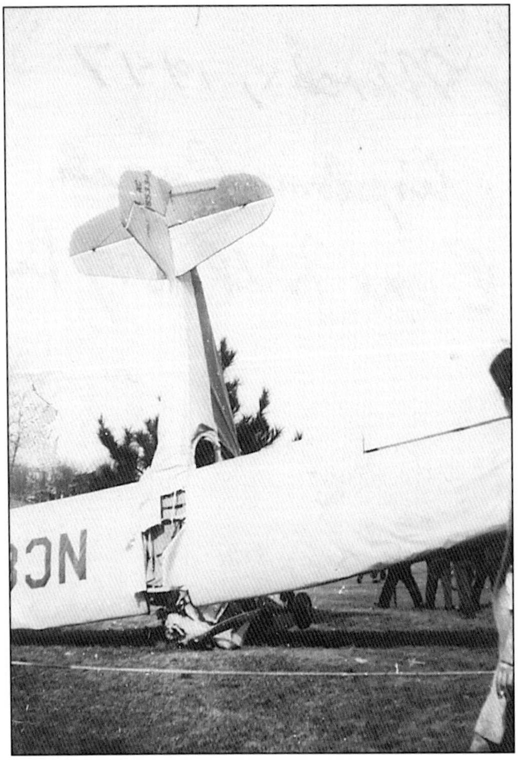

No, Stoneham did not have an airport. This was the fourth fairway at Bear Hill Golf Course on the morning of Saturday, March 8, 1947. A plane hired from the airport in Revere had motor trouble and attempted to land on the fairway. When only 75 feet from the ground, the plane took a nosedive, killing the pilot and seriously injuring the passenger.

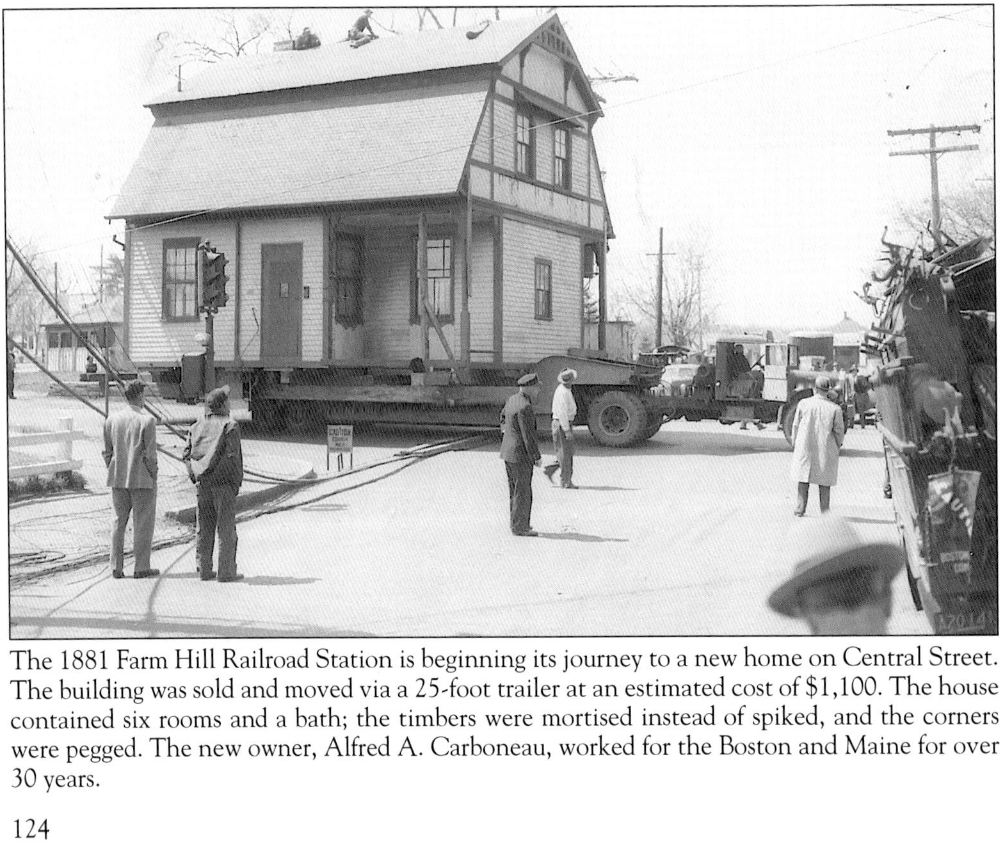

The 1881 Farm Hill Railroad Station is beginning its journey to a new home on Central Street. The building was sold and moved via a 25-foot trailer at an estimated cost of $1,100. The house contained six rooms and a bath; the timbers were mortised instead of spiked, and the corners were pegged. The new owner, Alfred A. Carboneau, worked for the Boston and Maine for over 30 years.

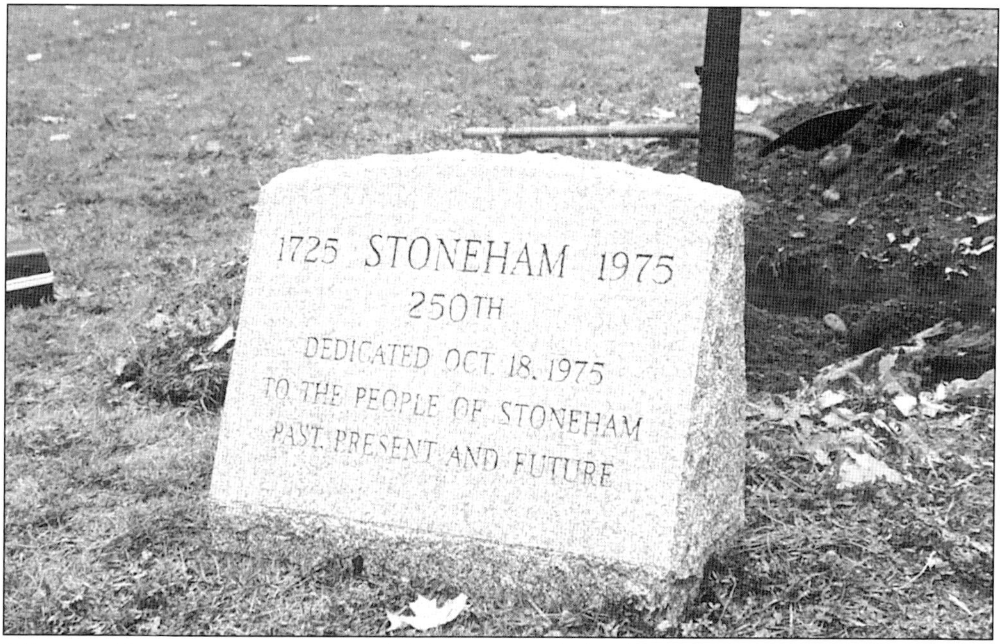

What would you put in a time capsule? A time capsule lies beneath this granite marker on the north lawn of town hall. Placed there during the town's 250th celebration in 1975, the capsule contains items pertaining to the celebration, including local newspapers, commemorative coin sets, and tickets.

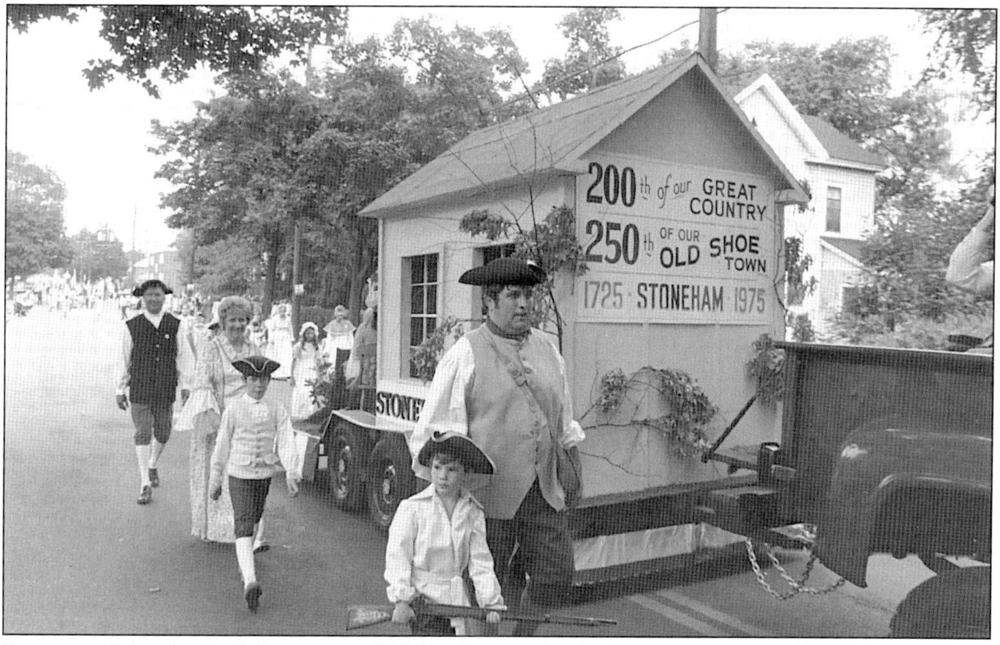

Because of the dual celebration in 1975 to honor the 200th anniversary of the United States and the 250th anniversary of Stoneham, the Stoneham float and committee participated in parades all over eastern Massachusetts. The float was a replica of the Ten Footer that stands on the grounds of the Stoneham Historical Society. In the foreground are John J. Hanright and his son John.

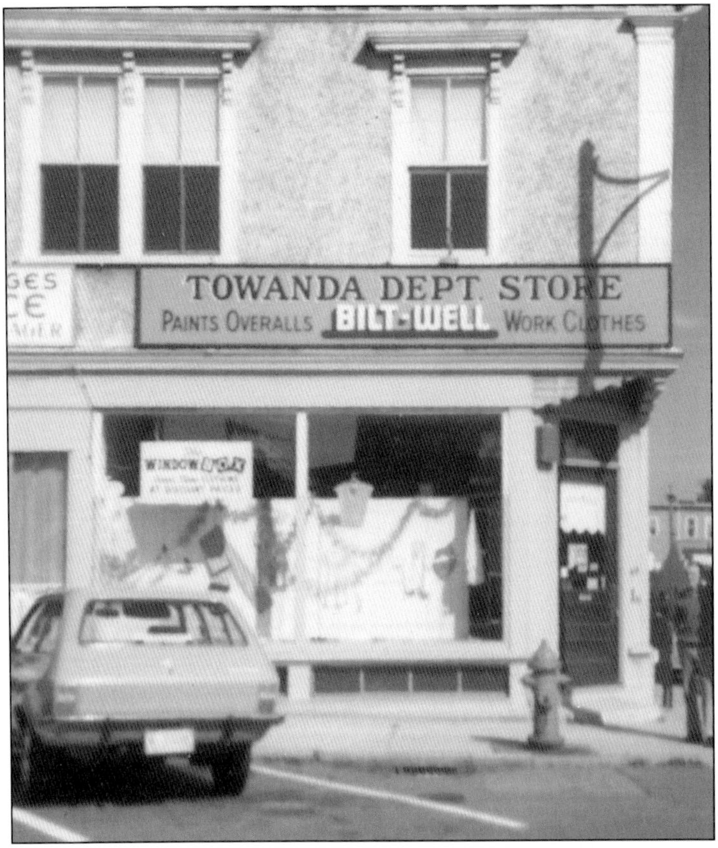

A portion of the movie depicting the Brink's Robbery in Boston (1950) was filmed in the Square in July 1978. Storefronts were remodeled and their signs changed to reflect the 1950s. Shown here is the Window Box Dress Store, located at the corner of Central and Franklin Streets, which became the Towanda Dept. Store.

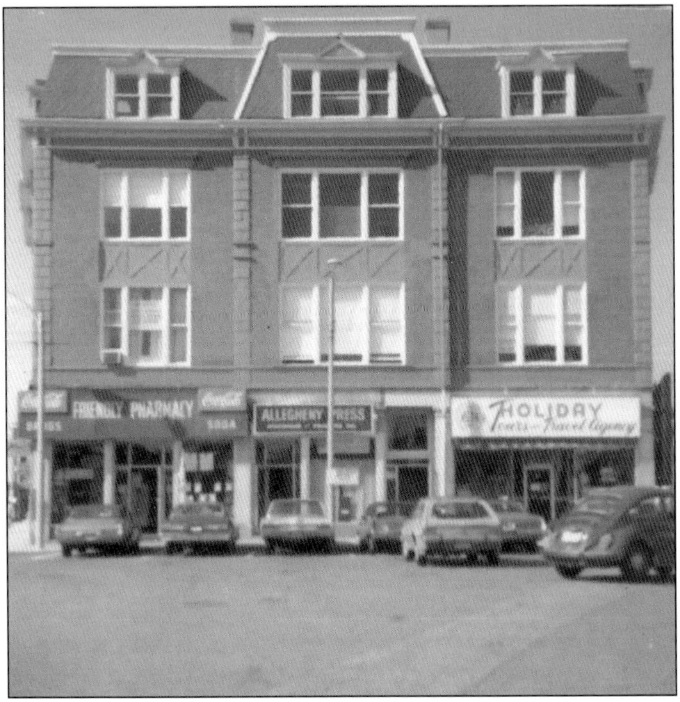

During the filming, the Square would have confused even a long-time Stonehamite. The most familiar landmark, the Dow Block, was disguised. Middlesex Drug became Friendly Pharmacy; Pro-Graphics became the Allegheny Press; and Aquarius Tours and Travel appeared as the Holiday Travel Agency.

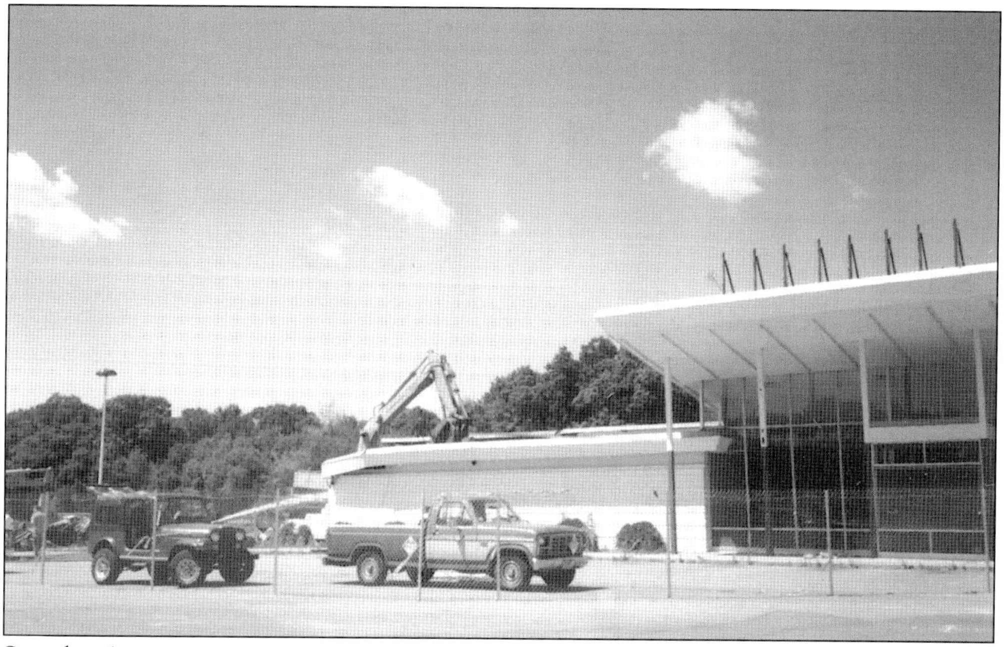

Stoneham's most recent operating movie theatre was the Cinema, which was created at the Redstone Shopping Center in May 1968 from the former Holiday Lanes Bowling Center. This theatre was up-to-date and so popular that in November 1971 it was remodeled into twin theatres each seating over 400 people.

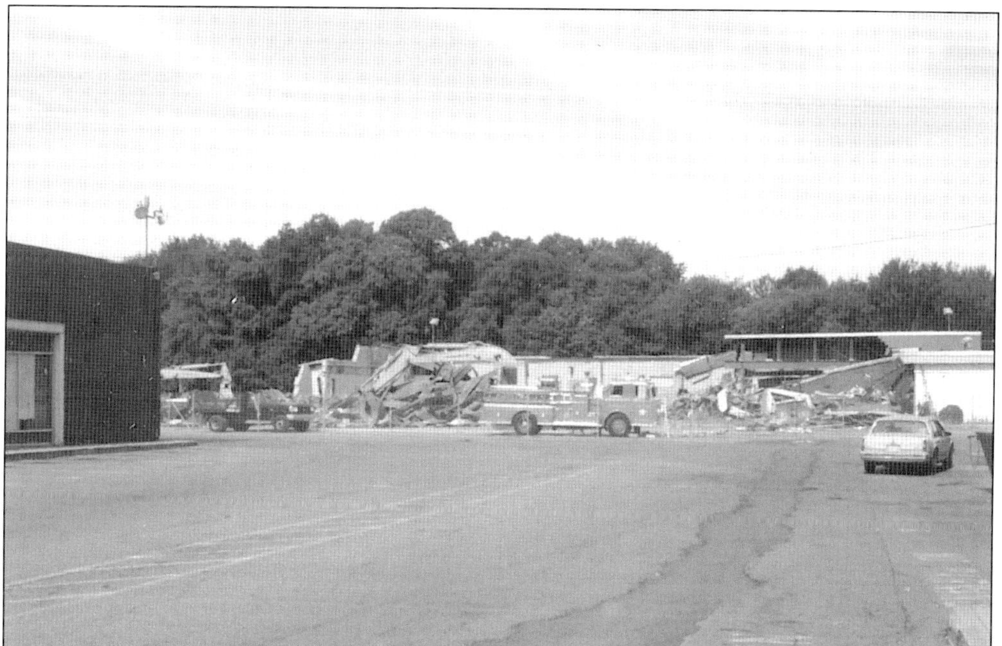

In 1991, the Redstone Shopping Center was redesigned and expanded, and the Cinema was closed. It was demolished in July to create a spot for the new supermarket and liquor store, leaving Stonehamites without a movie theatre for the remainder of the century.

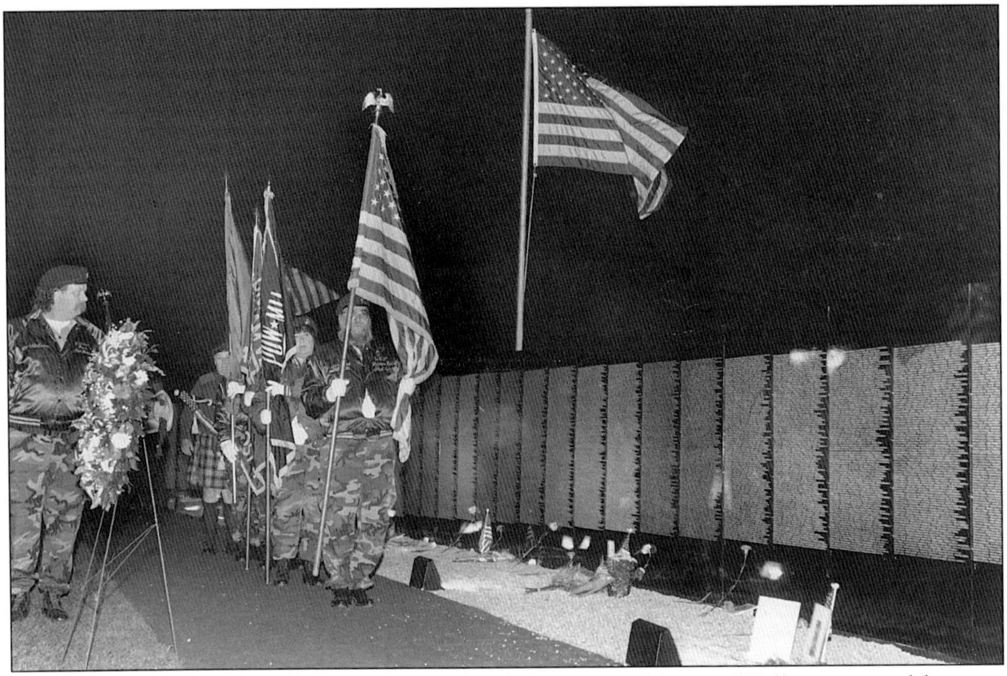

From September 22 to September 29, 1997, the Vietnam Moving Wall was visited by over 120,000 people in Stoneham. Residents paid tribute to those 58,209 men and women whose names were inscribed on the wall. Prisoners of war and those missing in action were also remembered as various Vietnam veterans groups came to place wreaths.

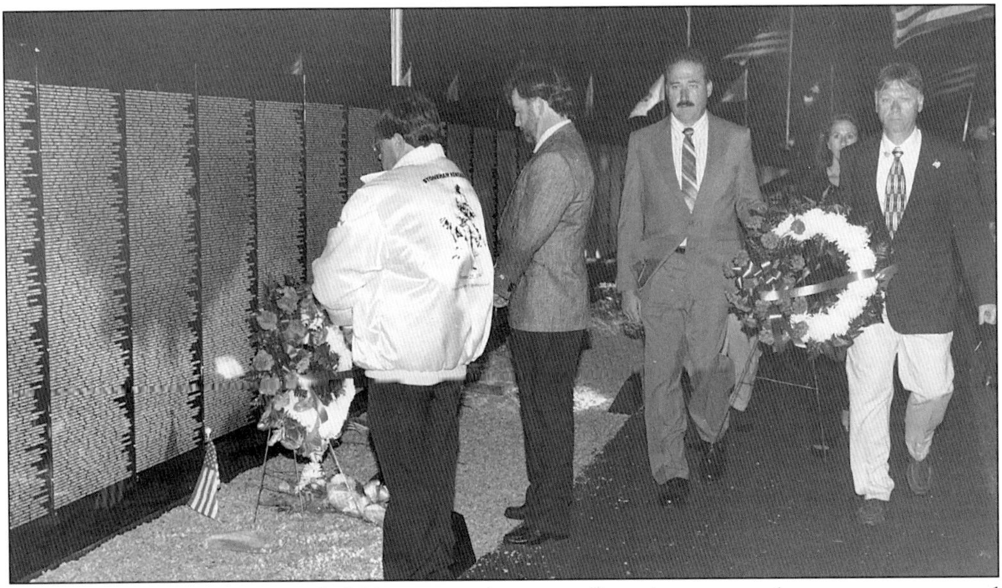

Each day special events were held honoring the seven Stoneham men whose names appeared on the wall. The men shown paying their respects at the wall are Charlie Chuisa (left) and Tom McDermott. Preparing to place another memorial wreath are Tom Marshall (left) and Ed Apalakis. The Stoneham men honored were Lt. Joseph T. Campbell, Sgt. Joseph C. Cerrone, LCpl. Robert P. DelRossi, SP4 James P. English, LCpl. Richard B. Fitzgibbon III, CWO Paul R. Moran, and CWO George C. Schultz.